RUFF STUFF

A WWII PILOT'S STORY
MAJOR NORBERT C. RUFF

SECOND EDITION

By
Tina Susedik
With Major Norbert C. Ruff

Cover Art
By
Emily Mikl

For Additional Copies Write:
Tina Susedik
PO Box 772
Hayward, WI 54843
Or order from
Website: www.tinasusedik.com

To order the Juvat Boys Choir Headhunters CD
Write:
The Headhunters
905 Arapaho Court
Columbus, GA 31904
www.mindspring.com/~jaybirdone/headhunters
CD Price: $20.00 which includes s/h

Table of Contents

Dedicated to all the men and women who fought and continue to fight for our country.
'Thanks' is just not enough.

Forward by Author

Since the first publication of *Ruff Stuff*, many exciting things have happened. When we realized that a second printing was necessary, we decided to make corrections to the first addition and add a few pages in Chapter Seven with pictures depicting these events.

When the book first came out on December 7, 2006, Norb and I were on TV13 in Eau Claire, Wisconsin the day the book was published. Since then Norb has been on television again, several newspaper articles have been written, we have had numerous books signings, both received letters from Laura Bush, I have given several speeches and Norb has had many, many people come to his house to talk about his experiences. To top this off, in April of this year, while in Fort Worth, Texas for his 80th Squadron Reunion, Norb, then eighty-eight years old, had the opportunity to go up in a Stearman plane like the one he flew in cadet training in 1941. Scott Purdue, the owner of the plane, not only took Norb up, but once airborne, let Norb take over the controls. Norb said it was like coming home again.

The biggest story came in December of 2006, when Norb and Mark took the finished book to Ron Fagen in Granite Falls, Minnesota. Ron rebuilds warplanes and is written about in the latter part of Chapter Seven. When he saw the book, Ron decided to take the P-38 he was re-building, paint it the colors of Norb's 80th Squadron from WWII and name it *Ruff Stuff*. Ron said, "I think *Ruff Stuff* will fly again." What an honor for Norb. During the winter Ron's crew, under the "Crew Chief" direction of Erik Hokof, worked diligently re-building the plane. Finally, on July 23rd, 2007, the freshly-painted plane was flown directly from Sturgiss Aviation, owned by Danny King, in Sturgiss, Michigan, to the annual EAA fly-in at Oshkosh, Wisconsin. The final nose artwork was done, *Ruff Stuff* added in orange to the already painted green spinners and the large X in bold orange. For further authenticity, four Japanese flags were added for Norb's confirmed kills. The plane was awarded "Judges Choice, Best WWII Fighter" at the air show. When we all arrived on July 25th, we were speechless when we saw the massive P-38 glowing in the summer sun. People were lined up waiting to look at the plane, one of only four P-38s flying to date. When it was known that Norb was on site, people were anxious to talk with him, shake his hand and have their picture taken with a real hero. On Thursday, the 26th, the plane was pulled to The Warbirds in Review presentation area. There, with crowds surrounding the plane, Norb and Roy Easterwood, another WWII pilot talked about their experiences and fielded questions from the audience. It was then Ron's intention to fire up the engines and take the plane up so everyone could hear the engines and see it fly, but a storm blew in right after the presentation was over and the idea was scrapped. Now *Ruff Stuff* will go on tour at various air shows throughout the country.

Introduction

When the Ruff family asked me to help write a book about their father, I was honored and nervous. Honored to put into words what life was like for a man who served his country so well; nervous that I would not be able to put into words what it was really like in the South Pacific during WWII.

To begin with, I realized my knowledge of WWII in the Pacific was very limited: the Japanese bombed Pearl Harbor, my father was in the Navy somewhere in the South Pacific, we bombed Hiroshima and Nagasaki and the war was over. I had no idea the extent of Japanese control, how little our men had to fight with in the South Pacific and how close we came to losing the war in the early years.

My generation, known as the "Baby Boomers," was raised by fathers who did not talk about their experiences in WWII. They fought, watched friends die, came home, married, raised families and went on with their lives. It was something they did not want to re-live and with good reason.

My father watched war movies, and we watched with him, but movies made in the fifties, sixties and seventies did not portray the true reality of the war in the Pacific. It also seemed that most movies were about the European theatre. We began to believe the men who fought in WWII were like John Wayne, Lee Marvin, Ernest Borgnine, Glen Ford and others, and not as the individuals who slogged through mud or snow, suffered through heat and mosquitoes or flew planes ill-equipped to enter battle.

Since starting this project, my entire attitude about WWII has changed. We have heard so much about the "Greatest Generation" and until I started this project, I did not fully understand what this meant. I realized the men and women who served are dying off at a rapid rate and a large part of what happened to the individuals who fought for our freedom was dying with them. The stories of those who survived and those who did not come back need to be told. I look at men in their late seventies and eighties and wonder if they served and where. Do they have hearing loss from bombs going off next to them without ear protection? What flashbacks enter their dreams at night? Do they still have problems with loud noises like fireworks? Do they think often of their buddies that did not come back and wonder why they made it and their friends did not?

To say my research was fascinating sounds morbid as no war is fascinating. Norb and I agreed that what we wanted to get down in writing was what these men and women went through to protect our freedom; the living conditions; lack of supplies, ships and airplanes; the use of WWI equipment and rations because that was all that was available; and the way the Japanese treated our men if captured. There was a saying I came across during my research that I feel is appropriate:

"If you're reading this, thank a teacher. If you're reading this in English, thank a soldier."

I did something I never in a million years would have thought possible. I read numerous books on the war in the Pacific. A list is at the end of the book. Some were used in the writing of this book. Many were read just to learn more about the war. One, which will be quoted a few times in the following brief history, was written in 1943, about as close to the time the war started as possible. I also found a surprising number of DVDs with original war footage, both American and Japanese.

My time interviewing Norb was a thrill. Norb's memory and knowledge is incredible. I looked forward to each and every Tuesday afternoon I spent at the table in his kitchen, papers and pictures strewn from one end to the other. His patience with my lack of knowledge made my job that much easier. I felt there was no question I couldn't ask, and I asked plenty. If I didn't understand something, I knew I could say, "Okay, Norb, you've lost me here. Could you say that again?" He never acted like I was incredibly dumb (which I was). Each time he had another book for me to read, letters to peruse, and more pictures to scan. The discovery that I was interviewing a man that started flying in bi-planes and six years later was flying the first jets, was amazing.

The day we went up to the Bong Memorial in Superior to see the reconstructed P-38 was surreal. Here I was standing next to a man who had flown a P-38 just like the one at the

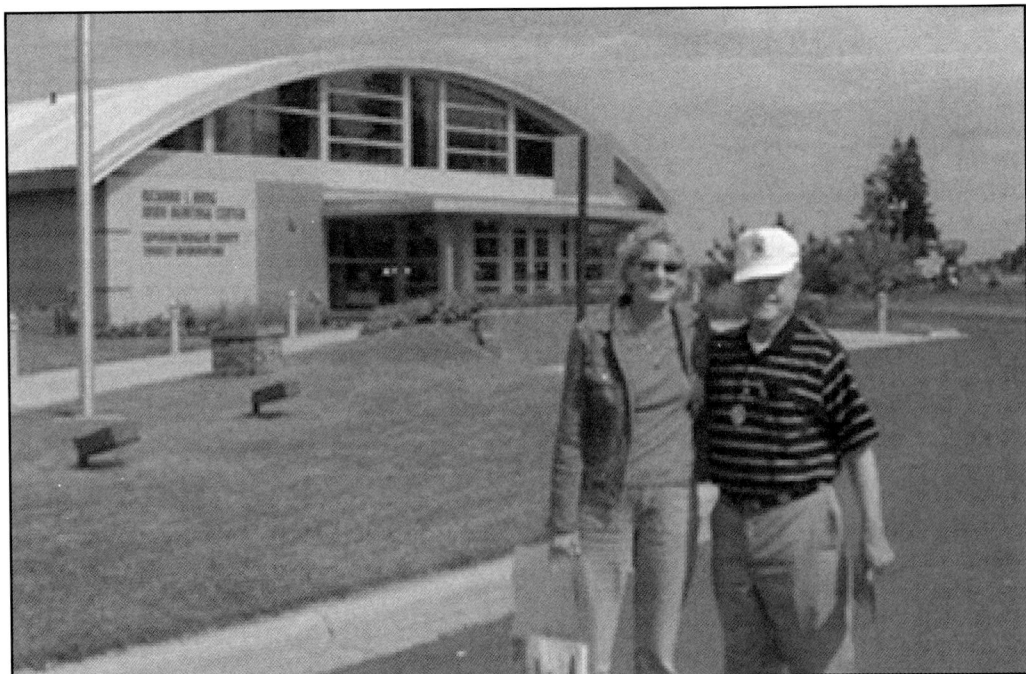

memorial, listening to him describe taking off, where the ladder came down, how they scrambled up to the cockpit, where the belly tanks were attached, how the plane was fueled and much, much more.

By the end of his service, Norb had flown many different types of planes including the P-400, P-39F, P-39D, P-38G, P-40E, P-38F, P-38H, AT-6A, P-47D, P-38J, BT-13A, P-59 and F-80. Whenever I brought up the subject of Norb's medals, he would answer humbly, "You just got medals for the number of missions you went on." He received the Distinguished Flying Cross, Air Medal with three Oak Leaf Clusters, the American Defense Ribbon, Asiatic-Pacific Campaign Medal with three Bronze Stars and a Presidential Unit Citation.

I want to thank Norb for steering me through what for me was a life-changing process. His wife, Eileen, was always gracious when I came to their house, and I feel I have made a true friend and someone who understood my need to show off pictures of my grandchildren. I want to thank Norb's son, Mark, for giving me the opportunity to take on this project. There are several others who need to be mentioned: Marion Kirby who fought with Norb and sent information and got in touch with other pilots; Jay Riedel, a past commander of the 80th, who supplied pictures of the 'old' Headhunters., and my youngest brother, Bill Peters, a Gulf War Veteran, whose interest in this project and our untold number of hours on the phone discussing it, helped make writing this book that much more fun. Last I want to thank my husband, Al, for sitting patiently time and again as I went on and on about the early days of the war in the Pacific to anyone and everyone who would listen.

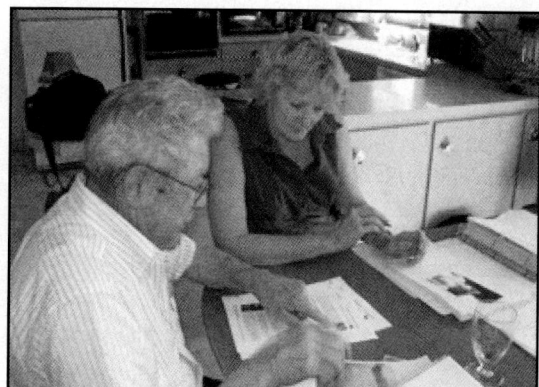

There was always more information to go over. Norb was looking over pictures of Salamua I printed from the internet.

A letter Norb wrote home to his brother, Dick, in 1942 sums up Norb's feelings about the war. "Well Dick, I've been out of school for six months now with five month's foreign service. I've learned a lot and have had a darned good time. We have lost quite a number of boys in my class from Ellington Field, but you get used to it, and after all, this is for keeps. Don't do any worrying because this is one boy that's coming back."

We also stopped at the Northern Wisconsin Veterans Memorial Cemetery the day we went to the Bong Heritage Center.

Just holding the controls of the P-38 was scary - and it wasn't even attached to the plane!!!

The Back Yard War

*B*efore getting into the life of Norb and his fellow pilots, it is important to get an idea of what those men in the early part of the war in the Pacific were heading into. The war against Japan was a totally different ball of wax than the war in Europe. The mentality of the Japanese military was completely foreign to the rest of the world. To serve the emperor, they would fight to the death; die rather than be captured. They were told that if they died in combat, they would go to heaven. They believed that any soldier that allowed themselves to be captured was not worth keeping alive – especially pilots. Their sole purpose was to fight for their emperor, an emperor who did not even care about his own military men. The Japs were out to kill as many Americans as possible.

With the war in Europe raging and the majority of the military's resources being sent in that direction, the bombing of Pearl Harbor by the Japanese caught the United States off guard. As General George C. Kenney, Commander of the 8th Air Force wrote in 1951: "We have fought wars of this kind since 1775, but it is hard to find a time or place in our history when we were less prepared to withstand an attack than we were to counter the Japanese invasion of the Philippines in the closing days of 1941. A well-planned and skillfully executed surprise air assault on the morning of December 7th had wrecked our Pacific Fleet at Pearl Harbor and stunned the nation with its revelation that the only barrier to the Japanese conquest of the Far East had been removed. That same day, December 8th Far Eastern Time, bombs rained down on Manila, Hong Kong and Singapore, and during the next five months an empire that the white man had held for four centuries was taken over by the Nipponese who boasted that they would organize all Greater East Asia into a 'co-prosperity sphere.'

"It was an understandable reaction by a nation that suddenly realized that it was in a war for which it was woefully unprepared. All hope of saving the Philippines had vanished. With our Pacific Fleet out of action, we could not send troops to reinforce MacArthur. As a matter of fact we did not have the troops available to send. We did not have the aircraft to replace the losses in the Philippines. Back in the United States we did not have a single fighter or bomber squadron up to full strength in airplanes." (*They Fought With What They Had*)

Even though the United States had been caught off guard, they had been forewarned years earlier by one of their best pilots. General Billy Mitchell, a decorated WWI pilot and top American combat airman of the war, tried to convince the government of the necessity of building an air corps within the Army and Navy. Having been the first man to fly over enemy territory during a battle, Mitchell realized the affect planes could have on shortening wartime and saving lives. No one would listen, even those whose names became famous, Coolidge, Roosevelt (a Navy man), Doolittle, Spaatz,

Arnold, and even General Kenney, also a WWI pilot.

Mitchell, a Wisconsin native, would not give up the battle. After he returned to the United States in 1919, he became the deputy chief of the Air Service. As he became more adamant about the need for airpower, he and his ideas became unpopular. The Army and Navy did not appreciate being told that airpower could better protect the US coasts than warships. In 1921 and 1923, to prove he knew what he was talking about, bombing tests were held. In 1921, off the coasts of Virginia, Mitchell's bombers sunk three German ships that had been captured during WWI. They also sank the U.S.S. Alabama, an obsolete vessel. In 1923 he again showed the importance of airpower by sinking two more U.S. obsolete battleships.

General Billy Mitchell

Even with the success of these tests and the support of others who believed in Mitchell, the Army, Navy and President Coolidge believed battleships and ground troops with their equipment was the right and only way to win a war. Mitchell was demoted to Corporal and sent to Texas. He was eventually court-martialed, found guilty of insubordination and suspended from active duty for five years without pay. He resigned from the military but continued to fight for airpower.

In a prophetic turn of events, in 1923, after a honeymoon tour of Hawaii, Philippines, China, Japan and India (provided by the Army to get him out of their hair) Mitchell predicted that Japan was becoming militarily strong and preparing for war.

He said of the Japanese: "They can fly, are going to fly, and may end up developing the greatest air power in the world. I think if we plunged into war tomorrow, it would take us at least two years to get on a par with Japan." He predicted that a Pacific war would start with a Japanese attack on Pearl Harbor by air and sea, along with an attack on the Philippines. "Attack will be launched as follows: Bombardment, attack to be made on Ford Island (Hawaii) at 7:30 A.M...Attack to be made on Clark Field at 10:40 A.M." With the attack at Pearl Harbor occurring at 7:55 A.M. and Clark Field in the Philippines at 12:35 P.M., Mitchell's prediction was eerily uncanny. He also said, "Japan never declares war before attacking."

Mitchell died in 1936 at the age of 57, never seeing his life's work vindicated. The fact that it did take nearly two years after Pearl Harbor for airpower in the Pacific to come up to strength, shows Mitchell knew what he was talking about. He was posthumously awarded a special Congressional Medal of Honor. The medal was designed specifically for Mitchell. It stated: "Award of the Congress, August 8, 1946 For Outstanding Pioneer Service and Foresight In Field Of American Military Aviation."

By late 1941 the Japanese had a major stronghold in the South Pacific and were attempting to take over New Guinea and Australia. Things were so bad that at one point Australia was ready to concede defeat and give up most of Northern Australia and use their resources to fight for the southern part.

General MacArthur was sent to stop the Japanese from gaining full control of New Guinea and to get our military onto the island. His arrival in Australia would be the start of the longest campaign fought during WWII. From July 20, 1942 to December 14, 1943 our men battled for Buna in New Guinea before the island was completely taken from the Japs. Without this territory, the Air Corps would not have a base from which to fly to other Japanese-held islands. It must be noted that since MacArthur was a cavalry man, even he did not understand the necessity of having an air corps. If not for General Kenney, the war in the Pacific would have been fought solely on the ground.

General Kenney

"When Kenney started serving as MacArthur's chief air officer and commander of the Fifth Air Force, there were exactly eight combat-capable Boeing B-17s in the bombing force. Kenney and his resourceful staff began working to build up a respectable force, salvaging parts from wrecks (some still in Japanese-held territory) and in some cases creating their own substitute parts. Kenney took any plane he could get. He proved to MacArthur that the Fifth Air Force could carry anything anywhere anytime MacArthur needed it and destroy Japanese air power while doing it." (*Aviation History*)

The lack of supplies and men for this offensive was a major frustration for MacArthur and frequent, urgent requests to Washington went unheeded. Materials and men were needed in Europe. It was only necessary for the men to hold the Japanese until the war in Europe was over and those resources sent to the South Pacific.

"There is a legend, probably apocryphal, that General Arnold, in explaining to some men who were fighting out of Australia why they could not expect more support until United States production was able to catch up with the demands from Europe, called the war in the Southwest Pacific a 'back yard war.' It is a phrase that sticks in the mind, for that is very much how the war was actually fought, by a handful of men with a handful of planes and never enough replacements to let them get ahead of the game. But surely it was the biggest back yard in history." (*They Fought With What They Had*)

The reality of Japanese control in the South Pacific seemed to not reach Washington until the attack at Pearl Harbor. At one time, "A thousand planes took off from England to bomb a German base, when he [MacArthur] himself at the start could rarely send more than a half dozen planes on a bombing mission to New Guinea. As a matter of fact, the maximum number of planes he was able to muster for one raid during 1942 was thirty-one, and this was late in the year then the boys gave Rabaul a good going over." -Robinson (*The Fight for New Guinea*) (Robinson was a war correspondent.)

"Consider for a moment the situation confronting him [MacArthur] when he landed in Australia. The triumphant Japs had swept down through China and across Thailand. They had banged through Malaya and Burma and captured what had once been regarded as impregnable Singapore. They had most of the Philippines and they lost no time in adding Sumatra, Java, Borneo and the Celebes to Hirohito's imperial realm. They had grabbed New Britain, New Ireland and many small islands in the Dutch East Indies. They had poured down in an avalanche into the Solomons. Only New Guinea stood between them and the projected conquest of Australia. Even in that jungle land they had already acquired more than one base of operations." (*Ibid*)

Suddenly the U.S. government was scrambling to gather an Army, Navy and Air Corps to send to the South Pacific, while at the same time fighting and reinforcing the war in Europe. Time was running out. The Japanese were moving quickly and fiercely.

When MacArthur arrived in Australia in early 1942 from the Philippines where he had been stationed before the war, he not only was faced with shortage of supplies and men, he had to deal with the political problems in Australia, the in-fighting of who should lead which group and the problem of where the Australian military should fight – Europe or at home protecting their own country.

"Never once did he [MacArthur] suggest that Australia should be defended from invasion. He never thinks in the terms of defense. From the very beginning he insisted that it was his intention to attack the Japs wherever he found them, and he added the assurance that he would one day take back the Philippines and move on to Tokyo.

"That pronouncement must have stirred up gales of laughter in Japanese military circles, and they had every reason to laugh. They had hundreds of thousands of seasoned, war-toughened veterans; they had complete air superiority everywhere and absolute control of the seas in the Far-Western Pacific. Yet here was an American who talked with certainty about driving them back with a handful of men and a few planes.

"In the eyes of the Japs, our predicament was hopeless. They had caught us napping at Pearl Harbor; they had torn the Philippines from us; and they had no reason to suppose that what they had done once they couldn't do again.

"How, the Japs must have reasoned, can MacArthur hope to start an offensive without a Navy? And hadn't they sunk or damaged most of our Pacific Fleet at Pearl Harbor? Of course, it was unfortunate that they hadn't followed up their Pearl Harbor attack with a second one the following day. Had the done so, they might have taken the Hawaiian Islands. That was the fault of their naval intelligence section perhaps. But, in any event, they had inflicted enough damage to make certain that MacArthur could expect no help from the American Navy. Well, then, what had they to fear from him?

"Such reasoning was militarily sound. It seemed virtually impossible for us to oust them from any island without the help of the Navy, and the Japs were fully aware MacArthur didn't have enough transports to move an army large enough to do them any harm in New Guinea. They overlooked only one factor in what they considered a simple and perfect equation. That factor was MacArthur himself.

"The Japs failed to take into account the genius and resourcefulness of the man. They simply could not attribute to him more daring and vision than they themselves had. How could they foresee that this man would have the ingenuity to use his Air Corps as a navy?

"That is exactly what happened. The only navy MacArthur had was his Air Corps, and he used it to the Japs' complete surprise and bewilderment. There were many ships around New Guinea and New Britain, but they were Jap ships—many cruisers, destroyers, torpedo boats and transports, but they all flew the flag of the Rising Sun. There were many barges to send thousands of Marines swarming onto beaches and into the swamps and mountains of New Guinea, but they were Jap barges and Jap Marines, not American.

General MacArthur

"MacArthur had no navy, but he had a small band of gallant American airmen, and to these youngsters, recruited largely from the small towns and farms of our South and Western States, must go the major award for turning back the Japs and saving New Guinea and Australia.

"The fight for New Guinea couldn't even have been started without these boys of the Air Corps; it couldn't have been carried on without them; and it couldn't have culminated in a glorious victory at Buna without them. It was these young bomber and pursuit pilots who sought out and sank Jap warships and transports, bombed Jap strongholds and blasted Japan's dreaded Zero's out of the

IX

skies. And when the Japs, heedless as always of losses in men and material sent their hideous green-clad hordes swarming onto the beaches of New Guinea, it was these same American youngsters who sank their landing barges, strafed and bombed their transports and escorting warships, cut their lines of communication and supply, and finally joined Australian and the Wisconsin National Guard – 32nd Division to crush Japan's bid for complete mastery of the Southwest Pacific.

"The Air Corps even flew the infantry from Australia to Port Moresby and then across the perilous Owen Stanley mountain range to the scene of action. But the Air Corps' task didn't end with the mere transportation of troops. Those troops had to be fed, clothed and armed. How these falcons of our Air Force did this job forms one of the most glorious pages in the annals of our military history.

"In years to come historians may analyze the exploits of these airmen and explain the physical and psychological factors that made it possible for a mere handful of them to block the might of the Japanese Empire." (*Ibid*)

Robinson, as a war correspondent, was able to meet and get to know many of these pilots, who, like Norb, were young, homesick and anxious to see action. "Pilots were flocking into Brisbane from the Philippines, Java, Bali, Darwin and New Guinea, and I had them all to myself because there wasn't another war correspondent within hundreds of miles of Brisbane. The pilots took me into their confidence as we sat in the lounge at Lennon's, drinking and swapping stories.

"They were all young; their average age could not have been more than twenty-three. Some were quiet, serious chaps, but most of them were talkative and cheery and always ready for a fight or a frolic. Nothing daunted them. They didn't care whether they faced a suicidal low-bombing mission, a battle against overwhelming odds with Zeros, a crashing landing or a long trek through the jungles. It was all part of the job.

"Many of them had had very few hours of flying time when they were sent on their first mission. They had to learn the hard way—in combat with seasoned Jap fighters who knew every trick of aerial warfare. Many didn't live long enough to learn at all. Those who did survive became what the Air Corps calls 'hot pilots.' Captain Al Schinz, a grand little fighter pilot from Ottawa, Ill., once defined a hot pilot as 'a damn fool gone haywire in an airplane.' The Air Corps would subscribe to that definition, but to me a hot pilot is a mixture of brains, courage, skill, daring and resource in about equal proportions, a lad who is willing to risk his life any time against any odds. Almost every pilot I met in Australia or New Guinea would fit that definition.

"Some of these lads had incredible adventures in the air and in the jungles. I often wondered what their lives would have been like if there had been no war. Undoubtedly, many never would have left the farms or small towns where they were born. They would have gone on to live happy, ordinary lives, content with their lot because they had known no other. But now they were in a strange land, thousands of miles from their towns and villages, and already becoming front-page heroes back home. I often wondered how many would be reconciled to the small town or farm after the war. Some admitted frankly that the war was a boon to them. They were making more money than they could have hoped to make in civilian life; they were learning something about the rest of the world; and, if they survived, many were confident that they would make their mark in civilian life after the war." (*Ibid*)

"At the time one wonders what they [pilots] accomplished or expected to accomplish. At time times they wondered about that themselves. They flew missions when and how they could with what they had on hand. A great many of their replacements came to them utterly green, but they used them anyhow. They had to. Unlike the Infantry, who were given months to train in, arriving Air Corps personnel were likely themselves in combat within forty-eight hours. Bombers often carried gunners who had never fired machine guns. Some pursuit pilots went into action after only fifteen hours' training in a fighter plane. It was wasteful war. It was disorganized. It reminds one a little of the old Indian wars on our forest frontiers, for the Japanese knew how to use the weather the way the Indians used the woods. It was a matter of ambushes and long hunts. There was no intelligence worth mentioning. After December 8, 1941, with one exception the first real intelligence briefing the men ever had came just before the Japanese attacked Milne Bay in August, 1942." (*Ibid*)

"…In victory the tendency is to forget the unhappy times before we started winning, and this is largely true among military men as well as civilians. The emphasis, even in the histories, is all on how we won, not on how close we came to losing; and we read about how unbeatable our men were, how resourceful their leaders, how superb their equipment. All that is true and it is proper that Americans should find a source of lasting pride in its truth. But there is a beginning to any history, and though it is not a pretty story, the beginning of this war should be remembered." (*Ibid*)

At the second 80ᵗʰ reunion in San Diego, Norb talked to General Kenney. They were now both civilians and Norb felt he could ask Kenney a question that had been bothering him for years. "What happened to all those pilots that had been trained at Randolph Field in 1936, 1937 and 1938? Why didn't we use them instead of sending in men who hadn't flown since training schools and had no other flying experience?"

General Kenney replied, "How many hours of flying time did you have before you went overseas?"

"Three schools of sixty hours each," Norb answered.

"So you had 180 hours of flying time in. Well, by the time I HAD THIRTY HOURS OF

FLYING TIME IN WWI, I HAD SHOT DOWN TWO PLANES AND WAS SHOT DOWN ONCE MYSELF!"

To help understand the workings of the Army Air Corps during WWII, Norb wrote the following brief description. It should hopefully help to understand the information in the following chapters. The Fifth Air Force under the Command of General Kenney was comprised of many Groups. Each Group consisted of three squadrons. This needs to be kept in mind when you read about Norb first being in the 49th Pursuit Group, 7th Squadron then eventually moved to the 8th Pursuit Group, the 80th Squadron. (To further confuse things, until May 15th, 1942, the Groups were known as Pursuit Groups, not Fighter Groups.) The 7th, 8th and 9th Squadrons belonged to the 49th Pursuit Group and the 35th, 36th and 80th Squadrons belonged to the 8th Pursuit Group.

Although the 35th, 36th and 80th Squadrons were 'Sister' squadrons, the 80th never fought, lived or ate with them. As the 35th & 36th quickly lost men, the 80th was used as replacements for those killed. The 35th and 36th were more cohesive as they were the first fighting Squadrons in New Guinea before the 80th arrived. The 80th was considered "Upstarts."

You may wonder why the 8th only had two Squadrons when they went to New Guinea. Originally the 8th consisted of the 33rd, 35th and 36th Squadrons. The 33rd was sent to Iceland and on January 6th, 1942, at Mitchell Field in New York, the 80th was formed to replace them.

A Squadron has about 400 men, with forty pilots with ten supporting men to each pilot. At that time all pilots were Commissioned Officers – one Major, who was the Squadron C.O. (Company Commander), about four Captains, some 1st Lieutenants and the rest 2nd Lieutenants.

Each department head was a Commissioned Officer in charge. These were not pilots, but ground officers. The Adjutant is in charge of all paper work, orders and records, intelligence, cooks, etc. Then there is an officer in charge of supply; one in charge of airplane mechanics, a Flight Surgeon or the Sqdn Doctor; one in charge of radio repairs and crews on all aircraft radio; an officer for guns, which included aircraft as well as side arms and guard duty; then one in charge of ordinances – the bombs, missiles, etc.

Under each department head are various sized crews composed of enlisted men, Sergeants, Line Chief, Sergeant Major, Master, Tech, Staff, Buck-Corporals, Private 1st Class and Privates.

Many things contributed to the early failures of the troops, from MacArthur's disdain of the air corps (he was a cavalry general and in New Guinea tanks or horses were of little use.) to the location of his headquarters in Australia which were too far removed from the fighting to understand the conditions in New Guinea; to lack of decent maps of the island; to his inability to make Washington understand his need for ships, aircraft and more soldiers. All of these made the fight for the Buna area, the longest battle the US government ever fought in any war - over one and half years.

Although Kamikaze's were not used during the time Norb was overseas, eventually there were over 5,000 used by the Japanese. If the United States had not bombed Hiroshima and Nagasaki, it is estimated that millions of additional soldiers and civilians would have been killed as Japan was still training their soldiers and citizens to kill Americans.

By the time the war was over, an estimated 300,000 American soldiers were killed in all theatres. Most of these were buried on foreign land. Many bodies were never found. In all, 27 countries were involved in the war, with over 57 million casualties, both military and civilian. Germany surrendered on May 7, 1945 and Japan on September 2, 1945.

"Let us hope that this story of another case of 'too little, too late,' will drive home a lesson to the people of this country. We must not again let our defenses down. The next time might be simply – 'too late.'" - General Kenney

Chapter One
Farmboy

$\mathcal{T}$he cruise ship's bow plowed through the warm Pacific waters, the blue water splashing on its hull, then slowed as it reached the San Francisco dock. With barely enough time to discharge its New Year's holiday passengers, the crew quickly refueled, restocked food and emptied the two swimming pools. The next set of passengers would not need such luxury. Instead, the pools were filled with coffin-like boxes containing folded up P-40 planes, their bodies devoid of wings.

One young man, just a few months short of his twenty-third birthday, stood at the railing of the Mariposa, his arms folded across the top of the railing, and gazed at those boxes. He, like many other pilots on board, wondered where they were going and which box held the plane that would bring him to his death. His gear, winter and summer, issued before sailing, was stowed near his bunk in the crowded quarters below.

Barely one month after Japan bombed Pearl Harbor, the young man felt the rumbling of the ship's engines under his feet as it took him further and further away from his homeland, his hometown and his home and closer to Australia and the war that would take so many of his buddies and forge life-long friendships with those that managed to survive the horrors that were soon to become part of their everyday life. There would be many more days and long dark nights watching the wake at the end of the ship waiting and wondering what his fate would be. As the days became longer and warmer they knew they were not headed for Alaska, but maybe the Philippines.

It has been written that WWII was fought by farm boys and boys from rural America. This is true of Norbert C. Ruff, who was born on June 4, 1919, when many young men from the village of Bloomer, Wisconsin were still overseas fighting the enemy in France during WWI. Several from the village gave their lives, including Martin Treptow, whose name became well-known when President Reagan used a quote Treptow wrote in his diary on December 13, 1917. It was found in his shirt pocket when his body was found after he was killed in action in July, 1918. "The end of a long journey, Now bring on your wars. 1918 Resolution: American must win the War. Therefore I will work, I will save, I will sacrifice, I will endure. I will fight cheerfully and do my utmost as if the whole issue of the struggle depended on me alone."

At the time of Norb's birth, Bloomer had a population of about 1,400. Automobiles made their first appearance a scant ten years before; the number of horses, cows and pigs nearly matched the number of residents and horse-drawn carriages and wagons out-numbered cars five to one. Ice was still cut from the local pond in the winter, put in ice houses, and covered in sawdust to keep frozen for the coming summer. On Saturday nights stores stayed open late and farmers came in to shop and visit with their neighbors in German, Scandinavian, Polish and Bohemian. The theatre still had a local pianist accompany the film. The train sounded its whistle at the depot a few blocks from Main Street. Doctors still made house calls, babies were born at home and in an emergency neighbors shared their phones with those who did not have one. Very few farmers had electricity with many not getting service until the mid-1940s.

Like many Northern Wisconsin villages, Bloomer was founded on the lumber trade. In 1858 a few hardy souls settled near the pond, where a dam and mill were quickly constructed. Logs from northern lumber camps floated down Duncan Creek and into what was quickly known as Mill Pond. In the summer, lumberjacks became farmers, and as soon as harvesting was over and the snow started, these farmers put away their plows and hoes, hitched up their horses or oxen and headed for the lumber camps north of the village. While they were gone, their wives and children did the chores. It was a time when a farmer could make a good living milking fifteen to twenty cows, have a few pigs for meat, chickens for eggs or butchering for Sunday dinner, and a garden for fruit and vegetables.

Unlike many lumber villages, Bloomer was lucky enough to not only have a good source of water, but a railroad that connected them to large cities south, such as Chippewa Falls, Eau Claire, Milwaukee and Chicago. As the woods played out, instead of the village rolling up its wooden sidewalks and heading for greener pastures, men turned their full attention to farming and the same trains that once carried lumber, now hauled animals and crops. Bloomer, once known as Vanville, after its first settler and founder, became well-known for its potato crops, shipping as many as 200 carloads a week. The ever resourceful citizens continued to find ways to over-come the twists and turns of the economy and turned Bloomer into a thriving agricultural shipping point. In 1890, 18 cars of lumber were shipped out. In 1902, just twelve years later, only two cars of lumber were loaded, but 191 cars of potatoes, 32 cars of grain, four cars of hay, seven cars of livestock and two carloads of miscellaneous items were taken from Bloomer to points south. It was truly a farming community.

Carl Ruff

Norb was born into such a farming family. In the early 1860's his grandfather, Carl Ruff, along with four brothers, Godfried, William, Antone and Joseph and two sisters, Barbara and Catherine, came from Germany to southern Wisconsin, then to an area northeast of Bloomer known as Brush Prairie. There, Carl and his wife, Magdalina, along with their son, Edward, born in 1879, homesteaded. Three older children had died during the black diphtheria outbreak in 1878 and 1879. Seven more children were born to the couple after Ed.

On April 9, 1907 Ed and Lena (Hassemer) married and rented a farm on Brush Prairie for five years before building a farm just outside of Bloomer. While the buildings were under construction they rented a home in town.

The Ruff farm circa 1926. Note the railroad cars in the upper right side. Main Street ran between the farm and the railroad tracks.

Finally, in 1914, Norb's father, Edward, his mother, Helena (also known as Lena) and his siblings, Herbert, Norma, Richard and Lorraine moved to their farm on what is now part of North Main Street. The sixty-acre farm, barely a quarter mile from the village line, was backed by a creek with its fields and pastures running along Mill Pond. The Ruffs milked eight or nine cows and had pigs, chickens and other stock.

Five years later, on June 4, 1919, Norbert Casper was born, the only Ruff child to be born on the family farm. A short time after, Norb's grandparents retired from their Brush Prairie home and built a house next to Ed and Lena.

Like many men of his era, Ed was a jack-of-all-trades, using his many skills to provide for his large family. Along with being a farmer, Ed was a drayman, delivering products from the depot to businesses and homes around town. He was also a butcher. In the fall of the year he would go out to farms to do the fall butchering. His regular route included Ed Lund, Charlie Miller and Wes Raven who all lived west of town. The farmers all worked together on each other's farms during butchering time.

On the first day the animals would be killed, dressed and hung up to cool. This might be three or four hogs and one beef. On the second day the meat would be cut

Ruff pasture along Bloomer Pond. Note the wagon tracks from the pastures to the farm. Today this is all built up with houses, including Norb's.

3

up, lard rendered and sausage made. Norb's father charged $5.00 a day for this service along with a lot of the equipment needed.

"Sometimes he would even let his youngest son, age four, spend the day and learn the trade. My job would be to help chase the pigs out to be shot and bled. If the evening and darkness arrived before we were finished, I might have to hold the lantern, just right, so he could split the hanging beef carcass down the center of the back bone from tail through to the neck. There was no electricity on farms at this time and naturally no refrigerators or freezers so the meat had to be taken care of differently than today. The splitting was done with a special two-handled saw which had a blade about two inches wide. I still have the saw of my Dad's and have used it many times.

At the end of the day, which would sometimes be at eleven at night, the men would gather, play cards, drink beer and tell stories. They also tested the day's sausage. After Ed left, the farmer would smoke his own sausage and cure the hams and bacon in salt barrels. The salt brine was regular non-iodized salt. The farmers added enough salt to the water to float an egg, then added some of the side pork to cure for a few weeks

When Norb was four years old, he and his father took the Chicago Northwestern from Bloomer to Chippewas Falls. Then they caught the Sioux Line to Boyd. His Uncle John met them with a large sleigh and took them to Edson, Wisconsin to learn to make maple syrup.

for bacon. When the meat was fully cured, the farmer would bury it in oats in the granary to keep until Easter. No air could get through the grain, which kept the meat frozen. Other pieces of the side pork would be sliced and fried out until nearly done. Then the fried pork would be put in crocks and the grease from the frying out would be poured over top. The same could be done for pork chops and pork steaks. The crock would be put in a cool location. The lard or grease would keep air from getting to the meat. At mealtime the quantity needed would be dug out, grease and all, and reheated. Lean pork trim went into sausage along with beef trim. The fat would be ground and cooked down then

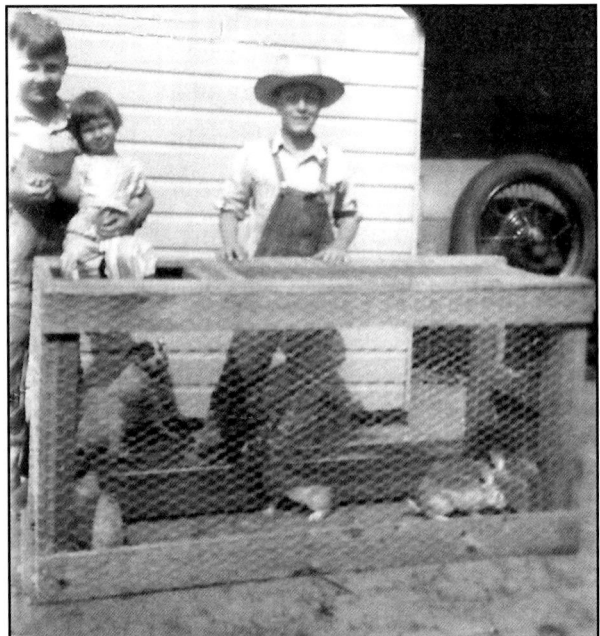

As many young boys did, Norb raised rabbits.

4

pressed out for cooking lard. Some children had lard on their sandwiches at school instead of butter or jelly.

"The halves of beef would be cut into quarters with some being sold to neighbors. The remainder was cut up for roasts, steaks and sausage meat. All the bones from the beef was used in soups.

Cutting and shocking grain with his father. This is about where the fairgrounds are located.

Some of the nice lean beef would be cut in cubes, browned in hot beef kidney suet either in hot water baths or pressure cooked in jars. This would keep for a couple of years. Some of the lean beef would be dried and smoked for jerky or dried beef."

In the winter Ed had space in the back of the local Farmer's Store Implement building where he sold sausage, chunk meat and cut up beef and pork. Ed would buy live animals from local farmers and butcher and cut them up at his farm. In the afternoons, after school was out, the family would butcher four hogs and one beef. Then in the evening until eleven or twelve, with each child assigned a job, they would make sausage from the prior day's meat. Norb's job was to wash casings for the sausage. Then the meat and sausage was taken to the shop. Because the building was not heated, it was perfect for keeping meat cold, but not so perfect for those working in the store.

"All through grade and high school classmates called me Butch Ruff. Some still do. My older brother, Dick, was big Butch, and I was little Butch."

The family owned about eight acres of open land at Keystone about twelve miles away. Besides cutover stumps in the fields, the rest of the forty acres was woods. There they cut wood and hay and during the winter, hitch horses to a sleigh and haul the wood and hay back to the Bloomer farm.

Their cows were herded, by the children, a mile to a pasture along Mill Pond that was part of the farm. The cows were kept in a corral and milked by hand. There was a small milk house that contained a cold water tank to keep the milk cans cold. In the morning, when Norb walked or drove the model "T" pickup out to the pasture to milk the cows, there were already people fishing along the shores of the pond. When the weather became too cold for the cows to stay in the pasture all night, Norb herded the cows out every morning then herded them back to the farm at night where they stayed in the barn. His mother sold this raw milk for six cents a quart at the house. Today Norb can look out the back and front windows of his house to that same pasture and farm land.

Norb had a horse that he raised from a colt. "After cultivating row crops like corn and potatoes with horses all day, I would tie up the other horse to a tree and Barney and I would get his harness off and we would go swimming in the pond. He would make a big circle and come back to the same spot we started from. When his feet touched bottom, he would just stand. I would crawl up on his back and dive off two or three times. Then we'd go to shore and harness up again, and I would put my clothes on. Nobody lived on the lake at this time."

As mentioned earlier, Bloomer was a large potato-producing area. Norb's family grew fifteen to twenty acres of potatoes, which were shipped on the railroad or sent to the local starch factory. Growing potatoes was a long process that included the entire family. In Spring the grandparents cut up last year's left-over potatoes for seed. Then the father or older son planted the potatoes in early May and once the potato bugs appeared, applied paris green (bug

Norb's First Communion
from St. Paul's Catholic Church
Bloomer, Wisconsin

poison), and then dug up the potatoes in October. When the potatoes were dug, the mother and children picked them up and put them in the potato boxes for their fathers to load into a wagon to take to town. School was closed for two weeks during which time most students worked on either their own family's farm or for another farmer. The city children could make $7.00 a day if they were good workers. This is how they bought their school clothes. Norb can still hear the clip clop of horses hooves and the creak of the potato wagons as farmer after farmer brought his crop into town, rolling past Norb's house.

Ed also planted peas for the local canning factory which the farmers had to harvest. To make life a little easier, much of the work was done with neighbors. Like the threshing bees, farmers went from farm to farm helping harvest crops. Then everyone had to go home and milk their cows and do chores for the day.

When Norb was four years old he had what was to be the first of many close calls in his life. Norb was with his father one afternoon while he drove cattle to the pasture. One cow was being particularly stubborn making Ed angry. He picked up a rock and threw it at the cow. The rock glanced off the cow and hit Norb in the head. Norb was taken to the hospital in Chippewa Falls, and during an operation, the doctors removed a small part of his skull on right side of his forehead.

6

He was in the hospital for several days. The newspaper reported it as "a very close call."

Squirrel and rabbit hunting when Norb was about four years old.
L-R: Brothers Herb and Dick, Paul Wolf, Ed and Norb.

The Sled Deal

"When I was nine or ten years old, I got just what I wanted for Christmas – a 'Flexible Flyer' sled. This was the Cadillac of sleds. The runners were flexible so it was easy to steer going down hill. My sister Lorraine, who was five years older than me, borrowed it to go riding down John Langer Hill with a group of girls. This is the same hill east of Bloomer on the way to the golf course. We used to use this country road since there was little or no automobile traffic in the wintertime. Most cars were stored in the garages without their batteries during the winter months.

When Lorraine got home I got the bad news. Some group of boys had stolen my pride and joy. The next day my older brothers and I went back to the hill area, but we didn't find a sign of it. Lorraine didn't know the boys' names, so we had little to go on. When spring arrived and the snow melted, my sled was found in a ditch on the side of the hill on this road. There was one broken board on the right edge. My Dad took it over to Albert Henneman's blacksmith shop and he repaired it. Naturally we never knew how the sled was damaged. It could have been hit by the county slow plow while in the ditch. You can bet my sister didn't get another chance to borrow the sled again. I still have this sled"

In May of 1931 tragedy struck the family.   Ed, then 52, spent the day planting corn, and, as he did every night, had a small lunch before going to bed. About midnight he suffered a major heart attack and died. At that time, Norb, his mother and his sister, Lorraine were the only ones living at home. His oldest brother, Richard was in college, Herbert had also left home and Norma was married. In a flash, Norb became the man of the family. He was twelve years old.

The next four years were busy ones for Norb. Having entered school at the age of four, he was

7

already out of grade school the year his father died. During high school he got up in the morning, fed the animals, milked cows, delivered milk to the local condensary and then went to school. At noon he came home, changed clothes, fed the cows, changed back into school clothes and walked back to school. At four o'clock he again came home, changed clothes, scooped up manure from the barn, hitched the horses to the sleigh and unloaded it in piles in the field, milked cows and did other chores, then did his homework. With the help of a hired hand, along with his regular chores, summers were spent plowing, planting, making hay, and harvesting the crops. It was a rough life for one so young, but this discipline served him well in years to come.

The mid-thirties, the years Norb farmed, were dry years all over the United States. Nothing grew. Norb planted corn and when it was time to harvest, instead of a corn binder, he used a grain binder because the corn was so short.

The local canning factory had farmers switch from growing beans to peas, since peas did not need as much moisture to grow. One year was a particularly dry season for all crops, and for the third year in a row, Norb planted peas. The crop was so poor that at the end of the season he owed $350 for seed.

Even though life was difficult, Norb did find time for one of his passions—fishing. With the farm running along the pond, finding time and a place to fish was as easy as standing on the banks and throwing in a line. This passion continues to this day.

Another pastime was taking target practice at the rats that congregated along the shore opposite the Ruff farm. One of the local meat

markets kept hogs penned up along the south shore where they fed them scraps from their shop. It was also a place to dump bones and other remains of butchered animals, making it an ideal place for rats. The south side of the pond had not yet been developed, so there were no houses, no boat docks, just the shore, ice-covered pond and those rats.

It was March 29, 1935 and Norb was a junior in high school. He decided to meet his best friend, Bob Koehler, and shoot some rats. But Bob was helping a neighbor dig a basement and would not be able to meet him until later. Taking his dog, Smokey, and his 22-caliber, single shot, bolt action gun, (which he still has) Norb cut along the creek and crossed the dam. The water level had been lowered so crossing the dam was not a problem. The short-haired, brindle-colored dog sniffed his way along, sometimes meeting up with Norb, sometimes running off in his own little world.

For some reason there were no rats around that day, so being a little bored, Norb walked further west along the shore. He noticed the upper portion of the pond was open and decided the tip of the open portion would be good for target practice. Norb took aim and pulled the trigger. The splash of the water excited Smokey, also known as "That Damn Dog," and he ran out onto the ice. Before Norb could stop him, Smokey broke through and landed in the icy water, his paws hanging onto the edge of the ice.

There was an empty crate on the ice, so Norb peeled off his jacket, took the crate and went out onto the ice, cautiously walking to within eight or nine feet of the dog. He knelt down on the ice, and as he reached out for the dog, both knees and hands broke through and he belly flopped into the water. Grabbing hold of Smokey, Norb lifted him out of the water and onto the ice. Norb was not so lucky as he kept breaking off ice, landing back in the water time after time. Finally getting a firm grip on the ice, he pulled himself out, grabbed his gun which was still on shore and headed home, the dog trotting behind. By the time he met up with Bob at the dam, everything on Norb was frozen except his joints. He needed to get warmed up fast.

Norb and Bob had built a shack along the pasture behind the farmhouse. It wasn't much, just two bunks, a stove, a calendar with a thermometer attached, several potato buckets under the bunks, a little hatch on the door that opened to see who wanted to get in and a padlock on the door. It was a perfect hide-out for young boys. This is where Norb and Bob headed.

Since they hadn't been planning on using the shack that day neither had brought along the padlock key. Bob crawled through a window and Norb slowly followed, his clothes cracking with each movement. Bob started a fire in the stove while Norb peeled off his ice-encrusted clothes. By the time Norb was in his birthday suit, the thermometer read 120 degrees, which felt great to Norb, but Bob, sweltering in his dry winter clothes, crawled back out through the window and stood outside. The temperature rose inside the shack and the air was getting smoky. Norb looked up. The entire cardboard ceiling was on fire. Norb grabbed his wet clothes and beat at the flames, but to no avail. Then he remembered the potato buckets.

Potato buckets were metal and had screens on the bottom. When potatoes were dug up and put in buckets, dirt fell off the potatoes and shifted down through the bucket through the screens. At this time the buckets were

Bob Koehler

filled with coal the boys had picked up along the railroad tracks to use in their stove. Norb grabbed bucket after bucket looking for one with a solid bottom. He finally found one and tossed it out the window to Bob who filled it up with water from the creek and passed it back to Norb. It took several buckets of icy water to put out the flames. Now, not only were his clothes wet again, but they were covered with soot from trying to put out the fire. After putting the stinky, sodden mess of clothes back on, he trudged back to the house. When he got home he told his mother he'd had a very bad day and was going to bed early.

On July 4, 1937, Norb and a group of friends went fishing on Long Lake north of Bloomer. As Norb was rowing, an eleven pound northern jumped into the boat, making Betty Norris scream. Norb is on the left, Eileen and Pork Erickson are next to him. Betty is in front of Pork. Doc and Mrs. Norris are the two on the right. Doc was a chiropractor in Bloomer.

While Norb was growing up, there was a Bloomer man who played a large influence on Norb's life, especially during the war. Martin Weber, Jr. lived in a small house across the creek behind the Ruff farm. He was considered the city photographer, taking thousands of pictures of Bloomer and the surrounding area along with other parts of Wisconsin. Martin befriended Norb and triggered his interest in photography. When Norb was sent overseas, he purchased an old bellows camera in Australia, along with developing supplies and took pictures of his life during WWII. The pictures were developed in a garbage bag in his tent. Norb and Martin remained friends until Martin's death in 1978.

Another person who played a huge influence on Norb was his brother, Herb. As the eldest, when their father died, and since Norb was so young, Herb filled the male role in Norb's life. In January of 1941 Herb had to have emergency surgery for appendicitis. The surgery did not go well and he needed a blood transfusion. At 10:00 in the evening Herb was given a direct blood transfusion from Norb. Herb lived about ten days. He was thirty three years old and left his wife and two children, Don and Marilyn.

Herb Ruff

Norb and his mother continued farming until 1936 when he graduated from high school at the age of 16. His mother, with the help of a hired hand ran the farm for another four years when Norb went to college. She then auctioned off the cattle and machinery and rented the land to a local farmer. She continued living in the family house until her death in 1964.

Chapter Two
From Farmboy to Pilot

Norb turned seventeen the summer of 1936, the year he graduated from high school. At that time he and his mother were still running the farm, but it was difficult. His brother, Dick, who had graduated from UW-Madison in 1933, was now working in Detroit for Young Brothers Industrial Oven Company. He had met his future wife, whose family was from Detroit, at Madison. Dick came to Bloomer for a visit and invited Norb to live and go to school in Detroit. His mother hired a man to help run the farm for a few more years so Norb could go to college.

Norb agreed to follow his brother to Detroit where Dick also taught at the Detroit Institute of Technology. When Norb arrived in Detroit he had eighty dollars in his pocket, just enough to cover tuition at the university. He took a full load of classes during the day which included general chemistry, organic chemistry, qualitative and quantitative math, zoology, biology and physics. Since he was still too young to get a job, Norb found covering bills a major problem. Between that and having no real interest in getting a degree, during his second year in Detroit he went to Ditzler Color Company, a division of PPG (Pittsburgh Plate Glass), and was hired to work in the lab washing glassware and doing

Ditzler Color Company aka Pittsburgh Plate Glass

general clean-up, for which he received twenty dollars a week while continuing his education at night at Detroit Institute of Technology. Four-year college graduates received twenty-five dollars a week at this same lab. Even though Ditzler wanted him to work throughout the year, during the summers Norb would go home and work on the farm.

In January of 1938, after two and half years in Detroit, out of money, the depression at its peak and no jobs available, Norb went back to Bloomer to farm, but by then his mother was ready to sell. Norb would need to find work elsewhere.

At this time, one of the oldest businesses in the village was the brewery, which was started in 1875 by John Wendland and Fred Adler. Despite several fires, changes of ownership and prohibition, during which time the facility was raided by the feds, the brewery struggled on. In 1935 it was purchased by Al Tankenoff. Al was Jewish, which the village citizens did not like so they boycotted his beer. Desperate to get his product known, he gave the beer away. The people of the village

Bloomer Brewery

realized beer was more important than bigotry and his beer, if not Al, was accepted.

Tankenoff was a proud supporter of the troops during WWII, and he earned a contract with the war department. It was the end of the war that finally caused the demise of the brewery. When he lost the war contracts, Tankenoff bottled what beer was left in the beer vats and shipped it to England.

In 1938, at age nineteen, Norb was given a job at the brewery by Al Tankenoff. At fifty-two cents an hour, Tankenoff was paying the highest wages in the area. Norb was hired to load and unload trucks, sometimes getting calls at all hours of the day or night for one to two hours of work. Eventually he also washed bottles, filled kegs and any other job that needed to get done. Except for one summer working for Leo Bischel, a local farmer, Norb spent his summers home from college working at the brewery. Norb and Al became friends, and when Norb came home from the service, there was a case of beer waiting for him at his house. Many years later, after the war was over, the brewery building would once again play a role in Norb's life.

The summer Norb worked at Leo Bischel's farm his day started at 4:30 am when he fed, curried and harnessed the horses. He had already had breakfast at home before walking the mile to the farm. His noon meal was taken at the farm. If the hay was dry, he would work until 9-9:30 at night, then walk home and have supper. He worked from haying time through the potato harvest, earning $1.00 a day.

In the fall of 1938, Norb made a decision that was to affect the next eight years of his life. He registered at Central State Teacher's College at Stevens Point, Wisconsin. During this time the Civil Aeronautics Authority gave a certain number of college men at many colleges a chance to get their private pilot's license. In addition to regular college courses, during evenings and other times off, Mr. Ritzel, a physics instructor, taught ground school. Since there was no qualified airport at Stevens Point, the students drove to Wausau, a city thirty miles away.

Ten men from Norb's class were chosen to take the first course. With three or four men to a car, they would drive to Wausau to fly under the instruction of Archie Towle, who lived at the airport in part of a hangar with his wife and seven or eight of his children. Archie's eldest daughter Marie, at the age of sixteen, was the second youngest woman pilot in the United States and was known as quite a hellion in the air. One time her father grounded Marie for doing acrobatics at low altitude over Wausau. One of the ten men selected for training, Lyle Grimm, married Marie. Many years after WWII Lyle and Marie managed the Wausau Airport after Archie's death from a flying accident at the home airport.

The first plane Norb flew was a Taylor Craft. One plane had a 55 hp bycoming engine, the other had a 65 hp Continental. They were basically the same aircraft, where the student and instructor sat side-by-side with dual controls. After approximately eight hours of flying time, the students would usually solo; after thirty-five hours (about which half was dual and half solo flying), they received their pilot's license. Most of the ten men from Norb's class ended up flying during the war. Before a student went up alone, he was instructed on what to do on that flight. It could include maneuvers,

This 40 hp Taylor Craft, owned by Bob Koehler, is much like the first one Norb flew, except the one at flight school was 65 hp and had dual controls for training. Fred Henny is standing by the plane.

flying to another town, strange field landings, etc. Norb did his first solo flying on 4/4/40.

"Around 1938 to 1941 there was a lot of local interest in private flying in Bloomer. The airport was east of town alongside of what today is the Pines Dance Hall. Bob Koehler, Elmer Rowe, Elton Krenz, "B-Y" Meindel (Vernon) and the Amenson brothers all had airplanes in hangars out there. The flying was pretty much self-taught. There were no licensed instructors in the area. Only a few had private licenses. Just before WWII started, Bloomer had over fifty people flying – five of which were women. Most would put skis on the planes for winter flying off snow or frozen lakes.

During Norb's second year at Stevens Point (1939-1940) he roomed with two friends from Bloomer, Herb Trankle and Harold Jenneman. Trankle's father was one of the village doctors and delivered Norb. Like Norb, Trankle and Jenneman had their private pilot's license through the second CAA program, but did their flying at Wisconsin Rapids under Al Pottage.

With the war escalating in Europe in 1940, the Wisconsin/Minnesota 32nd National Guard was called up and many of their classmates headed for the southern states for maneuvers and training. In October of 1940, the government started the draft. One night the three friends discussed their options. They all liked to fly and none of them wanted to be drafted in the army as a foot soldier. The government was sending Army and Navy recruiters to colleges near major cities to recruit aviation cadets. There was no Air Force academy at this time. In order to get into the Air Corps as cadets, men had to have two years of college or pass a written equivalency test. In mid December of 1940 one of the teams of doctors and nurses from the Army Air Corps was in Wausau giving physicals. At this time only one out of ten would pass the physical. The three men decided they would go to Wausau to see the Army Air Corps recruiter since the Navy Air Corps wasn't coming until the following week. Trankle went the first day and passed the physical. Norb went the second day and passed. On the third day, after Jenneman passed the exam, the recruiter asked him, "Where the hell is Bloomer?" because all three had passed the physical with flying colors. Lyle Grimm took the physical the same day as Norb, but did not pass the exam. He later became a flying instructor at a Primary Flying school during the war. Norb signed up to become a cadet on December 23, 1940.

The men thought that since they had joined at the same time, they would go into training together. Instead Trankle went in first. Ten weeks later, in April, Norb went, then ten weeks after that, Jenneman was called. The only time they would meet again was for one hour at Randolph Field near Stamford, Texas when Trankle was graduating and going to Advance Flying School, Norb was becoming an upper classman and Jenneman was just starting.

Cadet Pilots were never sent to flying schools near their hometowns. Too many killed themselves showing off by flying over girlfriend's homes, their hometown main streets, their own homes and so on. So men who were raised in Texas were sent to California or Arkansas and those from California to Texas or Arkansas, etc.

There were three flying schools a pilot went through before he became a Second Lieutenant; Primary, Basic and Advanced. Of the three men, Norb was the only to fly fighters. Trankle was too tall and flew bombers and Jenneman went into observation, hence they ended up in different schools after basic at Randolph.

Primary Flying School at Stamford, Texas, April, 1941. "We flew Stearmans, WACO, P-17s and P-18s." The building in the background is the barracks.

Norb's primary school was at Arledge Field in Stamford, Texas where he spent five weeks in the lower class. At that level the "dodos' were hazed until five weeks later when they moved to the upper class and became the "big honchos." This was true for all three schools. They took classes for half the day and flew Stearmans or Wacos with open cockpits the other half. Classes included weather, stress, navigation, Morse code, math and others. The civilian instructor sat in the front of the plane, the pilot in the back. A gosport tube was used to talk from the instructor to the pilot. The students listened and prayed they would not wash out that day or be sent up for a review flight with another instructor prior to wash out. Up to fifty percent of the students were relieved.

Primary Flying School, April 1941 Stearman Aircraft with dual controls. The instructor sat in front and using a gosport tube, was able to tell the student in the back what to do. If the student did something wrong, the instructor would whip the wooden control back and forth, smacking the student back and forth between his knees.

In a booklet, *The Plane Wrangler*, used for graduation for the classes of 41-H and 41-I, F/C Donald Hays, on staff at Stamford wrote about the cadets. Norb graduated in the class of 41-I.

"The Flying Cadet is emblematic of young American manhood. Herewith are set forth his duty, an objective as a future officer in the United States Army Air Corps.

To those who have not experienced previous military training, many of the regulations may appear stiff and absurd. To rise early, dress hurriedly, double time to Reveille formation, return to the morning shave, be off to breakfast, and through the day's work, are all part of a Flying Cadet's curriculum. The day's work may consist of flying, walking the ramp, ground school, or drill.

Throughout the entire day he is governed by the spirit of the Flying Cadets—honor, discipline and character. Each duty or sleeping hour is carefully directed to shape him into an officer and gentleman.

The life from which he came permitted laxity and non-conformity. In the Air Corps Training Detachment he learns to rise on call, dress neatly, appear on time, and obey orders from a superior officer. Mental and physical hygiene become a habit. Here he learns to become an individualist in conformity with other individuals.

In learning to fly, he learns caution, judgment, precision, and receives a training superior to any in the service.

He has been selected from the ranks of those men who are physically perfect and far above average mentality. He learns to incorporate these qualities, with the best of training, thus he is transformed into an air pilot of the first degree.

In the Air Corps Training Detachment, as a Flying Cadet, he avails himself of an education in aviation, one of man's great achievements. He learns to conduct himself as a gentleman. He serves his country with a zeal and perseverance beyond that of the layman. His is the duty to protect his country and fellow citizens against all that assail them."

Cadet Ruff

The booklet had several items that give a good idea of what life was like for the cadets hoping to stay in the Corps and not "wash out."

"General Procedure for Washing Out
(Dedicated especially to the Dodos.)

Never look around before turning.
Never pay attention to the 'T.' It's just an ornament.
Just jerk the controls, and don't forget to cross them occasionally.
Fly your rectangular courses with three corners.
Pay no attention to the weather, it's just for the farmer.
Smoke in the hangars or while sitting on the gas truck.
Taxi not less than thirty miles per hour.
Always practice maneuvers where there are no landing areas.
Fight for the right of way, you were there first.
When taking off make it resemble a pylon eight.
Call your instructor by his first name, never Mister.
Don't bother to know the regulations, don't even read them.
On check rides, don't pay any attention to Captain Arnold; he is just joking."

"The Most Around Our Post
Wanted: A ticket to Randolph Field.
Embarrassing: Running out of altitude during a spin.
Inexcusable: Roundhouse corners on rectangular patterns.
Enjoyable: Thumbs up after a check flight.
Tiresome: Dodo rest.
Exacting: Flight Instructors.
Extinct: Pretty girls. (for that matter, just girls.)
Dreaded: Elimination Check Flights
Disastrous: Washing out.
Common: Mud!!!"

"A Dodo's First Impression of Military Life

Altruistically speaking, a dodo's conception of life as a flying cadet might be described as that of a haven of paradixe [sic]—wings, adventure, the rank of an officer, excellent compensation, and a carefree life. Buttressing this haven were the many articles written, the radio scripts presented, and the colorful advertisements.

Upon induction and arrival at the Lou Foote Flying School, A.C.T.D. Stamford, Texas, however, a dodo's idealistic portrayal was subjected to barcellating moments of happiness and disappointment. The sudden change from an independent and personal existence as a layman to the strict obedience and precision required of the dodo, or potential Air Corps officer, made it difficult for a dodo to acclimate himself. Regulations and orders of all types and descriptions were issued and each dodo was expected to immediately obey each order and regulation. No flaw or error could exist. Mental precision and alertness became the dodo's life theme. 'Hangar' flying predominated in the various discussions carried on in each bay and the fear of 'wash-out' preyed on every dodo's mind.

Coupled with this mental torture was the physical torture exacted on a dodo's soft, layman physique after weary hours of marching squads, platoons and companies.

However, a dodo in his altruistic conceptions expected precise and intense military drill and military phraseology, but, in addition, he soon learned that he must be on the alert for blackouts, air raids, three point landings, dodo rest, etc. He soon became acquainted with such household items as brooms, mops, sheets, etc. His first and foremost thought became that of cleanliness and thoroughness, for one demerit means one hour's ramp-walking. At mess he became so intrigued by eating square meals, sitting at attention with eyes front, making square turns, calling the control tower, that his appetite was non-existent. He learned that spending three hours at ground school – awake – was mental hell. His ears became accustomed to the mournful sound of reveille and taps, and the shrill sound of a

17

whistle sounding formation call, which, of course, meant double time.

However, after two weeks, a dodo's readjustment and acclimation, guided by that definite hurricane spirit and dogmatic desire to become a full-fledged officer in the United States Air Corps, gives him a new determination to prove to all concerned that dodos still can take it!!!"

The following was written by Frank Wrigglesworth, who was from Eau Claire, Wisconsin. He and Norb rode the train together on the trip down to Texas. Frank retired from the military after twenty years.

"The Dodo's Lament
From Eau Claire, Wisconsin, my own home,
To Stamford, Texas, where the buffalo roam,
Came the order to go as Flying Cadet,
Here I am and the land's all wet.

The planes are on the line, and
Where is the one that I call mine.
It flies fairly fast and maybe to the moon,
But all that it lacks is a pair of pontoons.

We get our shoes shined and the whistle does blow.
We march through the mud and could use a good tow.
We take it and smile like the soldiers we are.
In hopes that some day we'll get a gold bar.

"STAMFORD DODO"

When the mess call does sound,
From the bunks we do bound.
We hustle and push to get out of our bay,
For if we are late we will see Mr. Bray.

We get our good food and circle the field,
We call out our name for someone to yield.
We follow the pattern and come in and land,
Then must remember to eat with one hand.

This all part of the life of a dodo,
We have to be glad or we never will solo,
Kelly is our ultimate, but not for the present,
To be upper-classmen would surely be pleasant.
                                 ---Dodo Wrigglesworth."

Randolph Middle School was called the West Point of the air and was located near San Antonio, Texas, where Norb flew BT-14s, a low wing mono plane built by North American. Norb was interested in flying fighters and luckily was sent to Advanced School at Ellington Field near Houston where he flew the AT-6. It must be noted that during their time in these schools, the pilots never received any training in gunnery, skip bombing, dive bombing, firing from plane, flying in formation or fighter tactics.

Later, after graduation, the pilots were assigned to a tactical unit. They read the plane's manual and had to be able to find the instruments, gun switches, etc. during a blind-fold test. Pilots also read the technical orders on that particular airplane and answered questions. After that they started the engines and took off. Since it was a one-seat plane, there was no one to tell them what to do once in the air.

While at flight schools, student pilots lived in quarters provided near or on the fields. They were paid $60.00 a month with $6.60 a month taken out for life insurance. Uniforms were dress blues, with the shirts being a lighter blue than the slacks. Like all military facilities, days were regimented and orders strictly abided. If a cadet broke a rule, he received demerits that he had "to walk off." Upper classmen "hazed" lower classmen, with such things as having to memorize the shows on base, who the actors were, what parts they played and then recite this information—backwards.

While at Randolf, Norb roomed with Stenstrom and Wakefield. Each room had four bunks, but they were lucky enough to have just three men in their room. On the door of each room was a list showing who was

B-14 built by North American. It was used in basic training at Randolph Field. It was a single-wing monoplane. The men in the picture were Norb's roommates, Stenstrum, Norb, Wakefield.

in the room and which bunk was theirs. A daily roster showing where the cadet would be at each time of the day was placed in the blanket fold on the bunk. That way if the cadet needed to be reached, the daily clerk could look at the roster on that cadet's bunk and know where to reach him.

Rooms were inspected and had to be perfect. No water drops in the sinks, no water dripping from faucet, no dust anywhere and bunks made up so tightly, you could bounce a nickel off them.

"The Saturday inspections were 'white glove' inspections. He (the inspector) would wear white cloth gloves and wipe the top surface of drawers and doors. He would check the faucet with gloves on—if any water showed up, you got demerits. It meant you had milked the faucet.

If anything was out of order, demerits were given. Each day Norb's bunk was made up to perfection—at least that is what he thought. Stenstrom on the other hand, was a rather sloppy fellow and his bunk showed it. Each time they had inspection, Norb would receive demerits for his bunk and Stenstrom would go on his merry way. It seemed the harder Norb worked to make his bed perfectly, the more demerits he received and would spend his Saturday evenings "walking" while Stenstrom and his buddies headed into town. This went on for some time until Norb noticed the list of names on the door. His name was written where Stenstrom's bunk was and Stenstrom's name was placed under Norb's bunk. Norb had been getting demerits for Stenstrom's sloppy work. Norb never did find out if the error was done on purpose or not.

"At Randolph Field, in the late summer, the upper class could elect to buy cars. If you lasted this long – you were a good bet you would finish training, as far as the National Bank of Fort Sam of Houston was concerned. So they would lend money to buy new cars. A 1942 Chevrolet would be about $750.00. (I did not buy a car since I had borrowed money from my mother to go to college and wanted to pay this back, which I did from New Guinea the following year.) The car salesmen were allowed to come on base and talk to the cadets. As a cadet you got $60.00 a month. As a Second Lieutenant, you would be paid $200.00 a month. The bank payment went directly from the government to the bank. Later when I was ready to graduate from Advanced Flying School I borrowed $250.00 to pay for uniforms. Pants were $16.00, blouses $65, wool shirts about $16.00. This was winter or formal uniform. Summer clothes were cotton and a little cheaper. Officers paid for their uniforms other than flying gear, which was issued."

Norb graduated from training school on December 6, 1941 in the class of 41-I Texas as a Second Lieutenant. The next day, Pearl Harbor was attacked and Norb's life, like millions of other Americans, would change.

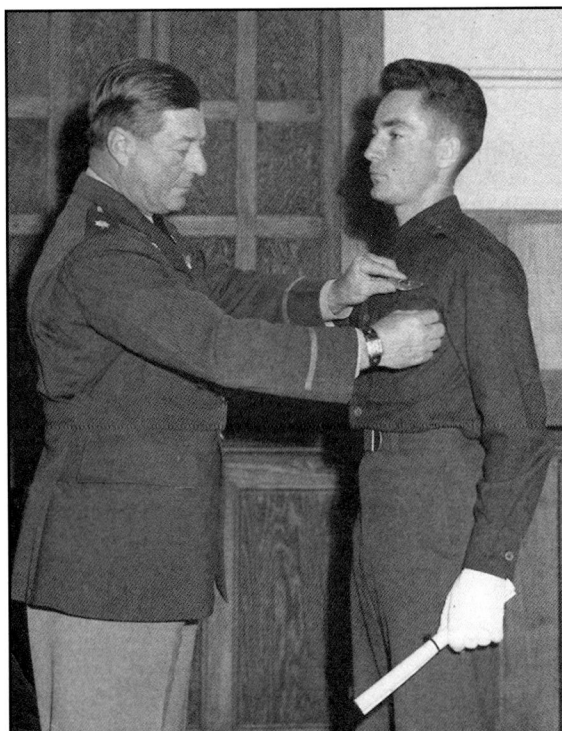

Graduation Day
Colonel Ried and Second Lieutenant Ruff

Chapter Three
Australia

*D*ecember 7, 1941, was a day that started like others, except Norb and his buddies were now Second Lieutenants for the Army Air Corps Reserves. Spirits still high from graduation most cadets were granted leave. Norb and one of his classmates, Jim Selzer, had dates for a picnic. Jim had a large Buick with leather seats and a rumble seat where Norb was riding. By today's standards he was not driving that fast, but while taking a corner one of the girls slid over, the door opened and she fell out. They had music playing on their portable radio at the picnic. Suddenly the radio announcer broke in and reported the attack on Pearl Harbor. They had no idea where Pearl Harbor was and thought maybe it was in Alaska, but knew things were bad when the announcer said, "Alert – all military personal immediately report back to your base."

People at Ellington Field were running around like crazy when the men returned to base. They thought the Japanese would attack within the hour. The pilots were told they were to receive new orders and when Norb told the Base Operations Officer that he already had his orders to fly to Selfridge Field in Detroit to fly fighters. The officer said, "Not anymore you don't," and tore up Norb's orders in front of him.

For the next nine days, Norb and his classmates waited for their new orders and for the cadets at the other flying schools to graduate. Most Advanced Flying Schools graduated on December 12th. Since the men were now officers and there were no quarters for officers at Ellington Field, Base Operations sent the men to the Blue Roof Motel in Houston and were told to report to base each day for new orders.

On December 12, 1941 the new cadets from all other Advanced Flying Schools across the country in the class of 41-I were rated as Pilots by the War Department. By December 20, 1941 orders were changed and some of this class of 41-I, Norb included, were sent by train to Morrison Field, West Palm Beach, Florida. On December 21 Norb was assigned to the 7th Pursuit Squadron of the 49th Group at Palm Beach, Florida. While there they were supposed to fly P-40s, but because of the necessity of getting the men and planes overseas, they never received any flight training with these planes. While crews disassembled the P-40s and crated them, the pilots were getting physicals, receiving shots, being issued flying equipment, and having parachutes fitted.

On Christmas Day orders were given for the 49th Group to ship out for California. On January 2, 1942 all personnel boarded a train bound for San Francisco. This included the pilots from the three squadrons of forty pilots, and the ground crews to support those planes; ten men to each plane. This meant there were four hundred ground personnel for each squadron, a total of 1200 men. This did not include group commanders, operations officers and other support troops. The train also held the crated P-40s, trucks and all other equipment necessary for the operation of a squadron. In other words—the train was packed. To feed all these men, cooks would go down the aisles with pots and slop food onto plates. The food was poor in quality and quantity and the swaying of the train made eating the slop difficult. The trip took five days.

Upon arrival in San Francisco, the men were herded to the Cow Palace in San Francisco. The Cow Palace, a brand new facility completed in 1941, could hold up to five thousand people and was built for rodeos and stock shows. The first show held in April of 1941 was the Western Classic Holstein Show. Its first major event was the first Grand National Rodeo in November of 1941. Only two weeks after the show closed Pearl Harbor was bombed. The United States Government then rented the large structure for $1.00 per year for the next five years to house troops getting ready to leave for war.

As the war moved on, the Ordinance Department took over the structure and turned it into a large garage for repairing military equipment.

The facility was dark and crowded. All the seats were removed and replaced with row after row of cots covered in olive-drab (od) blankets. Every level, as well as the football field, was filled with these cots used by the men waiting for deployment. No one could leave the building to view the sites of San Francisco because no one knew exactly when their ship would leave. To get to the bathrooms, the men maneuvered through the escape tunnels used for bulls during rodeos. With thousands of soldiers in the "palace" men were constantly in line. Noise was continuous; men getting sick, ambulances coming and going, voices over loudspeakers. "Some of the men with a sense of humor went around mooing plaintively and bellowed like bulls when they received the necessary inoculations for foreign duty." (*49th Fighter Group*)

While at the Cow Palace, Norb had to take his turn as officer of the day, which was like being a mother and father to these young men. MPs were at their beck and call. If an emergency telegram came for a soldier the officer of the day had to get the soldier on his way—after finding him in the mayhem. The loud-speaker system constantly bellowed out orders letting the men in their groups know when and where they were to be.

Finally, on January 11, 1942, the men of the 49th Group boarded the USAT Mariposa, one of the many cruise ships from the famous Matson line remade into troopships. On the day Pearl Harbor was attacked, the Mariposa was in Sydney, Australia, getting ready to sail back to San Francisco on

22

December 11. Like the other famous white ships of the Matson shipping line, the Mariposa was painted wartime gray. The entire personnel or

USS Mariposa, part of the Matson Line of ships taken over by the United States Government. (*Troopships of World War II*, Charles, The Army Transportation Association)

the line, ships (four passenger liners and thirty-five freighters, of which eleven were lost during the war) and other facilities were taken over by the government and used completely for the war.

Traveling alone, the ship sailed for San Francisco, arriving on December 30th. The next day the Mariposa "was delivered to the U.S. Maritime Commission under demise charter sub-chartered to the U.S. Army Transport Service, and workmen began to convert her into a troop ship. By January 12, 1942, she was fully converted, with permanent accommodations for 3,851 troops, and sailed for Melbourne with 4,550 aboard. In the same convoy were the S.S. President Coolidge (lost early in the war) and the S.S. President Monroe. She returned, unescorted, with 14,756 bales of wool." (*Matson's Century of Ships*) (Some sources state the Mariposa left on January 11, 1942)

The Mariposa continued its wartime service, ferrying troops, cargo, missionaries, and refugees to such places as Capetown, Karachi, Liverpool, Glasgow, Mers-El-Kebir, Rio de Janeiro, Arabia, Suez, Somaliland, Port Sudan, Bombay, Scotland and New York. "In 1945, before the war ended, the Mariposa uneventfully crossed the Atlantic ten more times, carrying troops both ways. By coincidence, the V-E and V-J Day announcements were both made when the Mariposa was in almost identical positions, passing through the Straits of Gibraltar. When the war ended, she continued on to Rio de Janeiro for disembarkation of Brazilian troops. The succeeding months saw the Mariposa still serving the Government, making several more trips in the Atlantic and later moving troops in the Pacific." (Ibid)

"The 127 officers and 999 enlisted men of the [49th] Group made up about one-third of the ship's passenger list. Members of the 35th Interceptor Squadron, the Headquarters and Headquarters Squadron of the 39th Pursuit Group, some miscellaneous units and a few civilians completed the list.

Part of the Group's aircraft rested in the ship's cargo hold. Among other items, the Mariposa carried nineteen crated brand new P-40E-1 Warhawk fighters. The Mariposa was part of a convoy made up of the SS Coolidge, loaded with thirty-two P-40Es and 3,270 passengers and the SS Monroe which carried another seven P-40Es as deck cargo. The convoy sailed at 1630 on 11 January, with the light cruiser USS Phoenix leading the naval escort. On the fourth day at sea, the Group celebrated its first birthday and was told of its destination—Australia. They were told that when they arrived thirty-seven of the P-40Es were to go to Holbrook and the remaining fourteen were to be stationed at Geelong." (*49th Fighter Group*)

The officer pilots were separated from the rest of the crew. They were given state rooms that normally held four passengers, but now held six pilots. The enlisted men slept below ship in trelais, which consisted of a standing pipe with a chain hanging down holding up four bunks on each side for a total of eight bunks. But no matter if officer or enlisted, the twenty-day "cruise" was boring. Men spent their time shooting craps, playing poker, writing letters, listening to the war news and telling stories about their hometowns, their sweethearts and families. Friendships were forged.

"There was one thing to be said, though, about the government taking over a cruise ship, crew and all. The food was out of this world, the best food during the war," Norb said. "Once we had roast pheasant under glass served by civilian waiters with cloth napkins and tablecloths. On this first trip made by the Mariposa, the food was already on board for the expected next luxury cruise. I'm sure it was not restocked for other war trips with the same excellent fare."

Church services were held on board with most men attending. Some men held boxing matches among themselves Each night an announcement was made: "Lights out. Black out. Close all ports. Refrain from smoking about the open decks." This was to keep the enemy from seeing the lights of the convoy.

Norb talked about the men's feelings while on the Mariposa. "Pilots were all over-confident, afraid the war would be over before we got there. Remember the Japs were not very good at flying, they all needed glasses. Their airplanes were not very good. They couldn't see in tight turns. We never mentioned the fact that these pilots had five years' experience in China. These first Jap pilots were so very good and we were so very poor and inexperienced."

On February 1, 1942 the convoy landed at Melbourne, making the 49th the first complete United States Army Air Corps Pursuit Group to enter a combat zone since the bombing of Pearl Harbor. After unloading the men, the Mariposa immediately left for Brisbane to unload the P-40s for re-assembly. The three squadrons of the 49th were split up with each going to a different RAAF station near Sydney.

After twenty-one days at sea, the Mariposa felt like home to the men. Before they had a chance to get their land legs, they marched twelve miles through Bacchus Marsh. Each officer had a mussette bag that held toiletries slung on his back as they marched in formation.

"February is a hot month in Australia. The flies were horrible. They are like a housefly, but so tame you couldn't swat them away. They would swarm all over the mussette bags, your eyes, nose, face, lips, everywhere and you couldn't brush them off. Luckily they didn't bite, but they were always on you. As you marched, you watched those flies thick on the mussette bag of the man in front of you.

"After spending twenty-one days on ship with nothing to do, we were out of shape, so the twelve mile hike to Bacchus Marsh was tough. We passed herds of sheep, some that crossed the road we were on; and taverns that we couldn't stop at. At camp our 'bunks' were in a one-story wood building. There was straw on the floor with blue Australian wool blankets for beds. The blankets had been used by others, so we got acquainted with Australian lice quickly. We were fed Australian food by the Aussie military—mutton stew for breakfast, lunch and supper. Lamb is not good cold no matter how you handle it. Beer, which was only available in town and not on base, was served warm. Butter came in brown cans about six inches in diameter and three inches high. On the side of the can was written, 'Guaranteed not to melt at 120 degrees.' It probably wouldn't have melted at 500 degrees. It made excellent axle grease." -Norb

Once, while spending time in Melbourne, Norb and two buddies, with no money in their pockets and no place to stay, headed for the USS Coolidge still in dock and sacked out in bunks. Luckily the ship did not leave during the night and they were able to get off the next morning.

The 7th's time at Bacchus was another hurry-up and wait situation. They did exercises to get back into shape and waited for the planes to be assembled. They played cards to relieve the boredom and waited to be sent to pick up the planes. They shot craps and waited anxiously to get into combat. A few weeks later, the 7th Squadron was sent to Bankstown, outside of Sydney. The other two squadrons were shipped elsewhere.

This is where they did their first checking out and slow-testing of a fighter aircraft, the P-40E. At this point they hadn't flown anything for four months, let alone a fighter. Just going from the smaller AT-6A with 300 hp to the larger P-40 with 1200 hp was a challenge. There was no training for combat formation nor firing of guns. The men were given a training manual to read over. After studying the manual and sitting in the cockpit, a blindfold test was given. The pilot sat in the plane and one of the 'older' pilots told them to touch various controls, as well as answer questions about the plane. After they passed this blindfold test, they were sent up in the plane—solo. "We were just not combat ready, yet here we were, sent to fight the Japs."

Meanwhile an event was occurring that was to cut into the already small supply of planes and pilots in the South Pacific.

"Less than a week after setting foot on Australian soil 1st Lt. Robert L. Morrissey, Commanding Officer of the 7th Squadron, was placed on detached service by Col. Wurtsmith [Commander of the 49th] and ordered to proceed to Perth. At Perth he was to arrange

Prior to the war, the USS Langley was a coal tender and then converted to the United States' first aircraft carrier. Note the seaplanes on board used for hauling supplies before the war. After the US government started building aircraft carriers, the Langley was again used as a seaplane tender. (*49th Fighter Group*)

for the transportation and loading of a number of P-40s aboard the USS Langley, which was due to put in at Freemantle on 14 February. The Langley was being used as an aircraft ferry and would deliver the P-40s to the 17th Pursuit Squadron (Provisional) on Java.

Arriving in Perth after a grueling transcontinental trip, Lt. Morrissey checked into a hotel and went to Headquarters for instructions. A Royal Australian Air Force (RAAF) officer was assigned to him in the project and they immediately got to work planning the operation. A quick survey determined that only one route would be feasible and that the P-40s would have to be towed some twenty miles from the landing field to the dock area. Taxiing them was out of the question due to the distance involved. And the strain such a trip would put on the engines. The only possible way was to tow the P-40s on their own landing gear, which meant that they had to be towed backwards.

Lt. Morrissey found a local machine shop to make a special towing attachment that would do the job and prevent damage to the P-40's tail. By working around the clock, enough attachments were completed in time for the P-40s arrival. Next they rounded up the necessary trucks and personnel to move the fighters and control the route. They had decided that the best time to move was after midnight in order to avoid traffic problems on the road. This left only two problems to be solved. There were two major obstacles along the route to the docks. At the dock entrance a large pair of concrete pillars barred the entrance and in the exclusive part of the town eight large trees (on private property) were too close to the road for the wings of the P-40s to pass.

Morrissey got the dock workers to dynamite the pillars, but when he wanted to contact the owners of the trees, the RAAF liaison office quickly vetoed the idea. He knew the locals and told Morrissey that they would never agree to losing their stately old trees. Instead he offered a simple and direct solution to the problem. He suggested stationing a crew of men with the proper tools at each tree with orders to fell the trees promptly at midnight! This was done and the move went on without a hitch. The convoy arrived and Langley docked at 0300, with the loading process being started immediately. By 0830 all the P-40s were stowed aboard. In all, thirty-three P-40s had been loaded in five and a half hours.

The P-40s had been flown to Perth from several locations. Initially twenty-five aircraft under Maj. Pell and eleven others under Lt. Boyd D. "Buzz" Wagner were to make the transcontinental flight from fields around Brisbane. The ferry route was Amberly via Richmond, Laverton (near Melbourne), Port Pirie, Forrest, Kilgoorie, and finally Perth. A number of planes were grounded along the route by mechanical failures and mishaps, such as blown tires, and of the thirty-six P-40s that started the trip, thirty-three arrived in Perth. Lt. Wagner was a well known pilot and was one of the few American pilots in Australia with combat experience. He had served in the Philippines with the 17th Pursuit Squadron, scoring five kills against Japanese fighters during the Philippines Invasion and became the Air Corp's first ace. [In the South Pacific]

When the loading was completed, Bob and "Buzz" were invited to have breakfast with the Langley's Skipper, along with some of the P-40 pilots bound for Java. They were thinking about staying aboard to get into action when a message arrived which ordered Wagner and Morrissey to report back and under no circumstances to go to Java. Morrissey bid the Langley people Bon Voyage, good hunting and good luck, then went back to his hotel room. Opening his room door, he was confronted by the highly agitated tree owners, demanding his scalp. He told them why it had to be done and promised that he would carry their complaints and claims with him and turn them over to Headquarters,

U.S. Forces in Australia. He told them he was sure that they would be compensated for the loss of their trees. When they persisted he told them that there was really nothing else he could do to resolve the matter, so they left and he finally got to bed.

Actually Wagner and Morrissey didn't realize how lucky they were by not being allowed to sail aboard USS Langley. On 27 February, just seventy-four miles short of her destination, the Langley was sunk by Japanese bombers. Although all of the P-40 pilots were taken off by the USS Whipple and USS Edsall, two were injured seriously enough to be transferred later to the USS Pecos. The pilots aboard the Whipple were transferred to the Edsall for a fast run into Java, however, the ship ran into a large Japanese Task Force and was sunk with the loss of all hands including the pilots and ground crews." (*49th Fighter Group*) (The Langley was the first US aircraft carrier to be sunk in the Pacific.)

Norb adds more to the episode. More will be written later about how the 80th factors into Norb's military career. "We have Col. Gerald Dix listed as a member of Headhunters and rightly so. He joined the 80th in P-39s about August 1942. He was the 1st pilot decorated in the 80th. He received the Purple Heart for injuries received on board the aircraft carrier Langley when it was sunk in the Java Sea on February 27, 1942. The Langley had been loaded with 32 assembled P-40s at Fremantle, Australia along with 33 pilots. Two pilots Dix and Ackerman were wounded on the bombing and were transferred to the Pecos, the remainder of the pilots, 31, were transferred to the Edsall. The Pecos was bombed a little later and sunk. This time Dix said they were in the ocean a matter of hours when they were picked up by the Whipple. This ship made it back to Fremantle on March 4, 1942. The Edsall was lost with all hands including the 31 pilots a few hours after the Langley bombing. Two Jap battleships sent her down. There had been 672 aboard the Langley and Pecos when it left port, 440 had been lost. No count of loss

Petrei Dix at 12 Mile after receiving the Purple Heart. (Picture by Norb)

of people aboard the Edsall. Some of this I remember talking with Gerald back in 1942." In a 2001 letter to Gerry, Norb wrote: "I've often remembered you were the first man decorated in the 80th. You rec'd the Purple Heart for injuries on the Langley. Do you still carry that piece of flack you had in your wrist? I also remember you telling about the P-40s rolling off the deck of the Langley as it listed to one side. Those kind of memories never leave."

Norb was at Bankstown with the 7th Pursuit Group, 49th Squadron until March, 1942. Before he had a chance to go into battle with the 49th, he was reassigned.

P-40N. The first fighter Norb flew when he was with the 7th Squadron of the 49th Group. It was built by Curtis Wright and used by the 'Flying Tigers' in China in the 1930s. It was the only plane that had wing guns with 3 - 50s on each side. The difference between a P-40N and a P-40E is the exhaust. The exhausts on the P-40N were flared back.

Different squadrons flew different type planes in the early days of the war in the Pacific. Until February of 1943, in the 8th Fighter Group, the 35th, 36th and 80th squadrons mainly flew P-39s and P-400s. The 49th Fighter Group, the 7th, 8th, and 9th Squadrons flew P-40s.

A lot of pilots did not like the P-39, thought it was an inferior plane, which it probably was compared to what the Japanese were flying. But Norb liked the plane. "To me you 'put it on and you took it off.' The engine sat behind the pilot. The nice wide landing gear, the nose wheel – you could see out ahead both on the ground and in the air – not like the P-40. Certainly it needed a super charger, but so did the P-40. Now when the first P-39 was delivered to the U.S. government, it did have a super charger, it was refused – a big, big mistake. We were pretty well dead in the air at 20,000 feet and the Zero's were up at 30,000. We could out-dive the Zero any time you had altitude enough, but *do not try to turn* with them. Just keep your speed up. I don't think there was much advantage of one airplane over the other. The big advantage was in the experience of the pilots. Those first Jap pilots were fantastic – remember they had five years' experience, and we had none. Some of us were lucky and that was so important."

"We had no gunnery practice, no formation flying up to this time. We were easy meat for the Jap pilots. They were experts, but after they were lost, the younger ones were not up to par. We didn't have anybody to tell or show us what to do or what not to do. I mentioned before that the 80th CO had been over to England flying "Spits." The tactics he learned were wrong for use against the Zero. We should have had German ME-109 pilots teach us tactics. Both the P-40 and P-39 were heavy non-maneuverable airplanes same as the German 109 or 190. The main thing, *stay alert* during the *complete flight*. Keep your speed up. Do not try to turn with Jap fighters. Pray a lot and stay lucky." Norb flew 75 of his 125 missions in P-39s and P-400s.

"The P-39 was definitely not an interceptor, nor was it a match for the Japanese Zero. Air warning usually was received too late for the slow-climbing Airacobras to intercept the bombers before they had dropped their bombs, and if Zeros were escorting, the American pilots had their hands full. All the Americans could do was make a head-on pass at the enemy and dive for the deck. The P-39 possessed good armament: a 37mm cannon and 2 .50 caliber machine guns in the nose, and 4 .30 caliber machine guns in the wings. It was a rugged aircraft and could take a lot of punishment, but it did not possess the high rate of climb or acceleration to be an interceptor, nor was its maneuverability good enough for it to be a fighter. It did prove to be a good ground-support aircraft if top cover could be provided, but nothing like this was available during the trying days in the spring of 1942." (*Pacific Sweep*)

"Maintenance was carried out under the most trying conditions. Mechanics and armorers were always under danger from strafing and bombing attacks. Spare parts were almost nonexistent, and wrecks were cannibalized to keep the Airacobras going. The mere fact that the ground crews were able to keep as many of the aircraft in the air as they did is

The P-400 was the British version of the P-39. The propellers and guns were synchronized so the bullets would go through the propeller. It was the only plane where the engine sat behind the pilot. There was armor plating behind the head, neck and shoulders of the pilot. The glass in front of the pilot was 2 1/2 feet thick. There was no protection from the sides. The British made changes to the P-39s before realizing this ground plane did not meet their needs. They needed interceptors not ground planes and gave the P-400 back to the United States, who sent them to the Pacific Theatre.

indicative of their skill, ingenuity, and devotion to duty."

The P-400s were the British version of the P-39. It was made in America for the British, but after flying the P-400 and making changes, they found it did not meet their needs as an interceptor. The P-400 had a 20mm cannon firing through the hub of the propeller instead of a 37mm. The speed indicator was in km (kilometers) instead of mph. It also had a different paint job. So, after rejecting the planes, they were given to the inexperienced American pilots.

Even though the P-39s did not work for the English, the Russians loved the P-39s and received a large number of them. They were an excellent ground support aircraft with seven guns firing.

The P-40 was a "tail dragger." The nose was up in the air with a little wheel in the back. This made it difficult to taxi because the pilots couldn't see above the nose. They had to perform a zigzag taxi to where their planes were parked. Other planes, like the P-38, B-25, B-26, P-59, F-80 and all later fighters had "nose gear" where the weight was in the nose, so it is not pointing up. This allowed the pilots to see over the nose to taxi. The P-40 had been used by the American Flying Tigers in China, as well as in the Philippines.

Some squadrons used numbers to identify their planes and others used letters. Planes in the 80th were identified by yellow letters. The tip of the tail and engines were green with white stripe. Norb was 'X' and 'K' in the P-400. As planes crashed or broke down beyond repair, mechanics scrounged parts from those planes to repair others, no matter which squadron they were from. That is why some planes have a letter as well as a number. Pilots were not assigned planes but flew whatever was available therefore they did not put their name or their crew chief's name on their plane. When a squadron was relieved, the planes were left behind. Later, when P-38s were issued, pilots were able to make their planes more personal by giving them names, having pictures painted on them and listing their name and their crew's names.

The 80th Pursuit Squadron

While Norb's group was nearing the end of the long ocean voyage to Australia, an event was happening in New York that would affect the majority of his time in New Guinea. The 80th Squadron, part of the 8th Pursuit Group, left by train from New York for San Francisco. Unlike the 49th, they, along with the 35th and 36th Squadrons, had no time to stay at the Cow Palace, but were immediately boarded onto another Matson liner, this time an old cattle boat, the SS Maui at Fort Mason, California. Because of sabotage to the ship, it did not sail with the rest of the convoy, and the men were given a weekend leave at San Francisco. When they were re-boarded, rumor was they were headed for the Philippines and many were surprised when on March 6, 1942, the 80th landed in Brisbane, Australia.

After six days, they were moved to Archer Field near Lowood to wait the arrival of their P-39s. Archer Field was nothing more than a cow pasture; a big grass field with no runway. When the planes finally showed up and were reassembled, the 80th started training along with pilots from other groups.

"At the same time the 80th Squadron [in March, 1942] was based at Lowood with meager staffing. The 80th was left behind as a replacement unit for the 35th and 36th Squadrons when they moved up to New Guinea. Phil Greasley was still commander of the 80th with George Austin as Operations Officer and Bill Greenfield, Bill Frank, Todd Dabney, David 'Pinky' Hunter, Harley Brown and Gentry Plunkett as assigned pilots. Plunkett was transferred to the 35th as a replacement pilot during the initial Port Moresby operations." (*Attack & Conquer*)

80th Squadron officers and pilots at Lowood
L-R: John Guttel, killed July 1943, Norb, Phil Cook, (with hat on), Gentry Plunkett (in front of Cook), who was attacked by crocs and survived to tell the story; Bill Greenfield, Operations Officer (face is in shadow); Todd Dabney, and Phil Greasley, CO. Guttel and Norb joined the 80th at the same time.

Non-pilots assigned to the 80th were: Matthew J. Buchele, Intelligence Officer; Ronald C. Mallock, Adjutant and Mess Officer; Paul F. Freund, Engineering Officer; James C. Bragg, QM and Technical Supply; Abraham Barocus, Communications; Robert T. Peters, Armament and Chemical Warfare; and Nicholas E. Patrick, Medical. All these men, plus the pilots listed above were First Lieutenants.

On March 17, 1942, after ferrying planes and training and without having yet seen any combat with the 49th Pursuit Group, Norb was assigned to this 80th Pursuit Squadron where he remained until October 1943 when he was finally granted leave to go home to Bloomer.

"Training went on during the early spring of 1942 in desperate hope of providing an adequate air shield against Japanese advances toward Port Moresby – and the coast of Australia. The greatest problem was that the new American pilots were not oriented toward the quirks of weather in the Australia and New Guinea area. The 8th pilots were traditionally geared toward professionally conducting themselves in military situations: they were disciplined and eager, but they did not yet comprehend the vagaries of meeting seasoned Zero pilots over the wild country of the Owen Stanley Mountains. There would be difficulty in simply reaching the operational bases around Port Moresby, as the young pilots would discover to their dismay in the coming weeks." (Ibid)

For the next few months the pilots of the 80th continued training in P-39s and P-400s while sending pilots and planes to replace those killed in the 35th and 36th Squadrons in New Guinea. Unfortunately their training did not include firing from the planes. There was no jungle training or what to do if they crash landed in the jungle. And any training they had at this time from their leaders was wrong because their knowledge was based on fighting in Germany. Here the enemy was different, their planes were different and their mentality was different. As Norb said, "We were pretty much flying by the seat of our pants. Never shot a gun from the plane until my first combat mission. My first flight was in a P-40 in the 7th Squadron – I didn't fly this airplane – it flew me. I survived the first fourteen to fifteen hours without damage to me or the 'kites'" (Australian term for airplane.)

Sydney Bay Bridge (Picture by Norb)

While pilots were waiting for combat, they trained as well as ferried planes from one field to another, which was no easy task in Australia. Like the United States, Australia is made up of states, but instead of fifty, they have five very large states. Since the P-40s were being assembled at Archer Field near Brisbane, men were assigned to travel there and fly the planes back to Bankstown near Sydney. Norb and six or seven other men were ordered to travel to Brisbane pick up planes, deliver them, then return "via the best commercial air route or by rail to their home station Lowood Aerodrome." Does not sound too bad, except the only way they could get to the planes was by railroad. The railroads in each state had a different gauge which meant each time they entered a new state, they had to switch trains. Sydney, where they departed is in the state of New South Wales and Brisbane is in Queensland. The trip was long and tiring.

On one particular trip 1st Lieutenant George Prentice was in charge of the inexperienced rookie pilots who, by this time, had a grand total of seven hours in a fighter. Prentice had one or two more years of flying experience, but no more time in Australia than the rest of the men.

Once they arrived at Archer Field and got their planes, the pilots all got off the ground except Stanley (Bow Wow) Borowski, who could not get his plane started. By the time he got it started, the others were gone. Not having any idea where Sydney was, he ran back to the Operations Building, tore a map of Australia off the wall and took off by himself.

Meanwhile the rest of the men are heading, they hoped, towards Sydney. None of the pilots had maps, and they were not familiar with the terrain. Norb was flying Prentice's wing when overcast came down and they overshot their destination. By this time they were running low on fuel and flying under the overcast one hundred feet above water. When they turned to head over land, they found a solid rock wall. They could not fly over the wall because of the overcast. In the wall Prentice found a narrow entrance and one-by-one, they all managed to fly through and landed in a field near the little town of Nora. The six planes spread out on the field. After spending the night in Nora, a gasoline tanker truck was sent out from Bankstown to refuel the planes.

In the morning they prepared to leave. A young local girl, riding her horse, stopped along the field to watch the American pilots take off. Lt. Prentice and Norb took off. Unknown to them, Lt. King's landing gear was damaged in the landing the night before. As his plane lifted off the ground, the damaged left landing gear snapped off. The plane veered into the horse and girl killing them instantly.

Borowski meanwhile had flown above the overcast and following his map, was the only one who landed at Bankstown.

The 80th also ferried planes to Port Moresby in New Guinea to replace planes damaged or lost by the 35th and 36th Squadrons. These two squadrons were the first units to take the P-39s into combat in the Pacific area. "While the sister squadrons were up in six weeks of combat, the 80th would supply replacement airplanes and pilots to the 35th and 36th from Petrie. There would be a list and a flight from the 80th almost weekly and the saying was 'Here today, gone to Moresby.' I made this list once. The flight leader was Bill Greenfield, a 1st Lt. and operations officer of the 80th. Earlier he and our C.O., Phil Greasley, had been assigned to England during the big air battle spraying 'Spits.' My flying ability was either a little better or worse than the 'trainees' we were sending up. Naturally since I had been assigned to be Greenfield's wingman for some time, he said I'd not be assigned to the 35th or 36th, merely deliver the airplane and return with him to Petrie."

Unfortunately, many of the early casualties did not occur during combat. With inexperienced pilots, pilots showing off, lack of experienced mechanics to repair malfunctioning planes, difficult

Operations building at Petrie

landing strips and weather, more men were lost at any given time prior to entering combat than in combat.

By May 10th, 1942, the 80th moved from Lowood to the Petrie Aerodrome. This airfield was on a deserted farm located near Brisbane. This difficult strip was situated in solid woods. Taking off from this airfield was not the problem as the planes took off against the wind, which was a straight shot for the pilots. Planes always land into the wind and in order to do this at Petrie, because of the trees, they had to make a sharp left turn as they were at low altitude. "Now on the base leg, the trees blanked out the strip and the pilots would over-shoot the last turn and "S" into the field at low speeds and doing the "S" siding turn the airplane would snap roll into the ground. Pilots killed at Petrie were Joe Cole, Causey, Nauman, Ferguson, (my tent mate) and Max Jones. We were usually two to a tent, sometimes three. I packed up personal equipment for five tent mates while overseas and in combat."

"May 26, 1942: 2nd Lt. Max J. Jones (80th), P-39. Killed in landing accident at Petrie, Australia area. He was an unusually short pilot who ordinarily used a pair of cushions in the seat of his P-39 to be able to see out of the windscreen. One of the disadvantages of the Petrie Field was that the strip was partially hidden during landing approach because of the tall trees surrounding the area. It was necessary at times to 'S' turn on final approach to keep the strip in sight. This was a dangerous maneuver at low speed and low altitude and proved fatal to Jones that day." (*Attack & Conquer*)

Max Jones' wreck at end of strip, May 1942.

35

Petrie Aerodrome from Norb's plane. This was an old farm. The farmhouse was converted into the Operations' building. It is the large one with the trucks and jeeps around it. The airstrip was over to the left. More men were killed here at any given time than in combat.

1st Lieutenant George L. "Whip" Austin was killed at Petrie in his P-39 on July 2, 1942. He was the Operations Officer and second in command of the 80th. "Flight Leader Lt. 'Whip' Austin, who often exhorted his charges to 'Close it up!' until his wingman on one mission closed it up a little too far and chewed away part of Austin's wing. Too much altitude was lost in the process and his parachute was not fully opened when he hit the ground." (*80th Fighter Squadron, The Headhunters Squadron History*)

The collision was with Milt Sponenberg, who survived the accident. "Spondenberg and I were very close, came overseas together on the Mariposa with the 49th Group and joined the 80th at Lowood. Sponenberg was a grand guy, very quiet individual. The accident really affected him. I don't believe he ever flew a combat mission with the 80th. I believe he was assigned to Fighter Command."

Norb flew a broken ship formation for Austin's funeral led by Bill Greenfield, a former "A" flight commander. In a broken ship formation one plane in the flight of four is dropped out. After the loss of Austin, Greenfield became Operations Officer. Norb was his wingman on all of his first combat missions. The picture to the next page shows Norb after the funeral. The jeeps and command cars in the background were used to take men to the funeral.

Norb after Whip Austin's funeral.

Some deaths came from just plain foolishness. The death of Tevis Ferguson on July 15, 1942, just five days before leaving for New Guinea, was just such a case. "Tevis came from Grass Valley, California. He and I were tent mates at Petrie; at that time just two pilots to a tent. As a cadet in flying school you could not marry. After graduation you were a 2nd Lt. and free to marry. Many pilots married the day after graduation.

"I heard of one pilot who graduated from flying school, got married the next day (home town girl). He was sent to Panama within a month, met another girl there, got married again. A month or so later he was sent to Australia, met another girl there, again got married to her. The guy that told me this story said he was invited to all three weddings.

Quite a few pilots married Australian girls – George Welch, Cy Homer. Some American girl wrote to her boyfriend, "What have the Australian girls got that the American don't have?" He wrote back, 'Nothing – but they got it here.'"

"In my class of 41I, most of us were on our way overseas in less than a month after graduation. Ferguson, Max Jones, Phil Cook, and Jasper were some of the just-married pilots. We had no electric lights in tents, so Ferguson would spend his evenings writing letters to his wife in front of a large photo of her by candlelight. We know we are soon going up to Port Moresby to relieve the 39th Sqdn. One day Ferguson shows up with this black cocker pup. I made some remark about the pup and what do we do with it when we leave. He said he just wanted something to write to his wife about. Shortly thereafter he's up flying a P-39. Decides to put on a little air

Norb and Ferguson's pup

show – unauthorized – over an Australian flying school near the ocean 30-40 miles away. He is at low altitude and hooks a wing in the ocean and kills himself. I go through his personal equipment, separate it from the military equipment, removing anything that the wife or family should not welcome and box it up for shipment home. Now I got this pup.

"We get orders to go up to Port Moresby and I keep the pup on my lap the whole flight. We had only ten airplanes to take up since we had already used up most as replacements to the 35th & 36th.

Fortunately the weather was good throughout the flight and we didn't have to go to altitude and use oxygen. It was somewhere about 1000 miles from Petrie to Port Moresby, 450 miles of it over the Coral Sea. I forgot who I gave the pup to."

Although Norb does not remember two men from Petrie being killed on the same day, *Attack &*
Conquer states that 1st Lt. Joseph P. Cole was killed in his P-39 in a flying accident at Petrie. The article goes on to say, "The base probably killed and injured more pilots than many of the operational combat bases."

A friendly game of volleyball to relax at Petrie.

James Griffen and the pup.

Upper left-DeJarnett, lower left-Jim Selzer, leaning on rail left-Pinky Hunter, arm on rail-Tevis Ferguson, in back-Guttel or Sponenberg, garrison cap-Charlie Able, right hand on rail-Joe Cole. Of these seven, four did not make it through the war, Guttel, Cole, Hunter and Ferguson.

38

In April, 1942, an incident occurred at Darwin, Australia, that showed another example of non-combative deaths. This one involved the death of one of Norb's classmates.

"Robert D. Jasper – 0-430929 was a classmate from Advanced Flying School at Ellington Field, Houston, Texas, Class 41I. He married right after graduation and was assigned to the 7th Sqdn, 49th Fighter Group at Morrison Field, West Palm Beach, Florida with me. Naturally, we made the train trip to the Cow Palace at San Francisco and the boat ride of 21 days and flew P-40s at Bankstown outside of Sydney. He was just as inexperienced in fighter planes as I was. Naturally we know how far from home we are and all are a little homesick. It must have been hard for those just married.

"Now we are having quite a few accidents in checking out in P-40s which were twice or actually three times the horse power of the A-T6 airplanes we flew in Advanced Flying School – and remember, we hadn't flown any airplanes for 3 to 3 ½ months.

"The war in the Pacific is going badly. Japs have Lae and Salamaua in New Guinea. We are still holding out in Java and the Philippines. As I remember they took over about April 15th, 1942 in the entire Pacific area.

"Now one day in late March or early April, Jasper makes an appointment to see Capt. Morrisey, Sqdn CO of the 7th Sqdn and told him he was not going to fly anymore. He would take any ground job he was assigned to. The Sqdn CO didn't know what to do with him – court marshal for refusing to do duty as trained? I imagine he would refer it to Group Headquarters. Anyway, he was no longer welcome in the group of pilots. I was still in the group at that time just before being reassigned to the 80th with many other classmates, some going to the 35th & 36th Sqdn.

"About this time part of the 7th Sqdn is sent up north and gets into their first combat with the Japs near Horn Island. Now the entire 7th gets sent to Darwin, Australia (in the northwest corner). This would be late February or March 1942. MacArthur is ordered back to Australia and other top officers are called back from the Philippines. They would fly out and land at Darwin for refueling. On one of these flights is General 'Pursuit' George, top leader of the fighter planes in the Philippines. [George had been an Ace pilot in WWI] Jasper escorts the group including, Melvin Jacoby, a Time war correspondent, back to their airplane, a C-45, which is parked near the runway. Lt. Edgar Ball, another of our classmates in the 7th Sqdn, is sitting 'alert' in a P-40. These two P-40s get orders to take off. Ball is the wingman and they take off in formation. Ball gets crowded by the lead plane and gets in the prop wash. This throws his airplane into the General's Lockheed and kills General George, Jacoby, and Lt. Jasper. Ball lives through the wreck. I think this made me carry on throughout the war. If your time is up, it's payday or you 'bought the farm'!"

The story, written up in *49th Fighter* Group said that two men standing in the area ran toward the C-45 trying to warn the men standing near the plane. "The warnings came too late – Ball's P-40 hit the nose of the C-45 ripping off chunks of metal and sending them flying in all directions like shrapnel. The Warhawk's propeller sheared off and spun directly into Mel Jacoby, killing him instantly. The P-40 reared up and over the C-45 and dropped directly on Gen. George and Lt. Jasper, who had driven up to pick up the General. Just before the P-40 hit General George, it clipped Reynolds [another pilot on the ground], tossing him head over heals. He landed, somewhat stunned, with two pieces of metal piercing his foot from top to bottom, although at the time he did not realize he was wounded. Reynolds got up quickly, shaking off his injuries, and helped the others load Gen. George and Lt. Jasper into his jeep. He drove them to the base dispensary, where the base doctor did what he could before they were transferred the twenty miles to the field hospital. Both men were pronounced dead on arrival at the hospital.

"The C-47 that was to take the pilots to Sydney [to pick up and ferry P-40s back to Darwin] finally arrived and now served as a hearse to take the remains of Gen. George and Mel Jacoby to Sydney." (*49th Fighter Group*)

"In May, 1942, I spent about ten days at Cooktown. We were ferrying P-39s and former 80th pilots that were being assigned to the 35th & 36th Sqdn at Pt. Moresby. The prop on some P-39s, being hydromatic, would leak oil which would coat the windscreen making it difficult to see out on landings especially when there was a dusty field. One of these P-39s flown by Bud Schultz was especially bad – my ship was okay. Bill Greenfield, the 80th operations officer was leading this flight and since I was coming back to the 80th at Petrie with him, he gave my ship to Schultz with me to stay at Cooktown for further orders.

"I really enjoyed my stay at an old frame hotel. I met the railroad depot agent and his wife. They invited me to dinner at their home which was on the second floor of the depot. He took me fishing on a small railway hand car up the tracks and north of Cooktown. I've forgotten their names – they had a son in the navy. He showed me how to use a cast net to get bait, also showed me which fish were good to eat and which not. One day an old wood sail boat came into the harbor, a native tribe and a German missionary, were put aboard and moved to another location. I assume it had something to do with the war.

"Each day I would go out and pre-flight my airplane. There was a small airline in and out of the airport. One day an old Aussie prospector came out to take the airline out and talked to me— wanted to know all about the guns. He was especially interested in the 50 caliber guns that fired through the prop and wanted a bullet. I ejected one round and gave it to him. He gave me a piece of quartz rock with gold flecks in the quartz. I still have this piece of ore. One day I got a telegram or a message, "Could I still fly the airplane in the present shape back to Townsville?" I did that and got a ride back to Petrie. The next day I went to the hospital for a ten-day stay with dengue fever. (Dengue "den-gay" fever is like malaria, but is not recurring.)

The plane Norb gave to Schultz was to be the last time it was flown. "May 26, 1942: 2d Lt. Arthur

R. Schultz (35th). P-39F (41-7221). Known as "Bud" Schultz in the 80th Fighter Squadron from which he was on temporary duty to the 35th Squadron. Was in a group of P-39s escorting transports to Wau. Engaged sixteen Zeros southwest of Mount Lawson, and Schultz was missing after the combat. He and Norb Ruff were on a ferrying mission to Port Moresby when Schultz's P-39 broke down at Cooktown, Australia. Since Ruff was supposed to return to Petrie, he turned his P-39 over to Schultz who flew it up to Port Moresby a few days before he was KIA." (*Attack & Conquer*)

"Bud Schultz was shot down over Pt. Moresby on one of his first combat missions on May 26th. We were very good friends thru flying school. His folks met my mother in Texas on graduation day. His folks lived in Illinois, we were from Wisconsin. Late 1943, about November, when I got home, his mother came up to visit me. His dad had died earlier."

Finally, after months of flying and ferrying planes to and from Port Moresby and sending men as replacements, the 80th was permanently assigned to replace the 39th Squadron at Port Moresby. The 39th and 40th Squadrons had already replaced the devastated 35th and 36th about six weeks earlier. On July 20, 1942, twelve pilots, including Norb, flew their P-39s to the 12 Mile Aerodrome, located twelve miles from the coastal village of Port Moresby, New Guinea. The remaining pilots and crew of the 80th (now known as a Fighter Squadron rather than a Pursuit Squadron) were shipped out to Port Moresby on the Dutch freighter, Maetsuyker. This was to begin a long and tiring battle to keep the Japanese, who at the same time had landed at Buna, from coming over the Owen Stanley Mountains. The Battle of Buna, which lasted nearly two years, was the longest battle ever fought by the United States.

Left to right: Cole, Causey, Hunter, Brown, Nauman, Austin, Jones, Greenfield, Boracas, Greasley, Cook, Hagar, Able, Borowski, Frank Buchele. Not all of these men were pilots. Boracas was head of the radio depatrment, Hargar was in armament and Buchele was a ground officer.

41

Ships of the Asiatic Fleet lost in battle between Dec. 7, 1941 and March 3, 1942.

SS PRESIDENT HARRISON

Hong Kong

(1) Scuttled at Corregidor

USS CANOPUS AS-9
USS QUAIL AM-15
USS PIGEON ASR-6
USS BITTERN AM-36
USS FINCH AM-9
USS NAPA AT-32
USS MINDANAO PR-3

(2) Lost or Destroyed

Motor Torpedo Squad. 3
PT-31, 32, 33, 34, 35, 36

PHILIPPINES

7-PATWING10 LOST

MANILA
LUZON
MINDORO
LEYTE
MINDANAO

INDO CHINA

Submarines sunk in battle.

USS SEALION SS-195
USS SHARK SS-174
USS PEARCH SS-176
USS S-36

PALAWAN

Tagilinog

(10) Due to hull damage on a reef ordered to return to U.S.

USS BOISE CL-47

HMS REPULSE
MALAYA
HMS PRINCE OF WHALES
Singapore

(3) Abandoned in Surabaya

USS STEWART DD-224

SARAWAK
BORNEO
Tarakan
Balikpapan

CELEBES
MAKASSAR

(9) The Japanese prison camp that held the survivors of the USS POPE, USS PERCH, and USS ASHEVILLE (1).

Sunda Strait
MADORA
(3) Surabaya
JAVA
Tjilatjap
BALI
LOMBOK
SOEMBAWA
FLORES
Makassar
TIMOR

(4) Sunk in the battle of Sunda Strait

USS HOUSTON CA-30.
USS POPE DD-225

(5) Sunk on way to Tjilatjap

USS LANGLEY AV-3

(6) Sunk south of Java

USS PILLSBURY DD-227
USS ASHEVILLE PG-21
USS EDSALL DD-219
USS PECOS AO-6

Sunk in Darwin

USS PEARY DD-226

Darwin

(7) Due to severe battle damage ordered to return to U.S.

USS MARBLEHEAD CL-12

The following ships, part of the ABDA forces in defense of the Dutch East Indies were also lost in the battles.

Australian
HMAS PERTH

Dutch
HNMS JAVA
HNMS DeRUYTER
HNMS WITTE de WITH
HNMS KORTENAER
HNMS VAN GHENT
HNMS PIET HEIN
HNMS BANCHERT
(12) SS TIDORE
7 MINE CRAFT SCUTTLED
Submarines KX, KXIII, KXII

English
HMS EXETER
HMS ELECTRA
HMS JUPITER
HMS ENCOUNTER
HMS STRONGHOLD

AUSTRALIA

(11) FREEMANTLE

Where most of the ships that were retired from the battle area headed for this port.

Perth
(11) Freemantle

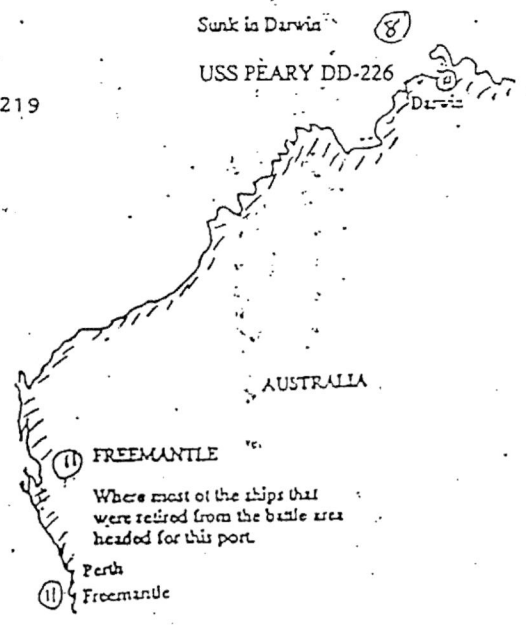

Ships of the Asiatc Fleet Lost in Battle
Between December 7, 1941 and March 3, 1942

1. Ships scuttled at Corregidor
USS Canopus AS-9
USS Quail AM-15
USS Pigeon ASR-6
USS Bittern AM-36
USS Finch AM-9
USS Napa AT-32
USS Mindanao – PR-3

2. Lost or destroyed
PT-31,32,33,34,35,36

3. Abandoned at Surabya
USS Stewart DD-224

4. Sunk in the battle of Sunda Strait
USS Houston CA-30
USS Hope DD-225

5. Sunk on way to Tjilatjap
USS Langley AV-3

6. Sunk South of Java
USS Pillsbury DD-227
USS Asheville PG-21
USS Edsall DD-219
USS Pecos AO-6

7. Severe damage ordered return to US
USS Marblehead CL-12

8. Sunk at Darwin
USS Peary DD-226

9. The Japanese Prison Camp that held the survivors of the
USS Pope
USS Perch
USS Asheville

10. Due to hull damage on a reef ordered to return to US
USS Boise CL-47

11. Lost north of Hong Kong
SS President Harrison

12. Lost or scuttled at Soembawa
SS Tidore
7 mine craft scuttled
Submarines KX, KXIII, KX II

Submarines sunk in battle
USS Sealion SS-195
USS Shark SS-174
USS Pearch SS-176
USS S-36

Australian
HMAS Perth

Dutch
HMMS Java
HMMS DeRuyter
HMMS Witte de With
HMMS Kortenaer
HMMS Van Ghent
HMMS BAnchert

English
HMS Exeter
HMS Electra
HMS Jupiter
HMS Encounter
HMS Stronghold
HMS Repulse
HMS Prince of Whales

American Warplanes at a Glance

AP Features

Here are silhouettes of the U. S. warplanes—Army, Navy and Marine—that will help you to recognize them at a distance. Shown are three views of the planes—when flying head on, when directly above in the sky, and as they look from the side. Given are the company names for the planes and the popular names for them which are now used in Army and Navy communiques.

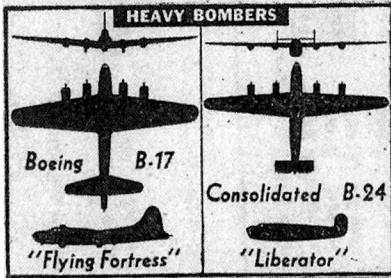

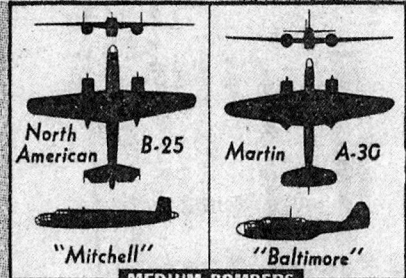

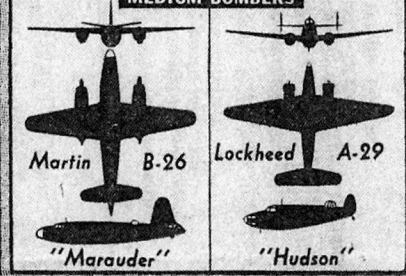

HEAVY BOMBERS

Boeing B-17
"Flying Fortress"

Consolidated B-24
"Liberator"

North American B-25
"Mitchell"

Martin A-30
"Baltimore"

DIVE BOMBERS

Curtiss (Army) A-25 (Navy) SB2C
"Helldiver"

Vultee A-31
"Vengeance"

Brewster SB2A
"Buccaneer"

TORPEDO BOMBER

Grumman TBF
"Avenger"

MEDIUM BOMBERS

Martin B-26
"Marauder"

Lockheed A-29
"Hudson"

PURSUITS

Lockheed P-38
"Lightning"

Republic P-47
"Thunderbolt"

NAVY PATROL BOMBERS

Martin PBM
"Mariner"

Consolidated PBY
"Catalina"

SCOUT BOMBER

Consolidated PB2Y
"Coronado"

LIGHT ATTACK BOMBER

Douglas A-20
"Havoc"

North American P-51
"Mustang"

Curtiss P-40
"Warhawk"

FIGHTER-PURSUIT

Vought-Sikorsky F4U
"Corsair"

Bell P-39
"Airacobra"

FIGHTERS

Brewster F2A
"Buffalo"

Grumman F-4-f
"Wildcat"

Chapter Four
New Guinea

$\mathcal{T}$here were many aerodromes or airfields in New Guinea. Most were named for fallen officers, but were generally referred to by the number of miles from the nearest town. During his time in New Guinea, Norb flew out of several different airfields at Port Moresby; 12 and 14 Mile from July to October 1942; at Milne Bay from November to January, 1943 and then back to Port Moresby at 3 Mile from April to October 1943. During February and March of 1943, the 80th was in Mareeba, Australia, receiving and training in their new P-38s.

It must be noted here that when the military referred to missions, they meant *combat missions*. In between flying these combat missions, pilots were assigned to other flights, such as picking up repaired planes, picking up other pilots or any other assignment they may be given by their CO. Some of these flights included going back to Australia, a long and hazardous 500 mile trip over the Coral Sea – especially when taken without escort. Even while on leave the pilots ferried planes. Although on Mission Reports it may look like they were flying every other day or with several days in between, they were actually taking on other assignments. A mission was considered complete if the pilots successfully escorted the bombers to the site to be bombed, not necessarily if the pilots used their ammo or not. Sometimes if there was ammo left, the pilots would strafe an enemy site on the way home.

"Down the center of the island through Kokoda area was the Owen Stanley mountain range that was well above 10,000 feet and only 50 miles from the ocean on each side. The Japanese made their landing at Gona and Bona (They already had strips at Lae and Salamua) about the last week of July 1942. Large transports and destroyers lay off shore five to six miles with many barges packed with troops between the transports and shore. The troops had rifles and the barges had one 35 mm gun." - Norb

The Japanese advanced along the Kokoda Trail to within twenty miles of Port Moresby. The Wisconsin and Michigan National Guards plus Australian troops held them. (Another Bloomer boy, Mush Turner, was part of the 32nd Division.) Two or three months later the soldiers tried to hike over the mountains to reach Bona, but the terrain, mosquitoes, lack of supplies, heat and Japanese snipers, made the going impossible and they came back.

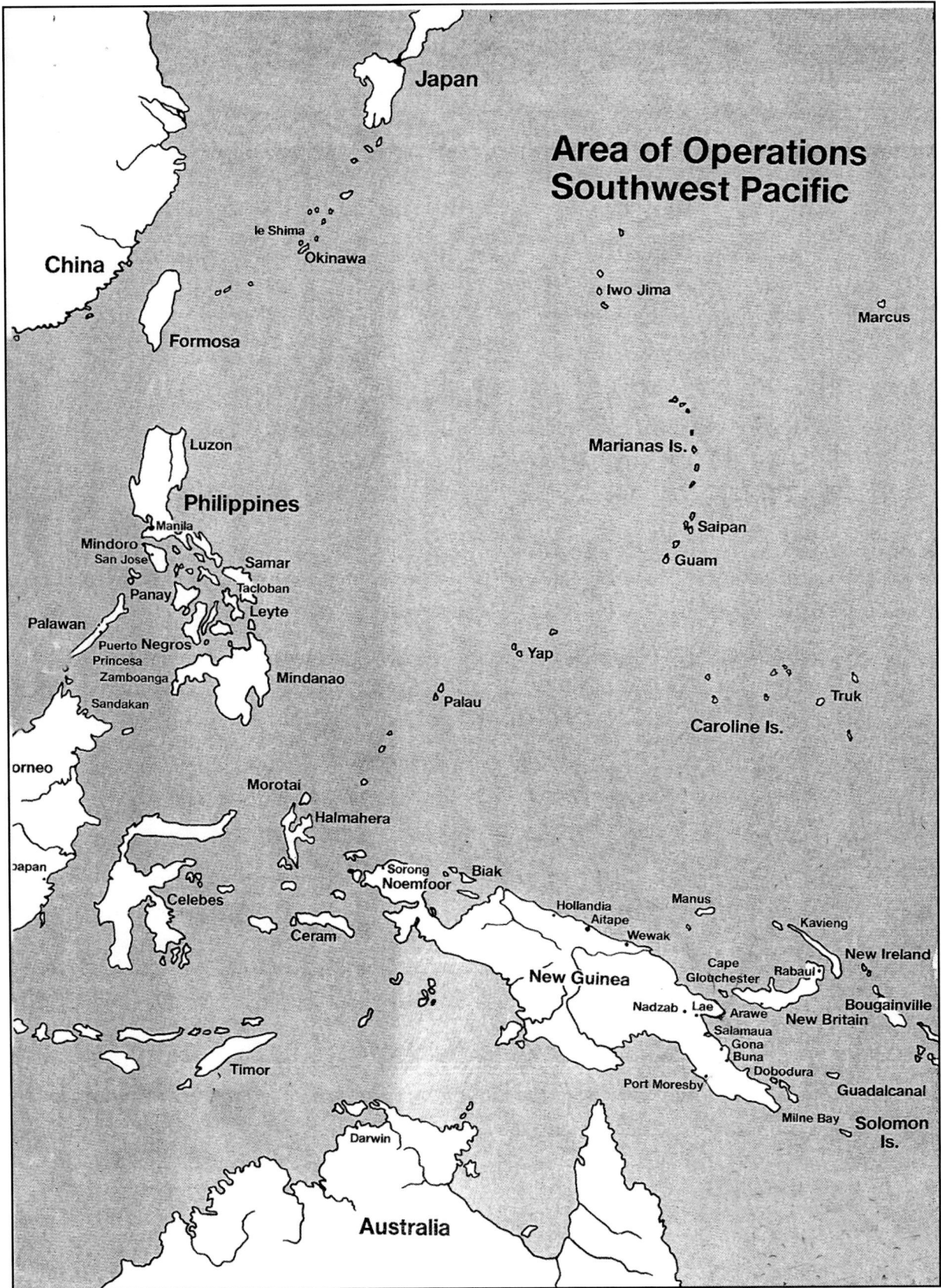

Area of Operations
Southwest Pacific

The entire northern coast of New Guinea from Biak to Doboduara was in Japnese control when Norb arrived.

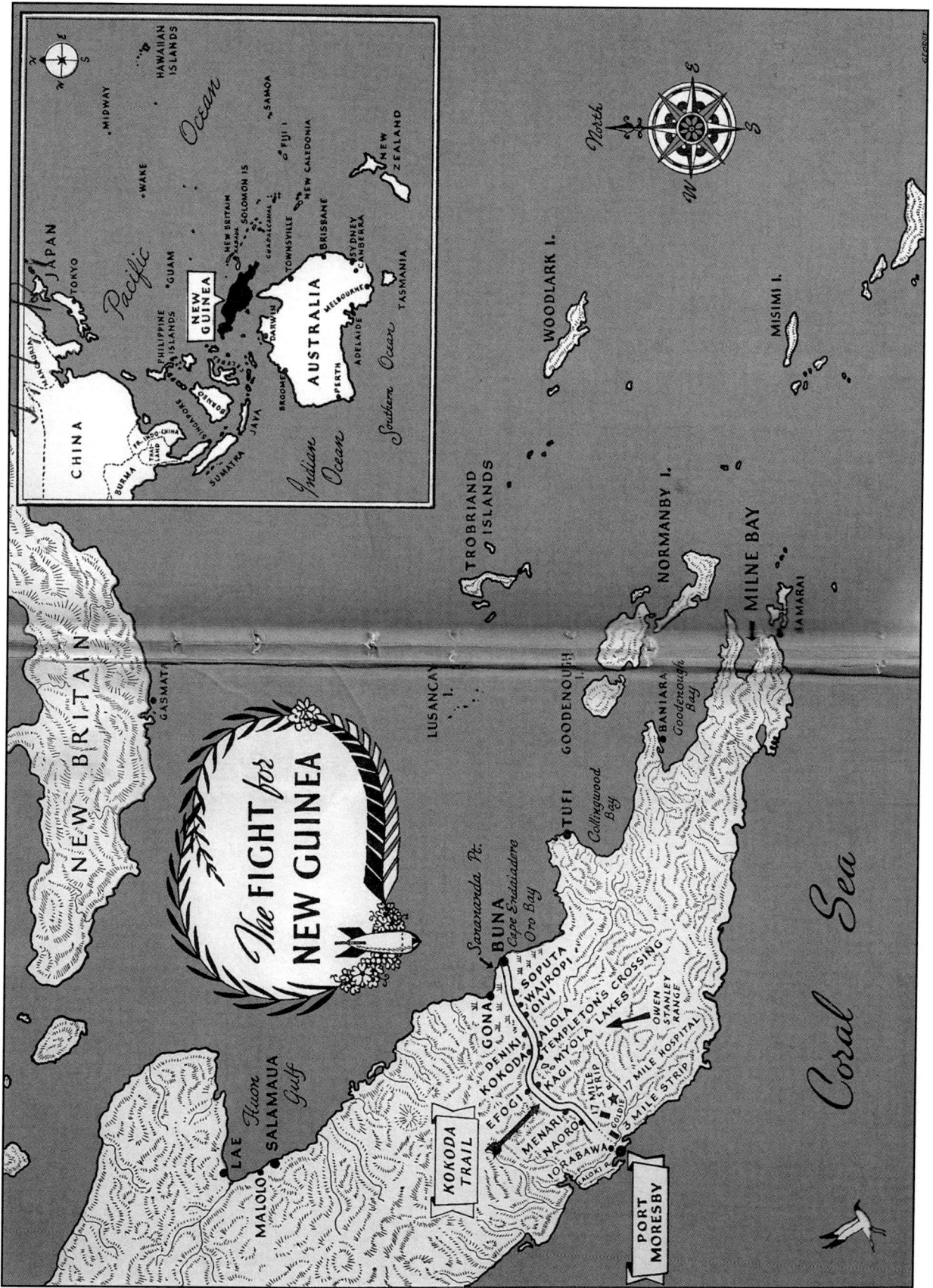

The Fight for NEW GUINEA

Inset map (top)
N E S W

HAWAIIAN ISLANDS
MIDWAY
WAKE
SAMOA
Pacific Ocean
FIJI I.
NEW CALEDONIA
NEW ZEALAND
JAPAN
TOKYO
CHINA
PHILIPPINE ISLANDS
GUAM
NEW BRITAIN
SOLOMON IS
RABAUL
GUADALCANAL
TOWNSVILLE
BRISBANE
SYDNEY
CANBERRA
MELBOURNE
TASMANIA
NEW GUINEA
BORNEO
FR. INDO-CHINA
THAILAND
BURMA
SINGAPORE
SUMATRA
JAVA
DARWIN
BROOME
AUSTRALIA
ADELAIDE
PERTH
Indian Ocean
Southern Ocean

Main map
North
North compass rose (N E S W)

WOODLARK I.
MISIMI I.
TROBRIAND ISLANDS
NORMANBY I.
BANIARA
Goodenough Bay
GOODENOUGH I.
MILNE BAY
SAMARAI
LUSANCAY I.
Collingwood Bay
TUFI
Cape Endaiadere
Oro Bay
Sanananda Pt.
BUNA
SOPUTA
WAIROPI
OIVI
GONA
DENIKI
KOKODA
ALOLA
TEMPLETON'S CROSSING
MYOLA LAKES
KAGI
EFOGI
MENARI
NAORO
IORABAIWA
LALOKI
GOLDI
3 MILE STRIP
17 MILE HOSPITAL
17 MILE STRIP
Owen Stanley Range

KOKODA TRAIL
PORT MORESBY

NEW BRITAIN
GASMATA
LAE
Huon Gulf
SALAMAUA
MALOLO

Coral Sea

GEORGE

47

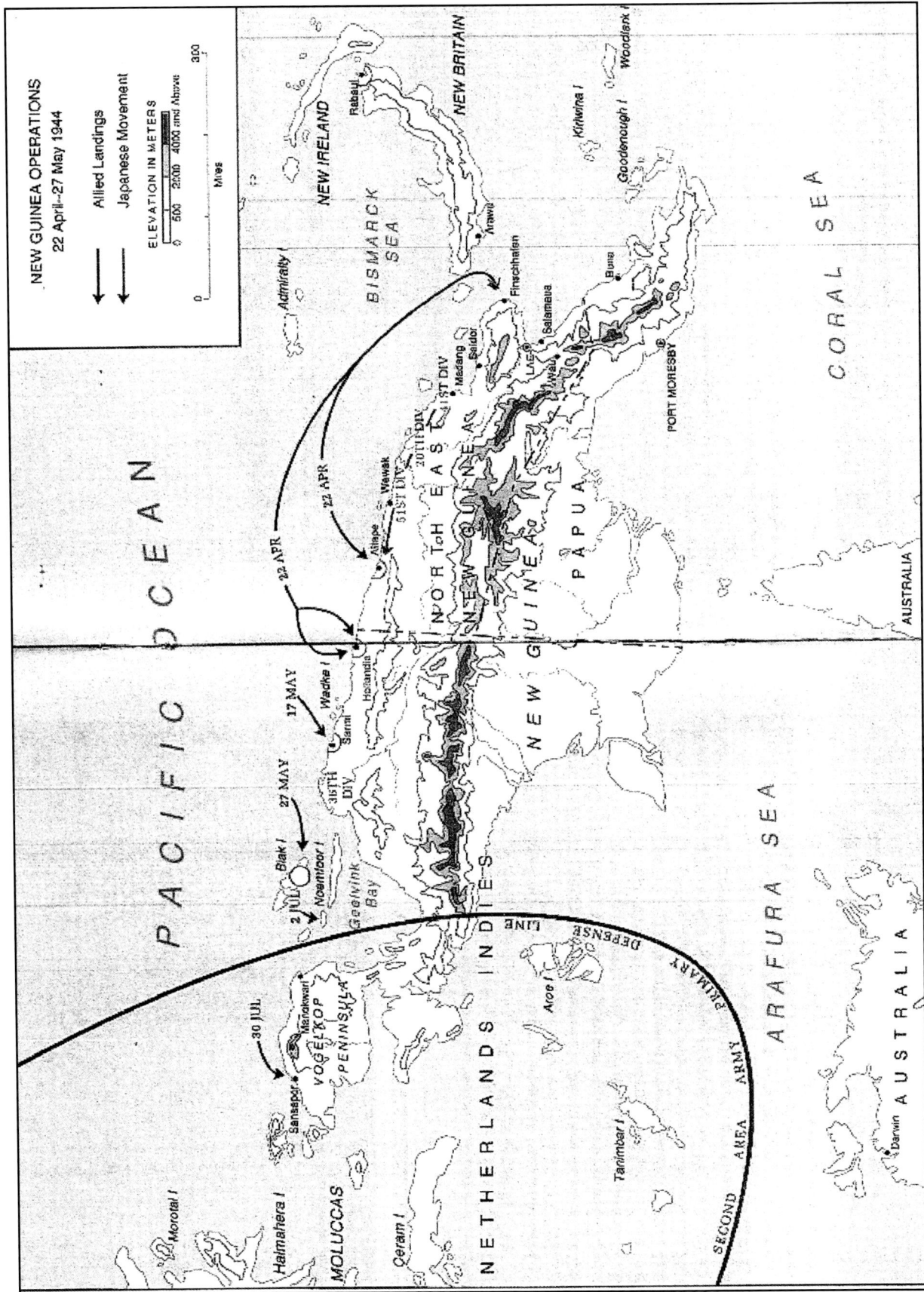

NEW GUINEA OPERATIONS
22 April–27 May 1944

Allied Landings

Japanese Movement

ELEVATION IN METERS

0   500   2000   4000 and Above

Miles

0   300

PACIFIC OCEAN

NEW IRELAND

Rabaul

BISMARCK SEA

NEW BRITAIN

Kirlwina I

Goodenough I

Woodlark I

Admiralty I

Arawe

Finschhafen

Salamaua

Buna

Saidor

Madang

31ST DIV

20TH DIV

Lae

Wau

22 APR

Aitape

Wewak

51ST DIV

PORT MORESBY

CORAL SEA

NORTH EAST NEW GUINEA

PAPUA

22 APR

17 MAY

Wakde I

Sarmi

Hollandia

316TH DIV

27 MAY

Biak I

2 JUL

Noemfoor I

Geelvink Bay

NEW GUINEA

30 JUL

Sansapor

Manokwari

VOGELKOP PENINSULA

PRIMARY DEFENSE LINE

NETHERLANDS INDIES

Aroe I

ARAFURA SEA

SECOND ARMY AREA

Tanimbar I

Morotai I

Halmahera I

MOLUCCAS

Ceram I

AUSTRALIA

Darwin

AUSTRALIA

48

Legend:

— International boundary
— Province boundary
— Line of separation (not a formal international boundary or territorial limit)
★ National capital
⊙ Province capital
— Road

Spot elevations in meters

Scale 1:6,500,000

0 50 100 200 Kilometers
0 50 100 200 Miles

Choiseul Island
Gizo
Northern Solomons
Bougainville
Shortland Island
TREASURY ISLANDS
Solomon Islands
Arawa
Kieta
Panguna
Buin
Teki
Tonolei
Haleta
Sohano
Konua
New Ireland
TABAR ISLANDS
Lihir Island
FENI ISLANDS
Namatanai
New Ireland
Kavieng
Konos
Rabaul
GAZELLE PENINSULA
Tanis
East New Britain
Pomio
Ewasse Balla
Hoskins
Talasea
Kimbe
Gasmata
New Britain
Kandrian
West New Britain
Gloucester
Sissi
Umboi Island
Long Island
Karkar Island
Bagabag Island
Madang
Kalkar
Saidor
Karkar Island
Bunabun
Sarang
Madang
Woodlark Island
Kiriwina I.
TROBRIAND ISLANDS
Losuia
D'ENTRECASTEAUX ISLANDS
Fergusson Island
Esa'ala
Normanby Island
Alotau
Goodenough Island
Rabe Itala
Abau
Mine Bay
LOUISIADE ARCHIPELAGO
Misima Island
Tagula
Rossel Island
Owen Stanley Range
Kokoda
Popondetta
Gona
Buna
Northern
Tufi
Itero
Ioma
Kupiano
Kwikila
Central
National Capital
Port Moresby
Sogeri
Kairuku
Madang
Finisterre Range
Bogia
Alexishafen
Cromwell Mts.
Finschhafen
Morobe
Lae
Bulolo
Wau
Salamaua
Mumeng
Markham
Wasu
Kaiapit
Menyamya
Garaina
Guari
Tapini
Woitape
Kerema
Malalaua
Gulf
Ihu
Kerema
Kikori
Baimuru
GULF PLAIN
Goroka
Kainantu
Kundiawa
Chimbu
Eastern Highlands
Western Highlands
Simbu
Mt. Hagen
Southern Highlands
Enga
Wabag
Laiagam
Wapenamanda
Mendi
Nipa
Koroba
Tari
Mussau
Palakau
New Hanover
ADMIRALTY ISLANDS
Lorengau
Manus
Manus
BISMARCK ARCHIPELAGO
Madang
Bismarck Range
Jimi
Central Range
West Sepik
Aitape
Lumi
Nuku
Amanab
Vanimo
Jayapura
Telefomin
Oksapmin
ORIOMO PLATEAU
Olsobip
Kiunga
Lake Murray
Daru
Western
Balimo
Morehead
Weam
Bula
Mabaduan
Boigu Island
Saibai Island
Mari
East Sepik
Wewak
Angoram
Pagwi
Maprik
Ambunti
Dagua
Aiome
Bogia

Indonesia

Australia
GREAT BARRIER REEF
Weipa

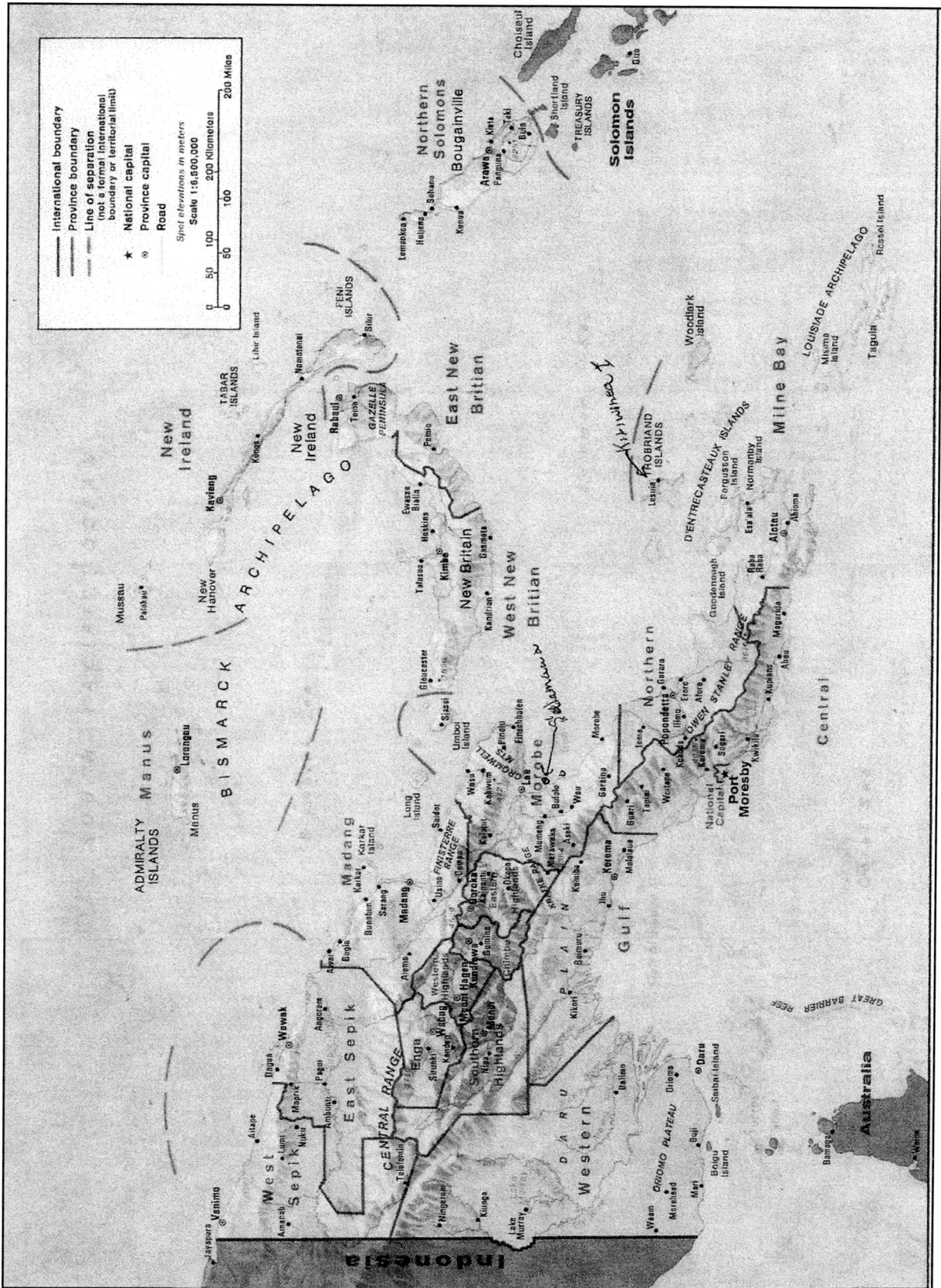

New Guinea today.

APO   929,
1   June,   1943.

Subject: Operational Flight Missions.

To   :   All concerned.

       1. The following is a true extract copy of Operational Flight Missions for 1st Lieutenant NORBERT C. RUFF, through 31 May, 1943.

No.	Date	Place	Type	Time	Remarks
1.	22-July-42	Port Moresby	P-400	1:40	Strafed barges-Buna Bay.
2.	22-July-42	Port Moresby	P-400	1:35	Strafed barges-Buna Bay.
3.	24-July-42	Port Moresby	P-400	2:15	Coverbombers-Moresby.
4.	24-July-42	Port Moresby	P-400	1:00	Interception-Alert.
5.	26-July-42	Port Moresby	P-400	2:00	Reconn.-Lae & Salamaua.
6.	26-July-42	Port Moresby	P-400	1:35	Interception-Alert.
7.	26-July-42	Port Moresby	P-400	1:30	Interception-Alert.
8.	28-July-42	Port Moresby	P-400	1:30	Reconn.-Lae.
9.	29-July-42	Port Moresby	P-400	2:15	Interception-Alert.
10.	1-Aug.-42	Port Moresby	P-400	0:25	Cover bombers-Moresby.
11.	3-Aug.-42	Port Moresby	P-400	2:00	Cover fighters-raid Buna.
12.	4-Aug.-42	Port Moresby	P-400	1:00	Reconn.-Fischer Is.
13.	6-Aug.-42	Port Moresby	P-400	2:10	Escort bombers from raid on Lae.
14.	9-Aug.-42	Port Moresby	P-400	1:05	Escort bombers from raid on Lae.
15.	12-Aug.-42	Port Moresby	P-400	2:30	Escort transports-Wau.
16.	13-Aug.-42	Port Moresby	P-400	2:00	Escort transports-Kagi.
17.	13-Aug.-42	Port Moresby	P-400	2:00	Escort transports-Kagi.
18.	13-Aug.-42	Port Moresby	P-400	1:10	Escort bombers Buna.
19.	15-Aug.-42	Port Moresby	P-400	2:30	Escort transports-Kagi.
20.	16-Aug.-42	Port Moresby	P-400	1:20	Escort transports-Kagi.
21.	16-Aug.-42	Port Moresby	P-400	3:00	Escort transports-Wau.
22.	18-Aug.-42	Port Moresby	P-400	0:50	Interception-Alert.
23.	18-Aug.-42	Port Moresby	P-400	2:20	Patrol Moresby.
24.	20-Aug.-42	Port Moresby	P-400	1:45	Interception-Alert.
25.	20-Aug.-42	Port Moresby	P-400	2:05	Patrol Moresby.
26.	21-Aug.-42	Port Moresby	P-400	1:15	Interception-Alert.
27.	21-Aug.-42	Port Moresby	P-400	2:10	Patrol Moresby.
28.	22-Aug.-42	Port Moresby	P-400	2:15	Patrol Kokoda.
29.	24-Aug.-42	Port Moresby	P-400	2:25	Patrol Moresby.
30.	24-Aug.-42	Port Moresby	P-400	1:00	Raid on Buna.
31.	27-Aug.-42	Port Moresby	P-400	1:40	Escort transports-Kagi.
32.	27-Aug.-42	Port Moresby	P-400	1:40	Patrol Kokoda.
33.	28-Aug.-42	Port Moresby	P-400	1:00	Escort transports-Kagi.
34.	31-Aug.-42	Port Moresby	P-400	1:50	Escort bombers from raid on Lae.

- 1 -

No.	Date	Place	Type	Time	Remarks
35.	2-Sept-42	Port Moresby	P-400	1:30	Escort transports-Kagi.
36.	4-Sept-42	Port Moresby	P-400	1:30	Escort transports-Wau.
37.	5-Sept-42	Port Moresby	P-400	1:30	Escort transports-Kagi.
38.	8-Sept-42	Port Moresby	P-400	0:10	Patrol Moresby.
39.	9-Sept-42	Port Moresby	P-400	2:00	Patrol Moresby.
40.	11-Sept-42	Port Moresby	P-400	2:10	Patrol Moresby.
41.	11-Sept-42	Port Moresby	P-400	2:20	Patrol Moresby.
42.	12-Sept-42	Port Moresby	P-400	0:45	Interception-Alert.
43.	15-Sept-42	Port Moresby	P-400	2:20	Patrol Moresby.
44.	20-Sept-42	Port Moresby	P-400	2:05	Escort fighters-raid-Buna.
45.	12-Oct.-42	Port Moresby	P-400	1:50	Patrol transports Myola.
46.	13-Oct.-42	Port Moresby	P-400	1:25	Patrol transports Myola.
47.	18-Oct.-42	Port Moresby	P-400	3:00	Patrol Wanigela.
48.	22-Oct.-42	Port Moresby	P-400	2:00	Patrol Myola.
49.	23-Oct.-42	Port Moresby	P-400	1:45	Patrol Myola.
50.	13-Oct.-42	Port Moresby	P-400	2:15	Patrol Myola.
51.	10-Nov.-42	Milne Bay	P-400	0:30	Interception-Alert.
52.	23-Nov.-42	Milne Bay	P-39D2	1:30	Patrol Moresby.
53.	27-Nov.-42	Milne Bay	P-39D2	1:15	Patrol Normanby Is.
54.	11-Dec.-42	Milne Bay	P-400	2:15	Escort shipping-Oro Bay.
55.	14-Dec.-42	Milne Bay	P-39D1	2:05	Cover shipping Tufi.
56.	15-Dec.-42	Milne Bay	P-39D1	1:30	Reconn.-Buna Bay.
57.	16-Dec.-42	Milne Bay	P-39D2	2:45	Patrol Milne Bay.
58.	17-Dec.-42	Milne Bay	P-39D2	1:20	Patrol Milne Bay.
59.	18-Dec.-42	Milne Bay	P-39D2	1:15	Patrol Milne Bay.
60.	18-Dec.-42	Milne Bay	P-39D2	1:10	Patrol Milne Bay.
61.	19-Dec.-42	Milne Bay	P-39D1	1:25	Interception-Alert.
62.	20-Dec.-42	Milne Bay	P-39D2	1:50	Patrol shipping-Tufi.
63.	22-Dec.-42	Milne Bay	P-39D2	1:25	Patrol Milne Bay.
64.	24-Dec.-42	Milne Bay	P-39D1	2:00	Escort shipping, Porlock Harbor.
65.	27-Dec.-42	Milne Bay	P-39D2	1:30	Patrol Moresby.
66.	27-Dec.-42	Milne Bay	P-39D2	2:30	Escort shipping-Normanby Is.
67.	5-Jan.-43	Milne Bay	P-39D2	1:45	Escort shipping Tufi.
68.	6-Jan.-43	Milne Bay	P-39D2	1:15	Patrol Milne Bay.
69.	6-Jan.-43	Milne Bay	P-39D2	2:00	Interception-Alert.
70.	9-Jan.-43	Milne Bay	P-400	1:00	Patrol Moresby.
71.	10-Jan.-43	Milne Bay	P-39D2	1:05	Reconn.-East Cape.
72.	14-Jan.-43	Milne Bay	P-39D2	1:30	Reconn.-Cape Nelson.
73.	15-Jan.-43	Milne Bay	P-39D2	1:00	Interception-Alert.
74.	17-Jan.-43	Milne Bay	P-39D2	2:50	Escort transports-Dobadura.
75.	17-Jan.-43	Milne Bay	P-39D2	1:55	Patrol Milne Bay.
76.	20-Jan.-43	Milne Bay	P-39D2	1:50	Interception-Alert.
77.	15-Apr.-43	Port Moresby	P-38G	1:00	Patrol Moresby.
78.	15-Apr.-43	Port Moresby	P-38G	2:00	Escort transports-Wau.
79.	20-Apr.-43	Port Moresby	P-38G	3:00	Escort transports-Wau.
80.	24-Apr.-43	Port Moresby	P-38G	2:00	Escort transports-Wau.
81.	24-Apr.-43	Port Moresby	P-38G	2:15	Reconn.-Lae.
82.	29-Apr.-43	Port Moresby	P-38G	2:25	Top Cover-Wau.
83.	2-May.-43	Port Moresby	P-38G	3:00	Top Cover-Wau.
84.	5-May.-43	Port Moresby	P-38G	0:30	Top Cover-Wau.

Operational F̲l̲i̲g̲h̲t̲ ̲M̲i̲s̲s̲i̲o̲n̲s̲, 1st Lt. _____, (Cont'd.).

N̲o̲.	D̲a̲t̲e̲	P̲l̲a̲c̲e̲	T̲y̲p̲e̲	T̲i̲m̲e̲	R̲e̲m̲a̲r̲k̲s̲
85.	13-May.-43	Port Moresby	P-38G	2:45	Top Cover-Wau.
86.	21-May.-43	Port Moresby	P-38G	2:25	Top Cover-Wau.

8̲6̲ ̲M̲i̲s̲s̲i̲o̲n̲s̲.   Total Time - - 151:05

FRANK D. TOMKINS,
Captain, AAF,
Operations Officer.

APO   929,
1   August,   1943.

Subject: Operational Flight Missions.

To   :   All concerned.

     1.   The following is a true extract copy of Operational Flight Missions for Captain NORBERT C. RUFF, for the period 1 June, 1943, through 31 July, 1943.

No.	Date	Place	Type	Time	Remarks
87.	2-June-43	Port Moresby	P-38G	3:00	Top cover-T-Wau.
88.	13-June-43	Milne Bay	P-38G	0:45	Alert-Milne Bay.
89.	16-June-43	Milne Bay	P-38G	1:00	Alert-Milne Bay.
90.	19-June-43	Port Moresby	P-38G	3:10	Top cover-T-Wau.
91.	19-June-43	Port Moresby	P-38G	2:40	Top cover-T-Wau.
92.	22-June-43	Port Moresby	P-38G	3:00	Recco-Wau-Lae.
93.	25-June-43	Port Moresby	P-38G	3:00	Top cover-T-Wau.
94.	25-June-43	Port Moresby	P-38G	2:50	Patrol Wau-Bulolo.
95.	29-June-43	Port Moresby	P-38G	1:30	Inter-Recco-Goodenough.
96.	3-July-43	Goodenough	P-38G	2:00	Patrol-Goodenough.
97.	8-July-43	Port Moresby	P-38G	4:00	Close cover-T-Bena Bena.
98.	11-July-43	Port Moresby	P-38G	1:00	Top cover-T-Wau.
99.	11-July-43	Port Moresby	P-38G	3:30	Top cover-T-Wau-Bulolo.
100.	13-July-43	Port Moresby	P-38G	3:10	Top cover-T-Guadacasal.
101.	14-July-43	Port Moresby	P-38G	3:50	Top cover-T-Wau-Bulolo.
102.	19-July-43	Port Moresby	P-38G	2:15	Recco-Madang.
103.	21-July-43	Port Moresby	P-38G	2:45	Escort-B-Madang-Combat.
104.	23-July-43	Port Moresby	P-38G	4:00	Escort-B-Madang-Combat
105.	25-July-43	Port Moresby	P-38G	4:00	Top cover-T-Bena Bena.
106.	28-July-43	Port Moresby	P-38G	3:00	Top cover-T-Wau.

                                                       53:25

      Total Prev. Time -   151:05
106 Missions - Total Time -   204:30

George S Welch

GEORGE S. WELCH,
Captain, AAF,
Operations Officer.

APO   929,
28 September, 1943.

Subject: Operational Flight Missions.

To   : All concerned.

1. The following is a true extract copy of Operational
Flight Missions for Captain NORBERT C. RUFF, for the period
1 August, 1943 through 27 September, 1943.

No.	Date	Place	Type	Time	Remarks
107.	11-Aug-43	Port Moresby	P-38G	4:15	Top cover-T-Marilinan.
108.	13-Aug-43	Port Moresby	P-38H	4:30	Top cover-T-Bena Bena.
109.	15-Aug-43	Port Moresby	P-38G	3:30	Escort-B-Salamaua.
110.	16-Aug-43	Port Moresby	P-38G	4:00	Top cover-T-Marilinan.
111.	18-Aug-43	Port Moresby	P-38G	2:45	Escort-B-Wewak-Incomplete.
112.	21-Aug-43	Port Moresby	P-38H	0:30	Escort-B-Wewak-Incomplete.
113.	26-Aug-43	Port Moresby	P-38H	4:30	Escort-B-Hansa Bay.
114.	28-Aug-43	Port Moresby	P-38G	3:00	Top cover-T-Wau.
115.	30-Aug-43	Port Moresby	P-38G	5:15	Escort-B-Wewak.
116.	10-Sept-43	Port Moresby	P-38G	1:30	Top cover-T-Nadzab-recalled.
117.	13-Sept-43	Port Moresby	P-38G	4:20	Escort-B-Wewak.
118.	15-Sept-43	Port Moresby	P-38G	4:20	Escort-B-Wewak.
119.	16-Sept-43	Port Moresby	P-38H	3:40	Escort-B-Alexishafen.
120.	20-Sept-43	Port Moresby	P-38G	5:00	Escort-B-Wewak.
121.	21-Sept-43	Port Moresby	P-38G	3:30	Cover Lae shipping.
122.	22-Sept-43	Port Moresby	P-38G	4:00	Patrol Finschafen.
123.	22-Sept-43	Port Moresby	P-38G	4:10	Patrol Finschafen.
124.	25-Sept-43	Port Moresby	P-38G	3:50	Escort-B-Kaiapit.
125.	26-Sept-43	Port Moresby	P-38G	0:30	Escort-B-Wewak-Incomplete.

67:05

Total Prev. Time -   204:30
125 Missions - Total Time -   271:35

CARL E. TAYLOR,
Captain, AAF,
Operations Officer.

54

Port Moresby – 12 and 14 Mile Aerodromes

*P*ort Moresby was a small native village on the southern side of the Owen Stanley Mountain Range of New Guinea. It was an area the Japanese coveted and fought hard to take control, bombing it at least 125 times and at one point getting within thirty-two miles.

Main Street at Port Moresby after the Japanese had bombed it 125 times.
Only the military and natives lived here.

A Fight for New Guinea, written in 1943, describes the New Guinea where our men lived and fought for so long. The author was a war correspondent stationed with the troops in New Guinea.

"New Guinea is a land of dark brooding mystery, unchanged by the ages. It offers a constant challenge to the mastery of the white man and still tolerates the black headhunters and cannibals who haunt its mountain jungles. Its swamps and rivers and rank forests defy both white and black alike.

The Portuguese discovered it about the time the Pilgrims were landing on Plymouth Rock, but it remains almost as impenetrable today as it was then. In the intervening centuries, explorers have managed to establish precarious footholds along its shores, but the vast island, larger than the British Isles, is as forbidding to us as it was to the first Portuguese settlers.

A glance at the map will reveal that New Guinea is formed like one of its own giant iguanas, with the head of the lizard pointing northwest to the Philippines and the tip of its long narrow tail stretching just beyond the northernmost point in Queensland, Australia.

There are many maps of New Guinea but none is accurate because much of it remains unexplored, even by natives. It is noteworthy that the maps refer to the probable course of certain rivers. They are not definitely marked because no white man has ever traced these rivers to their source. Even the narrow strip between Port Moresby and Buna, better known than most other parts of the island, was incorrectly diagramed on all the maps we could find, and Australian and American troops often found an impassable jungle wall where they expected to see a stream or a footpath.

The Air Corps was, therefore called upon to make aerial photographic maps of thousands of square miles of territory. To make these maps, they had to endanger their lives flying above the 13,000-foot peaks of the Owen Stanley Mountains, which split the long tail of New

Norb wrote on the back of this picture: "Now bail out and walk home over that Owen Stanley Range to 11,000 feet."

Guinea. This, the pilots always insisted, was the toughest flying front to be found anywhere on earth. Especially in the early days there, they were flying in what they themselves called 'old tomato crates' which had already seen too much service for safety and should long since have been retired to the home for the aged. When I left New Guinea the third B-26 ever built was still in service and, although often shot up, was still taking its turn on bombing raids.

The weather was frequently a greater peril than the enemy. Day after day a solid front of fog and clouds hovered over the eastern coast of New Guinea from sea level to an altitude of more than 50,000 feet. This front might be 1,000 miles long and 100 miles deep. Our planes could not get under it, over it, through it or around it.

The front usually built up in the afternoon. That was why so many of our bombing raids and dogfights were staged in the morning. Often neither the Japs nor our own pilots could get at each other because of the weather, and our transport planes sometimes were unable to carry food and munitions to the troops along the Kokoda Trail or around Buna because they could neither see the area to drop their loads nor find a place to land.

Some of our most daring and experienced Marauder pilots—fellows like Major Brian (Shanty) O'Neill and Captains Walter Krall, Graham Gammon, Hap Jolly, Arky Greer,

Bob Hatch, George Kahle and Dick Robinson—told me they would rather face fifty Zeros single-handed than try to go through one thunderhead. These thunderheads are cumulo-nimbus clouds containing up-drafts and down-drafts in which the plane's instruments are of no use. A pilot could see up and around a thunderhead in daytime, but there was little chance of avoiding one at night. If caught in a down-draft, a plane's nose could be pointed straight up, and still it would drop with startling speed. If a pilot tried to bull his way through a thunderhead, the currents were strong enough to rip his wings off. Robinson once was caught in a thunderhead on a night mission to Lae and dropped like a shot from 10,000 to 1,500 feet before he came out of it. Had he been over the mountains instead of the sea, he would never have lived to tell about it.

There are no large towns in New Guinea. Port Moresby itself probably never harbored more than 1,800 whites and about 2,000 blacks who lived in the largest native village on the island. Other little towns are scattered here and there along the coasts, but many of them are little

Port Moresby

more than names on the map. Buna, for instance, for which we fought so long and which cost thousands of lives, had only six European houses and a few native huts before the war.

Until then, the white man had made little, if any, impression on the island. There are a few rubber and coconut plantations and an occasional gold mine, but no extensive development anywhere. Hundreds of thousands of square miles are as untouched today as they were millions of years ago.

There are a few miserable roads here and there along the coasts, but none extends very far inland, even around Moresby. When the Australians took over Papua from the Germans seventy years ago, there were twenty-nine miles of roads around Moresby. When we arrived, there were still twenty-nine miles of roads. Our first need was for new roads. Our engineers built scores of them, and today you may see them fingering their way all over the region between Moresby and the mountains. We started to build a road from Rigo across the mountains to get at the Japs, but we soon found the task too formidable and abandoned the attempt.

The speed with which our engineers built roads and air strips was a never-ending source of amazement to the easy-going Australians. Major Herman Cox, gaunt engineer officer from Texas, supplied at least part of the answer. He told me that for a long time his boys virtually slept with their picks

Norb had written on the back of this picture: "Lonesome country to go down in." The two black spots in the picture are other P-39s.

and shovels after somebody had started a rumor that an Australian road digger had picked up a big gold nugget near Moresby. The Major, of course, smilingly denied that he had started the rumor.

A California or Florida real-estate promoter could, and probably would, turn Moresby into one of the loveliest seaside resorts on earth. The harbor is a paradise. A coral reef stretches across its mouth and there are several small islands between the reef and the mainland. The sea here deepens from the palest of greens near the reef to shades of deepest blue and green and purple.

Many homes are scattered among the hills which rise abruptly from the sea. Others are hidden by the tall cocoanut palms along the beach. The Australians had been content to use the town merely as a trading post and their troops thought so little of it that, after all civilians had been evacuated following the Japs' first raid there, they looted every home and shop and caused even more damage than the Jap bombs.

The main road from Moresby to Seven Mile skirts the base of the hills until an old native prison which stands on a hillock is reached. Here the road splits, one fork winding around hairpin curves for hundreds of feet before dropping abruptly into a valley leading out to Seven Mile, the other fork running level to Three Mile from which the bombers operated.

Between the forks stood our first hospital. This was a Catholic convent and chapel known as Koki Mission. Both were taken over by our medical corps. In the beginning this was entirely adequate, but after the Japs started their big drive for Moresby, this hospital was taxed far beyond its capacity, and within a few months hundreds of tents and huts were needed to care for the overflow of the wounded.

The Australians had a tent hospital in the foothills of the mountains at Seventeen Mile and we built one alongside it. Both of these continued to expand as the casualties poured back from the fighting fronts. As many wounded as possible were evacuated in hospital ships to Australia. Nevertheless, when the fight for Buna was at its peak, the hospital facilities everywhere were strained to the breaking point.

There were no towns anywhere near Moresby but various localities were identified by their distances from Moresby. Thus we identified our air strips at Three Mile, Four Mile, Twelve Mile, Fourteen Mile and Seventeen Mile. Newcomers had to learn to distinguish between Seventeen Mile hospital and Seventeen mile air strip, which were both approximately seventeen miles from Moresby but several miles apart from each other. Later every strip was named in honor of a fallen pilot, but these names were never widely adopted. The boys did, however, use the native names for some of the strips such as Laloki for Fourteen Mile because it was beside the Laloki River, Waigani for Seventeen Mile and Koki for Three Mile.

Eventually, Three Mile was given over to Havocs and Kittyhawks; Four Mile or Ward's Drome to Beaufighters, flown by the Aussies, Kittyhawks and DC-3's which were transport planes; Seven Mile to Airacobras, Flying Fortresses and Liberators; Twelve Mile to Airacobras and Kittyhawks; Fourteen Mile to Lightnings and Marauders; and Seventeen Mile to North Americans and Kittyhawks.

All planes were supposed to land at their own fields, but when in trouble, and that was often enough, they would land at the nearest field available.

Seven Mile Strip had been broadened since the time I first landed there, but there were still no revetments and no dispersal areas. Those were to come later. Meanwhile, our planes, huddled together, provided an easy target for Jap bombers and strafers. The engineers were being plagued on all sides. Every field was clamoring for revetments, and every camp was howling for roads. Day and night the engineers labored, trying to oblige everybody. The hillsides were scarred with broad brown gashes, where they had scooped out dirt for roads. Jagged stumps were all that remained of the trees which they had felled to construct bridges and culverts. Out near Twelve Mile, one high tor [mount] had been gradually leveled to supply rock." (*The Fight for New Guinea*)

If Norb's introduction to Port Moresby on July 20, 1942, was any indication of things to come, he was in for a hair-raising time. "It was in the evening in July 1942 that the 80th arrived in Pt. Moresby at Seven Mile, was shortly after a raid, fires and smoke – you would navigate over the

500 miles of Coral Sea from Horn Island to New Guinea. The Japs would come over daily 10:00 am, 2:00 pm, and 4:00 pm, with evening raids as well. I remember looking down at the mess and thinking, 'This must be what the gates of hell look like.' We had to fly a lane of entry pattern or the ack-ack would shoot you down. We flew up with all the P-39 & P-400 flyable, a total of ten. We landed shortly after an air raid, lots of black smoke, many things burning. I am on the ground taxiing behind Harley Brown, dust and smoke so bad you can't see. I kept Harley Brown's airplane ahead of me, as he moved up, I followed. Now, his right wing tip hits a 55 gallon drum of petro, catches fire, he goes out the left door and off the wing tip. I blindly taxi off to the right away from the fire and taxiway and cut off my engine. I get out and there is a little sign about five feet from where I parked. I get around so I could read it – 'Unexploded bomb 4:30 pm.' I look at my watch, it's 5:15 pm."

The lane of entry to Port Moresby was to go around an island near Port Moresby and swerve in so the pilots wouldn't be shot down by the ack-ack of their own men. Marion Kirby described the approach to Port Moresby: "We would be forced to

The harbor at Port Moresby before heavy raids by the Japs.

look for holes in the clouds and worm our way back to the south side of the island. Once we arrived on the south side there was a common rule…If you encountered reefs…Turn Right…If not reefs…Turn Left. This would take you right into Port Moresby."

Two days later Norb was in his first combat mission.

"Just before dusk on the evening on July 21 six of the 80th's Airacobras flew up to Fourteen Mile from Twelve Mile to operate with the 39th. The next morning Captain Greasley led the six P-400s off on a strafing mission against the landing at Gona.

The others in the flight included Lieutenants Cleve Jones, David Hunter, Danny Roberts and Norbert Ruff flying the wing of Bill Greenfield. It would take only about twenty minutes to reach the target area, so the pilots would not have much time to think about the odds against them. Their 37mm cannons were not charged which must have helped to dampen the pilot's enthusiasm.

Another factor that did not serve to bolster their spirits was that some of the radios were not functioning very well, but when the six Airacobras came roaring over the white beaches there was no question about the next action to take. Five or six barges were outlined on the bright coral and sand shore and there were three other craft lying in the water nearby that looked like motor torpedo boats. In their excitement some of the pilots also believed that they could identify two destroyers farther out to sea: in retrospect the more experienced pilots decided that they were just large transports.

The attack itself was short and sweet. Six angry Airacobras went in on a low pass with every machine gun firing. White fountains of water erupted in the midst of the barges while surprised Japanese either ran for their guns or jumped over the side. Some quick thinking gunners on the transports fired heavy anti-aircraft guns which fortunately threw heavy, but inaccurate fire around the marauding Airacobras.

There were twelve to fourteen barges in the water between the transports and for the moment panic was the order. Some of the barges turned their sterns toward the attack to offer the 80th strafers the most protected part of the vessel. One result was confusion that gave the Airacobras even more opportunity to send their punishing lances of machinegun fire into the iron sides of the landing craft.

At least one of the transports was badly hit, also, and emitted heavy black smoke. Unfortunately, this portion of the attack cost the 80th its only casualty of the raid when Lieutenant David 'Pinky' Hunter was hit, probably by a 37mm gun from one of the barges. (It was reported that Hunter was hit by an escorting destroyer which suggests that guns on one of the transports may also have been the villain. [Hunter was the first 80th pilot to be killed during enemy action.]

Danny Roberts was flying Hunter's wing and was almost hit by the jettisoned door of the damaged Airacobra. Apparently Hunter was alive enough at that moment to try and get out, but his fighter smashed into the water from the very low altitude about a hundred yards from shore. The other 80th pilots felt that he got out okay even though no word was ever heard of him again. Ultimately, he suffered the same fate as Durand on the April 30 mission when the Japanese caught him alive and subsequently executed him. [After the war Ken Gerrish of the 36th Squadron learned that Hunter's ring had been recovered from Rabaul with the news that he had been taken alive and beheaded after being transferred to New Britain.]

The loss of Hunter left Danny Roberts in something of a fix. He had not even looked at a map of New Guinea before the mission and was depending on the navigation of his leader to get him home. When the Airacrobras left the area at high speed, after each of them had expended an average of 600 rounds of machinegun fire, everybody took a different direction to get out of the way of aroused flak and fighters as fast as they could. Roberts desperately tried to tack onto someone's wing before they all disappeared, leaving him looking silly while he circled around in enemy territory trying to find the way home alone.

Somehow he did find the way home and never mentioned if he did manage to follow one of the other strafers or did a bang-up job of dead reckoning. When he was asked later in the war about his most frightening mission, Roberts unhesitatingly and unsmilingly mentioned his first one.

The pressure on the beachhead had to be maintained so missions like the first one were repeated with increasing regularity. A-24s attacked the Japanese with less than heartening results and the 39th Squadron flew its last mission [with the 80th] before being officially relieved by the 80th on July 24. Whatever damage was done to the Japanese invading force became largely dependent on the 80th's ability to adapt to the existing combat conditions."

"We (80th) with a couple of the more experienced 39th squadron pilots were sent over to strafe this landing. This was the first and second combat missions of the 80th. Eight airplanes would go down and work over the barges with all seven guns (one cannon, two 50mm and four 30 mm) firing and eight stayed up as top cover and then changed places. Lae airdrome was only 40-50 miles away and had many Zero fighters, but received no opposition from them since their field was not in operation. Pinky Hunter was lost here.

"We should have come back time and time again—only we had only two missions on this day. We were flying off of 12 and 14 mile airdromes, many times giving top cover to C-47s transporting men of the 32nd Division of the Wisconsin National Guard over to Buna." - Norb

The first planes the 80th flew in New Guinea were P-400s, a British version of the P-39. The plane was not a good plane at altitude, and very poor against the Jap's highly maneuverable planes. "When you shot from the plane, you could feel the bullets leave the plane, especially when you shot 20mm. They practically made the plane stop. The cockpit would fill up with smoke and the smell of gunpowder." -Norb

"The P-400 proved to be so bad that when Kirby's Squadron [80th] would be scrambled on word of a bombing raid on Port Moresby they would take off and climb in a direction away from the attacking aircraft in an effort to get to altitude. They would struggle up to

62

23,000 feet out over the ocean and only then turn back to face the enemy airplanes. The Japanese would come over at 27,000 feet and bomb unopposed because the U.S. fighters could not

Note the 20 mm cannon in the nose of the plane. Two 50 cals fired through the prop. Two 30 cals shot from each wing.

get that high. Fortunately for Kirby and his mates, because they could not threaten the bombers, the Zeros at that time in the war were under orders not to break close escort formation with the bombers and attack. Kirby remains convinced that had they attacked he would have been just another dead P-400 pilot shortly after it started." (*Kirby Files*) Norb's comment to this was, "Amen."

"We were flying P-400s at this time…The P-400 is nothing more than a P-39 which the English purchased before the war, and as hard up as they were they still realized that they had made a mistake and backed out of the deal…When war came along that was all that we had…it was designed for close support ground operations, for which it was real good. But we were using it, or trying to use it, as an interceptor…it never was designed for that and no stretch of the imagination could you make it fit that mold. The English altered the radio, changed the 37mm cannon firing through the nose to a 20mm. [They had Bell, the manufacturer make the changes.] As an interceptor, the absolute maximum ceiling was 23,000 feet. The enemy would come over at 25,000 feet…the bombers flying perfect formation (it was almost a pleasure to get bombed so you could watch them fly formation) and the fighters in trail having a big rat race. They would not come down… and we could not get up. If we had been able to reach their altitude all that we could do is make one pass then run like a spotted assed ape." -Kirby

Besides the poor planes the men were flying, they had to contend with the weather on the ground and in the air. Mud-filled runways, pilots lost or combat missions cancelled, all because of the weather. "Weather. The most feared word in the dictionary. Weather might have sealed the fate of more fighter pilots than the enemy. Very simply, fighter aircraft were not equipped to cope with bad weather and instrument flying. We had no automatic pilot or radio compass to help guide us through weather fronts and to the safety of home. Also, we had not received enough training in instrument flying to have the skills and confidence to fly blind and trust what instruments we did have available. A golden rule when flying blind was 'TRUST YOUR INSTRUMENTS." All we had to trust was known as needle, ball and air speed. Also, a magnetic compass was a must and hopefully had been properly calibrated for accuracy." –Louis Scribner

Keeping the planes in flying order was no easy task. The mechanics were hard-pressed getting the right parts, getting those parts into the planes and getting it done quickly to keep enough planes ready for combat. The use of different planes was also a challenge for the mechanics. Others on the ground worked just as hard to keep the pilots safely in the air and get them safely on the ground.

Roughhouse Bradley

One such person was Roughhouse Bradley, At age fifty, he the oldest man in the squadron. He never learned to read or write. Roughhouse was a signalman who made sure the runways were clear when the pilots came in to land. Roughhouse stuttered, but he wore sidearms that everyone knew he would use if he had to. One day a big car came roaring onto the runway. It stopped in front of Bradley. The window went down and a man stuck his head out and presented his hand to Bradley. "Hi, my name is MacArthur." Bradley looked at MacArthur and stuttered, "My name is Bradley. Now get the hell off this runway. I have pilots coming in to land."

In a pocket in each aircraft was a Form #14 which the pilot filled out after each flight—date, time, destination, type of flight, etc. The pilot would also list anything wrong with the aircraft. Squadron Operations would make a monthly list of flights as part of the pilot's record which he took with him from base to base.

The Crew Chief then read the pilot's notes and would make any necessary repairs. If planes were damaged beyond repair, the mechanics would take parts from those planes to fix those that could be fixed. There were times the mechanics worked around the clock trying desperately to get planes in flying condition.

"I must tell you at this point that the enlisted men were as much a part of this combat unit as the squadron pilots. They were so excited when they saw that a couple of their aircraft had fired their guns. They wanted to know the details immediately and we told them.

I have to compliment and praise our men. They

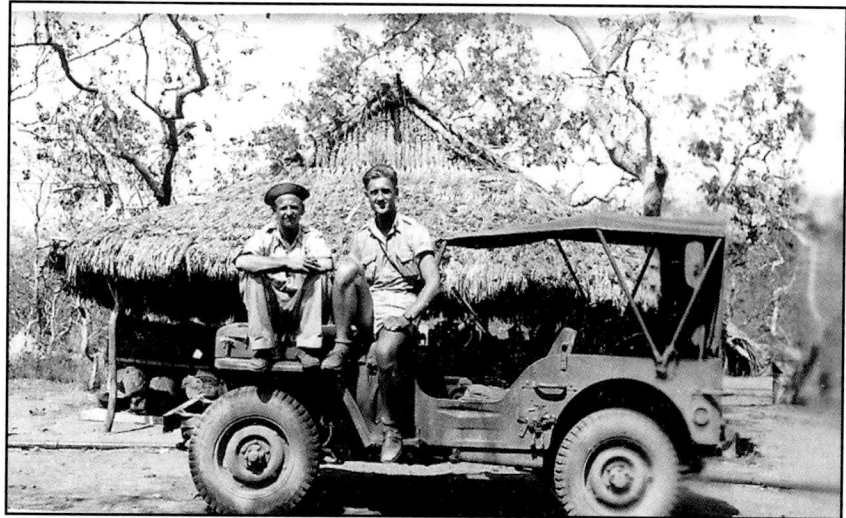

Salty Peters was a commissioned officer in charge of armament.. Bill Pruss, also a commissioned officer, was head of the mechanics.

worked so hard and often late into the night to make sure their aircraft were ready for the next morning's mission. The same praise goes to the other service men, such as the cooks and others who arose way early in the morning to make sure that the combat pilots had a hot meal before taking off at dawn. As tough as the conditions were, you never heard a complaint. To a question, you only heard 'Yes sir, no sir, no excuse sir or why don't you do it this way, sir?' They were so loyal, faithful, courageous and hard working. Man, how I loved, respected, and admired them." –Marion Kirby

Crew Chief Bill Myers

"Bill Myers joined the 80th after we received P-38s. He was a corporal when we first met and had been to school earlier on P-38s. Our older crew chiefs had some problems with the P-38s since the landing gear on P-38s operated on hydraulics, whereas the landing gear on P-39, which they were

Bill Meyers is standing next to Norb.

used to, was electric. The props on the planes were controlled just the reverse as the hydraulics.

"After a mission I was having trouble in my P-38 and couldn't get my landing gear down. I flew over the home strip for about one-half hour pumping the gear down manually, which got a little old. After the third time I made it known that something or somebody was going to change! This is when the young new corporal, Bill Meyers, shows up. He had just arrived overseas to the 80th. He fixed the problem, and I made sure he was assigned to my plane. I got him up to Tech Sergeant and my crew chief before I left after 50 missions in P-38s. After I went home he became line chief (top mechanic) under Jay Robbins.

"August 21, 1943 was my one-hundred twelfth mission and the day we lost my flight of Feehan, Krisher & Guttel. I came back home on a single engine from Wewak. Per Squadron rules all single engine landings had to be made at the long bomber base at 7 Mile. We are on 3 Mile not too far away. Naturally I flew low over our strip to show my airplane letter and have somebody pick me up at 7 mile. It wasn't long when Sergeant Myers showed up in a jeep. He had been down with malaria, but had to come over himself."

Virgin Lane

The first place Norb and the 80th lived during July, August and September of 1942 at 12 Mile was known as Virgin Lane (probably because no one had lived there except natives before the Americans arrived). The hut had already been erected on the hill by an earlier squadron, probably the 40th. There were eight to ten men in the hut. They slept on army cots with mosquito bars with zippers on the side. The men crawled in and quickly zipped it shut. Once inside on the cot, they didn't dare put an arm against the cloth or the mosquitoes, which were a terrible nuisance all over

Sign posted to tree says, "Virgin Lane."

New Guinea and carried malaria, would nail them through the netting. Their gear, except for life vest and parachutes which were kept down on the flight line, was kept under their cots. The men preferred the grass huts to the tents because they vented better. The tents would get hot and if left open, the mosquitoes would swarm in for attack. The mess hall was down below the hill where squadron cooks made their 'specialties.'

"Virgin Lane was not a ravine, but was built on the side of a small hill. A very steep grade accessed the area. Immediately upon entering was a relatively large area that was relatively flat. This was where the Officer's Club, Orderly Room, Mess Hall, and Dispensary was located. Each of these buildings were grass hutments constructed by native labor prior to our arrival. This had been the 40th's quarters before our arrival. Then all over the side of the hill were slit trenches with further small grass shacks for living quarters, about five or six men per hut. They were nothing more than a roof, with sides open. We slept under

This hut was already at Twelve Mile when the 80th arrived. Note the slit trench in the middle of the picture. Slit trenches were 'L' shaped and depending on where the Jap bombs were dropped, the men went into one part or the other.

mosquito netting with our personal gear in a foot locker beneath the cots. The 80ᵗʰ had hospital cots, the only outfit on the island to have such. It was a subject that was never discussed as to where they came from. They were there, so we didn't ask any questions. The Mess Hall was a tent. The sides were of canvas but the front and back were of netting for ventilation. Each Friday they served canned salmon. You could always tell when Friday arrived because the flies gathered at the tent in such numbers that they would almost cause it to collapse. Our showers were of the outdoor variety, that is, until the nurses started arriving, which was about when we left for Milne Bay." -Bob Peters

Food at Port Moresby was what one would expect in a combat situation. "When the enemy was on our side of the mountains, food became very sparse…Quartermaster knew how many troops we had, consequently they knew how much food to dole out. Friday was always fish day. [Canned salmon] We ate in a tent beside the kitchen… if you had forgotten the date,

This picture gives a better view of the 'L' shaped slit trench. The aerodromes were bombed day and night.

you were always reminded when it was Friday…The flies would land on the mess tent almost to the point of collapse…We had two or three flaps on the tent so that we could work our way into the dining area flyless...Bully beef, I think was a misnomer. It was mutton canned for the Australian troops during WWI. Powdered eggs were a standby... The Aussies occupied an old building in Port Moresby and converted it to a bakery. All of our bread was baked there and delivered with our food. The bakery had no screens... consequently we received raisin bread...so many flies were baked into the bread that it had the appearance of raisin bread...you had to cultivate a taste for it...but it did have a high protein content...sitting on the [flight] line was a can of cookies...it was a large can, in excess of 5 gallons. You would take a bayonet, pry the lid off, remove one cookie, put it in your canteen cup of coffee...and let it start to soak...if you had an early mission possibly the cookie would be out of the tooth breaker mode by the time the mission was completed...The cookies were also WWI vintage...but good." (*Kirby Files*)

Norb also remembers the "raisin bread." "You would hold the bread up to the light to see where the black spots were, then try to pick the flies out. Even after I came home, for a long time, I would hold my bread up to the light to check for flies and other bugs. We also had canned hot dogs and other rations from WWI since that was all that was available at the beginning of the war." Later they received "C" and "K" rations

Norb in a slit trench. Note the WWI helment. Because supplies were being sent to Europe, the men in the Pacific were issued WWI helments, gas masks and rations.

issued all over in WWII. "C" rations were canned and had to be cooked. "K" rations came in a box and were more like snacks that could be eaten while in the field. While the pilots were flying, they did not eat, so staying alert was a real problem when they were in the air for six to seven hours at a time.

The second accommodations at 12-Mile. Note the hospital beds in the hut. Instead of being up the hill, it was down in the squadron area.

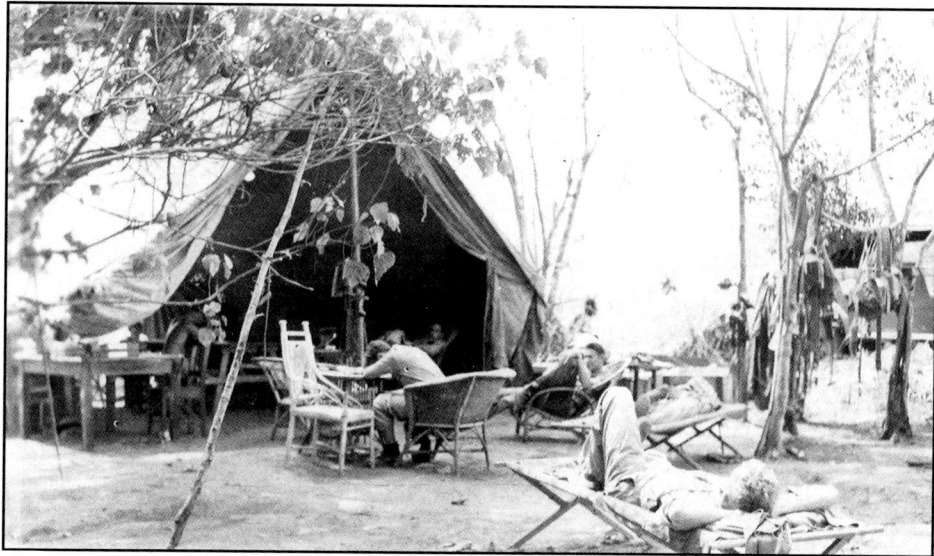

Alert Tent at Twelve Mile Aerodrome.

The alert Tent at Twelve Mile Aerodrome, was twelve miles from Port Moresby and two miles from Virgin Lane where the pilots of the 80th were living. Each morning a command car took eight pilots to Twelve Mile and eight to Fourteen Mile Airdromes from their living quarters to the alert tents. There they would nervously wait for the phone to ring either telling them they needed to go intercept or cover a returning shot up B-17 with enemy planes still attacking or searching an area for someone missing or a hundred other reasons. The calls were made every half hour to assure the line was open and not cut by infiltrating Japs from Buna. As the day wore on, each ring made them more edgy and the men would have to run outside to relieve themselves. It was a tiring, nerve-racking way to spend a day. Eventually they killed all the vegetation around the alert tents.

Notice the mae west vests hanging on the tree. Sometimes they wore their vests all day. When a call came that Jap planes were sighted, the pilots grabbed their vests as they ran to their planes. They needed to get their planes up quickly before the enemy strafed the runways and destroyed the planes. Parachutes were issued and fitted to the pilot's size and had their names on them. They were put in the aircraft the pilot was assigned to for the day. At this time pilots did not have their own planes – they just flew what was available. The chute made up part of the seat. On the bottom part of the chute was a folded life raft and the back part contained the survival kit – 38 caliber pistol, first aid, morphine, fish line, matches, Bowie knife and compass.

At 14 Mile the alert station was a grass hut. There was the same half-hour line check. An open box of hand grenades was under a table to take as needed if Japs came too close to the aerodrome.

"We were in this shack when two Jap Zero's followed a shot-up B-17 back to 7 Mile. They strafed our shack with us inside – grass leaves came floating down from the roof. We lost a P-39 or two, but no pilots were injured. There was a dugout with a slit trench

69

outside with a radio operator in it. We all dived head first into this dug out, one on top of the other. We had a helluva time getting back out.

"Our day would start before sunup, get dressed and go to the flight line, stow our gear in our assigned plane, return to the alert shack and wait. The waiting was one of the most difficult things that you could do…nervousness set in immediately…breakfast would arrive shortly, powdered eggs and coffee that [tasted like it] was made from the bark of some tree grown in Australia. After breakfast the wait would resume…cards, letter writing with nothing to say." -Kirby

The teams of four were color-coded. A pilot's team could be red one day or blue the next. When the phone rang for a real mission, the pilots would hear: "Red scramble two, or blue scramble four or all scramble." This let them know who was to go up and how many planes. "Each squadron was given a name – maybe it would be Plover or something else for a week or two. In the shack was a board listing each flight, who the flight leader was, his wingman and the second element. An element is two planes in the flight of four. The first element is the flight leader and his wingman and the second element is the third plane and his wingman."

"Never was the squadron referred to as the 80th on radio conversations. Our ground control would maybe be 'Madam' on the radio. They would call me 'Clover Red One' and direct you. 'Angels 12 you go to 12,000 feet.' You received this message on the plane's radio while taking off."

On the way to a combat mission, the pilots did not use their radios because the enemy could pick up the transmissions. After the fighting started the pilots opened their radio lines and the shouting started. "Look out number four, dammit, I told you to look out!" was about all there was time to say before a plane went down. "There was none of the long-drawn out things like you see in the movies. You prayed the pilot who went down, if he survived, would not be captured by the Japs because you knew he would get beheaded. They did not keep our pilots as prisoners of war. Another conversation I remember during an engagement over Wewak regarded a P-38 going down. "One P-38 pilot said, 'Look at the poor bastard going down in flames.' Back came a message, 'Dammit, I'm not dead yet!'" -Norb

When men are thrown together in stressful situations bonds are formed. Once the war was over, many men lost track of each other as they went on to get jobs, marry and raise families. Some, though, remained life-long friends. Danny Roberts, an Ace pilot who was a tent-mate of Norb's while he was with the 80th, was someone who probably would have remained a close friend if he had not been killed during a combat mission. Marion Kirby, another Ace, came from Panama to join the 80th in July of 1942. He still keeps in touch with Norb and they see each other at 80th reunions and have phone conversations every week.

But one man, a young Second Lieutenant, came into Norb's life at Port Moresby in September, 1942 and forged a close friendship that lasted nearly sixty years. Jay Robbins, one of the top ten-ranking P-38 Aces from all theatres of operation was trained by Norb as his wingman in New Guinea as a 2nd Lieutenant right out of flying school. Norb also trained Cy Homer, who was a top ten P-38 Ace, and Corky Smith, a top twenty P-38 Ace. Robbins made the military his career and became a Three-Star General and Corky Smith retired as a Colonel. Norb is more proud of these three men that he trained and their achievements than he is of all the awards he received while in service.

"The 80th was still at 12 Mile, Port Moresby, flying P-39 and P-400 type aircraft. I was a flight leader and a 1st Lieutenant. This would be about September, 1942. A real tall, thin 2nd Lt. reported to me that he had just joined the 80th and was assigned to my flight. I asked if he had seen Dr. Patrick who was the flight surgeon for this squadron. He answered "No," but he was on his way to do so. He had just arrived with Richard Bong who was assigned to the 9th Sqdn and Robertson, who also was assigned to the 80th. Within an hour I was called to the field telephone for a call from Dr. Nick Patrick. He said the Robbins boy who I had sent over was not going to fly because of a heart murmur. We had a heated argument, we needed pilots badly. I knew he'd had a '6-4' which is a pilot's physical before coming over. I guess I also questioned Doc Patrick's ability, where he was able to find a problem which hadn't been found earlier by other doctors throughout the many, many exams cadets are given while in training. I didn't win and Jay was sent back down to Regent Hospital at Melbourne, Australia for treatment.

"While at the hospital he met a nurse named Ina Priest. She came out of Winchendon, Massachusetts, off a small farm and had helped put her brothers and sisters through college, she being one of the oldest children. Now Jay is down at the hospital a few weeks. The doctors ran many tests. Yes, he did have a slight heart murmur, but they gave him his choice either to go home or up to combat. He elected to join the squadron. I believe he reported back to my flight in about November '42 after we moved down to Milne Bay." -Norb

"I first met Norb when I joined the 80th at Twelve Mile – Yancy, Bennett, myself and I forget who else, July 1942. Anyway we 2nd Lts. were not sure what was up or down, but a nice 1st Lt. came up to us and offered to show us around – that was Norb. We became good friends. I flew his wing a few times and was glad to have him as my flight leader. I had 75 missions, when in a two-week period I lost two tentmates,

Norb and Glen Hope

71

Adams and Thompson and my brother, Dean, from the Fifth Bomb Squadron B-24 pilot. That sent me home as he was my only brother. I was home in Glendale, California teaching new Lts. how to fly combat at Grand Central Air Field and who should come by to see me on his way home from New Guinea, but Norb. It was so great to see him, but again that shows you just what a thoughtful and great man my buddy Norb Ruff (God bless him) really is." -Glen Hope

"Glen Hope was flying Griffin's wing in a four-ship formation. Whenever you have to fly through weather the Flight Leader is the only one to fly by aircraft instruments. The remainder of the flight fly close together to keep their wingmen in sight. This is true either going up or down through an overcast. If the flight leader flies into a mountain, the entire flight goes into the mountain. In Hope's case he got too close and cut off part of the tail of Griffin's aircraft with his props. Hope always said Griffin 'backed into him.' An impossible maneuver in any airplane." -Norb

Stanley "Bow-wow" Borowsky

Stanley "Bow-wow" Borowsky was first with Norb in Advanced Flying School then in the 7th Squadron of the 49th group. They came over on the Mariposa together, then Bankstown near Sidney. Later they were in the 80th at the same time.

Before the men got on the Mariposa, they were issued full winter flying gear – sheepskin jackets and pants and overshoes, as well as tropical clothing, since it wasn't known where they were going. Their winter flying gear and winter dress uniforms included a woolen tunic or blouse and gaberdeen pants. As the ship sailed and the days became warmer, they realized they were not going to Alaska. When they were sent to the jungle and tropics, they had no need for their winter gear.

Each man had two foot lockers (small trunks). They could not take their woolens with them to the jungle because they would deteriorate within six weeks, so before going to Lowood near Brisbane, Norb and Borowsky stored their belongings in Sydney in a store called Dave Jones Large Department Store.

"A year and half later, the squadron pilots maintain an apartment in Sydney for pilots on rest leave. Each pilot paid a pound, about $3.00 toward this apartment; with forty pilots that was about $120.00 a week. Now we have enough pilots to keep three a week on rest leave. Your turn would come up every three or four months. The law of average was that you would live long enough to make one trip. Each pilot would draw out $500.00 for that week from his wages which were kept with the Squadron. There was nothing to spend money on in New Guinea outside of playing poker. There was always a big stake's game and a small stake's game.

"Now it's about Borowsky's turn to go down to Sydney on rest. Before leaving he told me he would be sending his stored foot locker home while down there since he felt he would be relieved and sent back shortly to the states and did I want him to do the same with mine. I said yes and thanked him. I am in the habit of sending a letter home every week so they know I'm okay.

Norb and Stanley Borowski. They had been classmates at Randolph Flying School.

Now when the locker arrives in San Francisco weeks later, my mother gets a telegram, "The personal effects & flying equipment of the late deceased Capt. Ruff have arrived in San Francisco for claimage." Well, the Red Cross gets going and sends a rep up to New Guinea to check on me. I was on a mission that day and he was so advised. He came back the next day to make sure I was alive, and I had to identify myself."

Gerry Rodgers on the day he walked into the 80th camp at Port Moresby in July or August

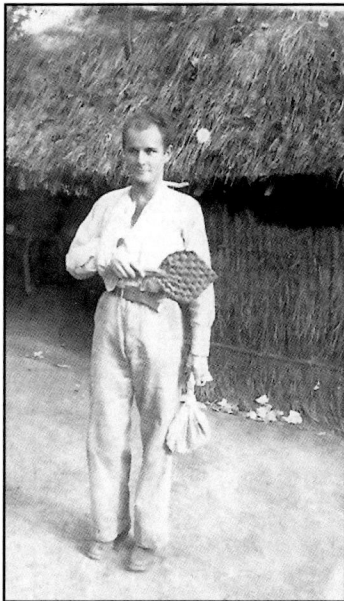
Gerry Rodgers

of 1942. After bailing out of his plane off Buna, he spent thirty days in the jungle trying to get back to friendly territory. Note the missionary shirt and sack he is holding. The sack contained the sum total of his belongings.

"Gerry was different. Before this mission he told me he would love to spend time in the back country of New Guinea – well, he got his wish. Before he went down, he would shoot birds with an air rifle, take the innards out, pack them with chemicals and cotton and send them back to the U.S. to some museum. As I remember I wasn't on the mission he got shot down on, believe it was on the coast between Buna and Milne Bay. He belly landed the P-39 in the ocean. The Zero came down and tried to get him in the water. He said he'd dive under water as the plane made passes firing at him."

Pilots were issued survival kits that were carried in their parachutes. Along with their survival kit they also carried a kit for trading with the natives. Not all kits had the same items, but could have beads, gold, rings or whatever could be used to help keep the natives friendly if the pilot crashed or was shot down and survived.

73

The pictures below show Norb and Dodo Brown at 3 Virgin Lane in early July or August of 1942 cooking up one of the two laying hens that Major Perry had purchased and brought with him from Australia. Major Perry was C.O. of the 39th Squadron. He was up flying on a test flight in a P-39. He crashed just out of the harbor mouth. Norb flew a search mission, but could not find any sign of him or the plane, no oil slick or anything.

After Perry was killed, Norb and Dodo dressed out the chickens because they did not have any chicken feed for them. Dodo is holding a wire with an egg attached, which doesn't show up well in the photo, but it is right up against Norb's upper right leg. Norb is in the rear of the picture. When they dressed the chicken, they found the egg inside. The garbage can had a couple inches of water. The chicken was cut up and put in a can and boiled. Just about the time the chicken was ready, Norb received a call that a repaired plane was down at Townsville (Australia) and he had to go down and get it. He took his chute bag and went down to the harbor to catch a Martin Flying Boat. Norb didn't get to eat the chicken, but Dodo said it was very good. (A Martin Flying Boat is a big four-engine boat, like the hull of a boat with the wings of an airplane.)

Norb, DeJarnette and Cobb on rest leave near Brisbane, Australia.

Norb, DeJarnett and Cobb (picture left) on their first rest leave in Brisbane. While in Brisbane, Cobb and Norb went into an ice cream shop. There was a row of metal bins that contained various sauces and malt powders. Cobb and Norb sat at the counter watching a girl cleaning these bins. One by one she opened the lids as she cleaned them. When she was done, she walked down the row, pushing the lids down with her arm in rapid succession, the sound of the metal lids hitting the metal bins. To the two men it sounded like guns going off, and thinking they were being attacked, hit the floor and headed for cover.

During one mission, Cobb's engine malfunctioned and he couldn't get back over the Owen Stanley Range. Norb covered him, but Cobb's plane couldn't make it back. He finally bailed out in the mountains where he lost his leather, sheep-skin lined Aussie boots when the impact of his chute opening popped his boots off. He cut material off the cover of his mae west, which was made up of rubber and fabric, and made a pair of sandals. He was found by natives and was passed on from native to native until he was finally returned to friendly territory.

"Cobb's aircraft started to lose power and he couldn't climb the 10,000 foot high Owen Stanley Range. I forgot what the mission was, he could have had some ground fire damage." -Norb

When Cobb bailed out, Norb went back to 12 Mile at Port Moresby, refueled, then flew back to find him. Cobb should have built three fires so pilots looking for him would know where to drop supplies, but Cobb never built them.

After he was found, Norb asked him why he hadn't built a fire and Cobb said, " I was so angry and lonesome already, I used up all the rounds of my 45 shooting at you, trying to bring you down to be with me."

For his missions while at Twelve Mile, Norb received the Distinguished Flying Cross, one of several medals he would receive. His mother received the following letter from General Kenney:

"Headquarters, Fifth Air Force APO, April 12, 1943. Dear Mrs. Ruff: Recently your son was decorated with the Air Medal. This award was made in recognition of his courageous, fearless service to his combat organization, his fellow American airmen, his country, his home and to you.

Your son was decorated for meritorious achievement while participating in aerial fights in the Southwest Pacific Area from July 22 to August 20, 1942.

He participated in more than twenty-five operational flight missions during which hostile contact was probable and expected. These flights included interceptions missions against enemy fighters and bombing planes and aided considerably in the recent successes in this theatre.

Almost every hour of every day your son, and the sons of other American mothers, are doing just such things as that here in the Southwest Pacific. Theirs is a very real and very tangible contribution to victory and to peace.

I would like to tell you how genuinely proud I am to have men such as your son in my command, and how gratified I am to know that young Americans with such courage and resourcefulness are fighting our country's battles against the aggressor nations. You, Mrs. Ruff, have every reason to share that pride and gratification. Very sincerely, George C. Kenney, Lieutenant General, Commanding"

Dodo Brown and Charlie Abel at Twelve Mile with P-39s. Note the iron matting on the right-hand side used for the runway.

P-39s peeling off to land. Whatever the flight leader does, the rest of the planes in the flight do.

"The cockpit of a standard P-39D. The Airacobra's cockpit was designed specifically for a 5 ft 8 in pilot who weighed 200 lb when equipped with his parachute and full flying gear. For larger pilots the cockpit was defintely on the cramped side, but the wind-down windows in the entry doors helped a little bit when the aircraft was on the ground. This unique window layout was one thing about the P-39 which really stuck in the memory of most pilots that flew it. 'Bud' Anderson remembers, 'You could taxi the thing while resting your elbows on the sill, like cruising the boulevard on a Saturday night.'" (*P-39s in the South Pacific*)

The lever on the right hand side was the control for the ammunition. The front button triggered the guns and the top button triggered the cannon.

Willett and Swede Hansen. Hansen above and in the picture to the right did all the barbering. The men paid him to cut their hair. Both Willett and Hansen were pilots with the 80th.

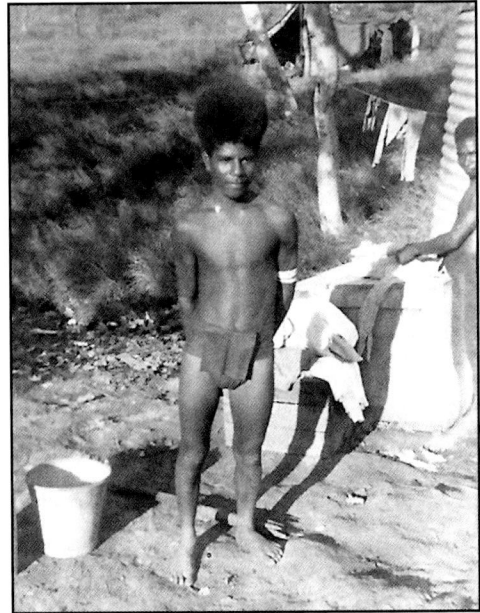

Many native boys hired out as 'camp boys' doing odd jobs such as cutting bananas, coconuts, and doing laundry.

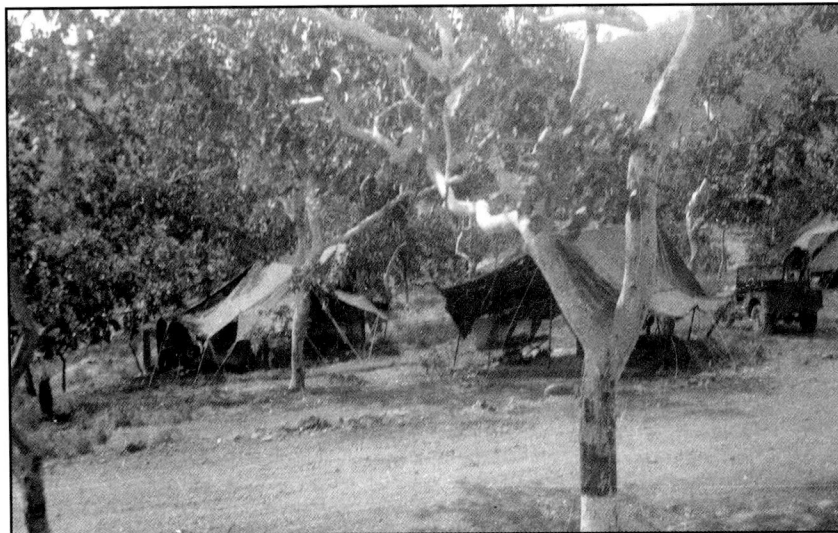

Tents at Virgin Lane. The sides had to be propped open to let the heat out--which then let the mosquitos in. The men did not like the tents as well as the huts. Virgin Lane is where the 80th pilots lived when they were flying out of Twelve Mile Aerodrome.

Swimming in La Loki River at 14 Mile.

P-39s at Twelve Mile Aerodrome

A P-40E that nosed in on landing. Note the bent propellar. The men are probably trying to figure out if they can fix the plane and if they can't, what parts they can salvage for repairs on other planes. Compare the exhaust (near the nose) with the P-40N.

Norb and his P-400.

Norb sitting by a slit trench. Note the WWI helmet which was issued to the men along with WWI gas masks, and WWI hardtack in tins. The helmets protected the men from chunks of metal raining down on them from their own anti-aircraft. Note the Aussie flying boots. Although these boots were extremely comfortable, they were not practical for flying. If a pilot had to bail from his plane, the boots would fly off his feet, leaving him in his stocking feet in the jungle.

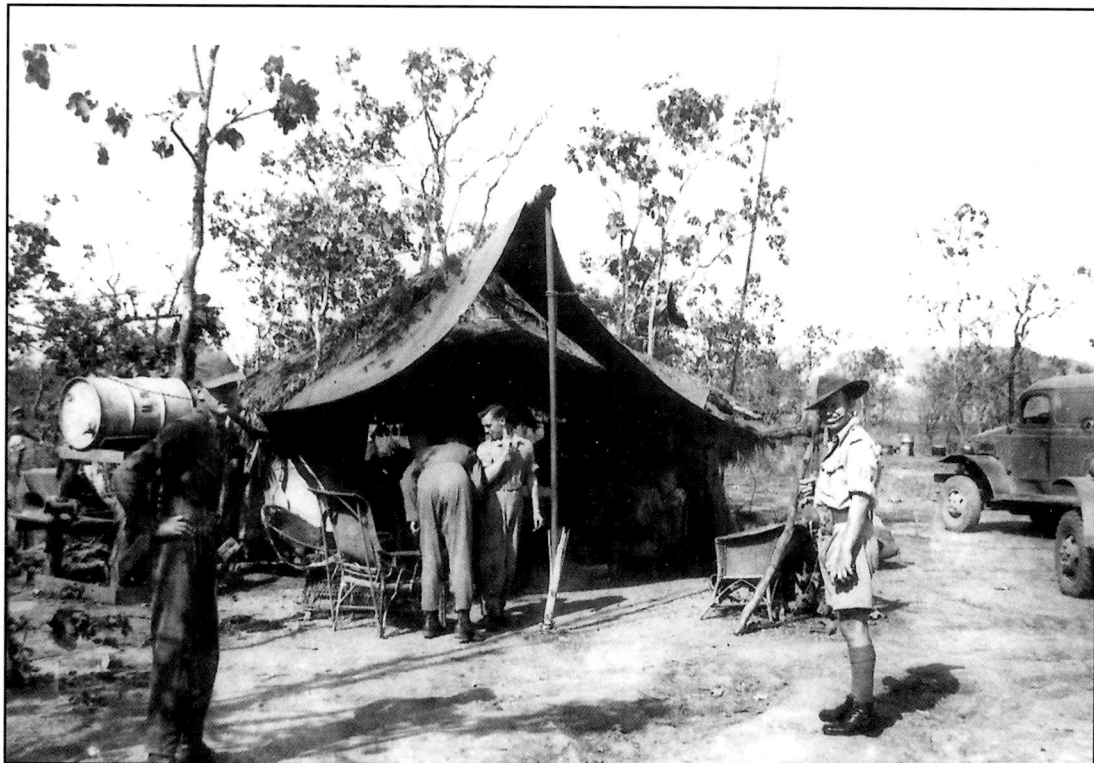

Alert tent. Man standing to the right is an Autralian named Anderson who was with the 80th for seven months and let the men know where Australian soldiers were located in the jungle.

Milne Bay

*W*ithout rest leave, the 80th moved the 225 miles from Port Moresby to Milne Bay in November of 1942. While the crews were sent down by ship, the pilots flew their P-39s, making them the first ones to bring P-39s to Milne Bay. They settled at Turnbull Field. Infested with mosquitoes, mud, more mosquitoes, more mud, along with sweltering heat, Milne Bay sat at the tip of New Guinea in the hook of the tail of the island. The bay was twenty miles deep and seven miles wide with hills that swept up from the shore. Before the war it was a coconut plantation owned by Lever Brothers.

"During the day there was heat and mud and rain; during the night there was cold and mud and rain. The mud was a foot deep and the rain drifted off heated bodies as steam during the daylight hours and stuck to freezing clothes like an ice bath at night. There were no roads as such and the only solid ground seemed to be the steel runway matting that settled into the ooze and made for hairy takeoffs and landings." (*Attack & Conquer*)

"By 10 November, 1942, the 80th had moved from 12-Mile Strip to Turnbull Field at Milne Bay, New Guinea, traveling in the Motorship *Karsik*. [Some of the pilots, like Norb, flew planes to the strip and did not travel on the ship.]

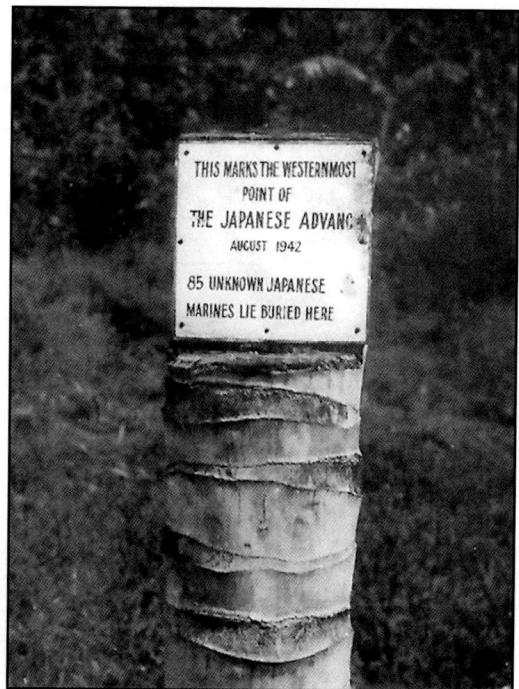

Alongside the dock at Milne, a Chinese freighter lay on its side, the result of a visit from a Japanese cruiser which had come to conquer the port only days before the 80th arrived, but was forced to depart with its tail between its legs. After sinking the ship, the cruiser had shelled the entire area incorporating the port and airstrip, then landed a detachment of its Imperial Japanese Marines, who were among the world's most elite troops, all six feet or more in height. Australian troops had put up a spirited defense as the Marines landed and fought their way inland. The return fire from the Aussies gradually dwindled away as the Japanese reached the Strip. Confidently, the Marines proceeded to march in loose order the length of the Strip, where-upon hidden US Army 50-calibre machine guns fired into their midst. There was an immediate scramble as the Japanese rushed from the middle of the Strip to whatever cover might be available

83

at the sides. The eastern side, however, was an almost impenetrable barrier formed by the bulldozers which had cleared the area, and offered no solace to the stricken Marines. Suddenly, as those Japanese who were trying to escape westward neared cover, additional machine guns opened up from one end of the cover to the other. It was a slaughter as the 50-caliber bullets, capable of enough force to kill two men at once, ripped into the troops caught in the savage cross-fire. It was a decimated group that was able to make its way back to their boats and, still harassed by American and Aussie fire, returned to their cruiser. Defeated, the cruiser commenced to vent its frustration with a parting barrage of shellfire." (*The 80ᵗʰ Fighter Squadron 'Headhunters' Squadron History*)

Runway at Milne Bay. They took off and landed toward the water. The runway came between the forks of Milne Bay. The bodies of Japanese Marines were located in the trees to the left of the runway. American and Australians held Milne bay on the right side. Note the steel runway matting which was not put in until the battle was over.

View away from the Milne Bay. The pilots' camp was to the upper right of the runway.

Although the land was not very productive, it was an important piece of property strategically. Whoever had control of Milne Bay had excellent position for their planes to take off for Port Moresby or up the coast to Lae, Salamaua or other islands like the Solomons. For the Japanese it meant easy access for attacking Port Moresby. For the United States it meant keeping the Japs from attacking Port Moresby and for having an air strip that made it easier to reach other islands in the enemy's hands. Remember the Japs attempted to make a landing. This was the Coral Sea Battle between Australia and New Guinea in May 1942 where we lost an aircraft carrier and so did the Japanese. Another one of the American ships was damaged.

"The Japs had to have Milne if they wanted to conquer New Guinea. They could hardly afford to send their ships around the narrow tip of the island while we sat there and blasted them with land-based planes. That would have been suicidal for them, and, despite what you may have heard of the Japs' eagerness to die for dear old Hirohito, they gave little evidence of wanting to commit suicide through sheer stupidity.

McArthur knew the value of Milne Bay to the Japs. He also knew its value to us. And he foresaw that ultimately the Japs must try to take it." (*The Fight for New Guinea*)

As mentioned, in August of 1942, the Japanese set out to take Milne Bay landing on the north side of the harbor. They were met with resistance by two Australian P-40 fighter squadrons, several

Both pictures show Jap remains.

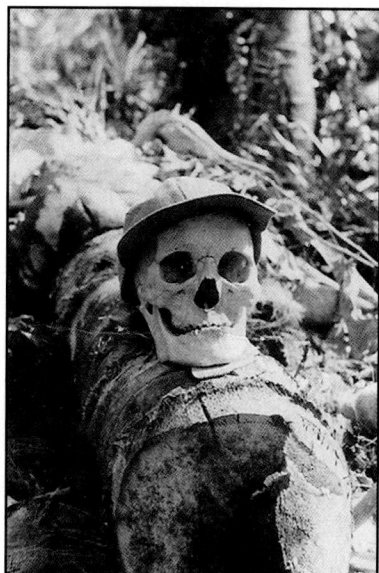

thousand Australian ground troops, some American engineers who were building a new airfield, along with a medical unit and some other American troops who built defenses against the attack. The Australian squadrons would take off, lift their gear and start strafing the enemy. On September 26th, 1942 close to 400 Japanese were killed by the 75th and 76th Australian troops. Area natives helped the troops by giving them information about where the Japanese were located. By the time the 80th arrived, the battle was over, but the effects remained.

Even though the Japanese lost the battle, they came so close that there were still many bodies lying within a close distance to the servicemen's camps. The smell was horrendous. In the heat and

humidity, bodies and clothing rotted rapidly, taking as little as two months for there to be nothing left but bones. Japanese boots were like gloves with the big toe part being separate from the rest of the boot. Norb mentioned how it eerie it was seeing bones sticking out from still perfectly-tied boots.

"Milne Bay – This was the best runway we flew off in the nearly two years I was with the 80th. Steel mats. Airplanes parked off south side of the strip in revetments. There was a mountain along the north side. We didn't use the north side for anything. Naturally 300 plus men required many tents (the 35th & 36th Sqdn were on another strip southwest of us.). We had to cross a little stream to get to the strip and our planes. This place marks the western most advance of the Japs. They made their landing along the narrow fork. The strip was cleared of trees etc, but not yet finished. The American engineers and Aust. Troops on the south side of the strip, the Japs on the north side. P-40s of Aust. Sqdn 75 & 76 would take off, lift their landing gear & fire their guns along the north side just beyond strip. One of the Sqdn COs was killed here – believe his name Rodger Turnbull. The end of the strip towards the ocean had many mines planted when we were there and many Jap bodies rotting in the jungle. The smell was bad. These areas put many pilots & crews down with malaria. It wasn't a base, just a strip with tents – no name except Milne Bay. Sunken Jap barges still along the shore." -Kirby

Jap landing barge left over from the invasion. The runway is just to the right of this picture. The mountains in the right background mark the other fork of Milne Bay. Directly behind from where this picture was taken was where Rodger Turnbull crashed on August 26, 1942. The belly tank from his P-40 with his name on it marks the site.

86

Coon Dog Connor

"Now the 80th had been in New Guinea over five months; we expected to be up six weeks like former squadrons and then rotated back to Australia. The 35th and 36th and Headquarters were all at the little strips formerly occupied by the Australian units. Our food was bad – no milk, no eggs, no fresh meat of any kind, no fresh vegetables and no deserts of any kind. We started getting many cases of malaria and all of us had lost weight. With so many sick, the rest of us were overworked. I flew ten days in a row once. Our C.O., Coon Dog, was evacuated with malaria and 104 degree temperature.

"Now there were no civilians left in the area, even though we were camped in one of the Lever Brothers largest cocoanut plantations on the island. Copra is the dried meat of the coconut which is used in soaps, margarines, etc. This was the chief export of the island.

"When the civilians left, they left behind a herd of mixed-breed cattle that wandered about on this end of the island. Sometimes they would even wander onto the runway since there were no fences. On our

Living area at Milne Bay
To the left is the officers' mess. The river they crossed to get to the runway is at the rear of the picture at the end of the road. Note the sandbags in front of the tents.

bulletin board was a notice signed by the 8th Group C.O. 'These cattle shall not be molested in any way.' Since the Group C.O. was based 20-30 miles away and didn't visit us often, something was bound to happen.

"Late afternoon you might hear a rifle shot or two. Then Dr. Patrick, the Flight Surgeon, would leave the

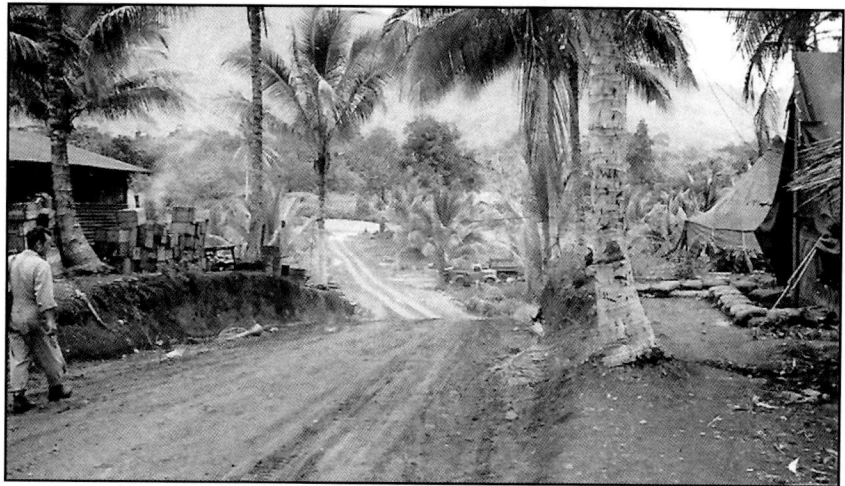
Native boat at Milne Bay. Any cities that existed were along the coasts.

area in his jeep to inspect the meat. The bomb service truck that had a winch on the back would follow. That night some of the pilots would get an invitation to dine out over on this little river bank. The cook had moved the gas stove down there and we feasted on steak."

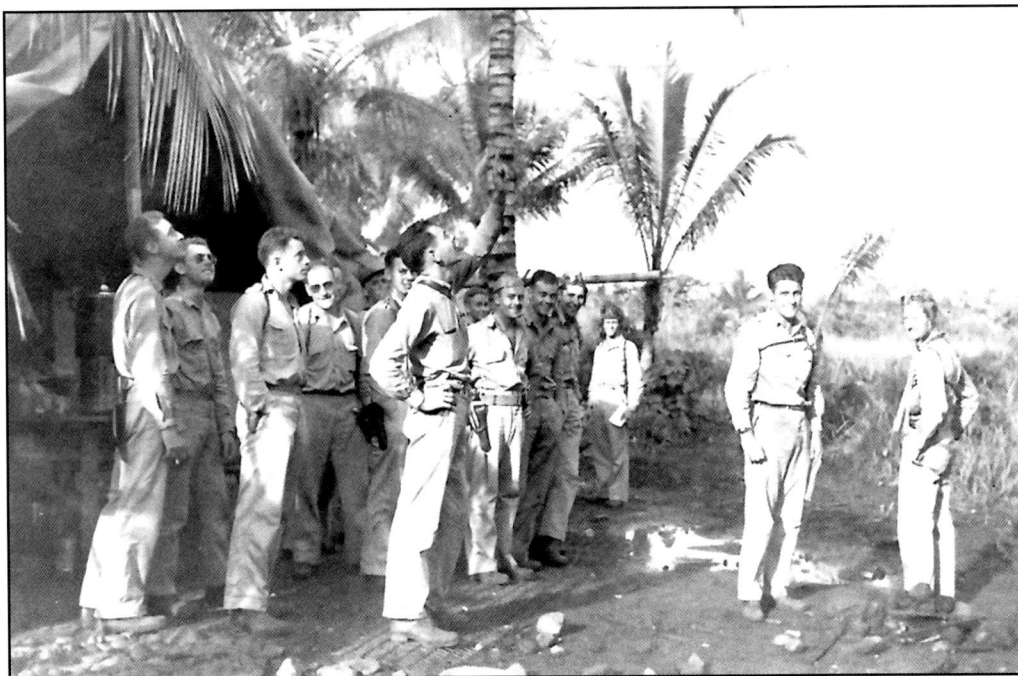

The above picture was taken by Norb in front of the alert tent at Milne Bay in late 1942 when the 80th was still flying P-39's. The man third from the left with his hand in his pocket is Charlie Bateson, who was beheaded by the Japs. Left to right is Lundy, who was shot down in P-38s in the 432rd Squadron and died. Next is George Neater, who was lost in the 80th in a P-38 on July 11, 1943 when he hit the top of a palm tree on Goodenough Island flying Griffin's wing. Griffin is the one pointing up. Dejarnette is facing the camera on the right and Hailey is to the right of him. Others are Dan Roberts, rear right; Corky Smith, with his hands on his hips; Kirby, to the right of Smith; Hanson, Willett, Daly, Baldwin, and Bennett behind Corky Smith.

The picture on the next page is the alert tent down by the airstrip at Milne Bay. The man walking towards the camera was an Australian Army Officer, by the name of Anderson. He was with the 80th for seven months at Twelve Mile, Milne Bay and also at Mareeba in Australia. Anderson would brief the pilots on where the Australians were in the jungle, so the Americans would not accidentally bomb or strafe them. Griffin and Bennett are in the background in the first picture. Cobb is facing the camera in the second.

Anderson had not been home in three years and had been through over 120 bombings at Port Moresby. While the 80th was being switched to P-38s at Mareeba, he was given permission to go down to Melbourne and marry his girlfriend. While on their honeymoon, he drowned.

88

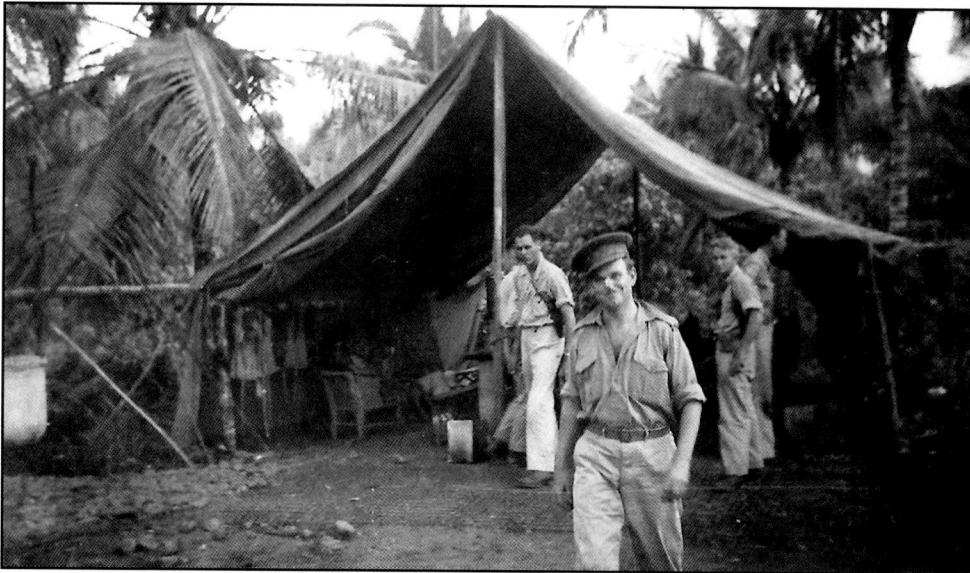
The man walking towards the camera is Anderson, Australian officer with the 80th.

People in any tense situation need a place to try to relax. The men on New Guinea were no different, so officers clubs or relaxation centers were built by the different squadrons. The 80th Officers' Club at Milne Bay was built using local natives. The frame was put up. Then the natives made shingles using vines to sew coconut fronds to sticks. The over-lapping fronds kept the incessant rain from pouring into the building. Note the officers' tents in the background.

Natives working on the 80th's Officers' Club

The finished officers' club

The Whiskey Run - November 11, 1942

"Phil Greasley was the first C.O. of the 80th when it was formed in 1942. He later was assigned to Group and Coondog Connor, from one of the sister squadrons, became the second C.O. Down at Milne Bay, he developed malaria and was shipped out with an extremely high temperature. Now Do-Do Brown is next in command. He had been an operations officer. He called me into

his tent and said he was getting orders cut for me to go back down to Australia and pick up a repaired P-39 at Charters Tower. This aircraft was going to be assigned to the 80th. Now he starts giving me further instructions. Catch the Martin flying boat. Naturally, take your parachute, which also contained your survival kit with rubber boat attached. Take an extra parachute bag since you will do some shopping. He instructed me where the liquor store was in Townsville, Australia. Old Cerio is a scotch type whiskey in a rectangular-shaped bottle. Each bottle is enclosed in a woven grass skirt. The complete package will fit in the 30 cal amo trays nicely – you will get three bottles in a row in each of the four trays. Of course you have to get rid of the amo. Hide it the brush. Now you have two-50 cal guns that fire through the prop. These have their

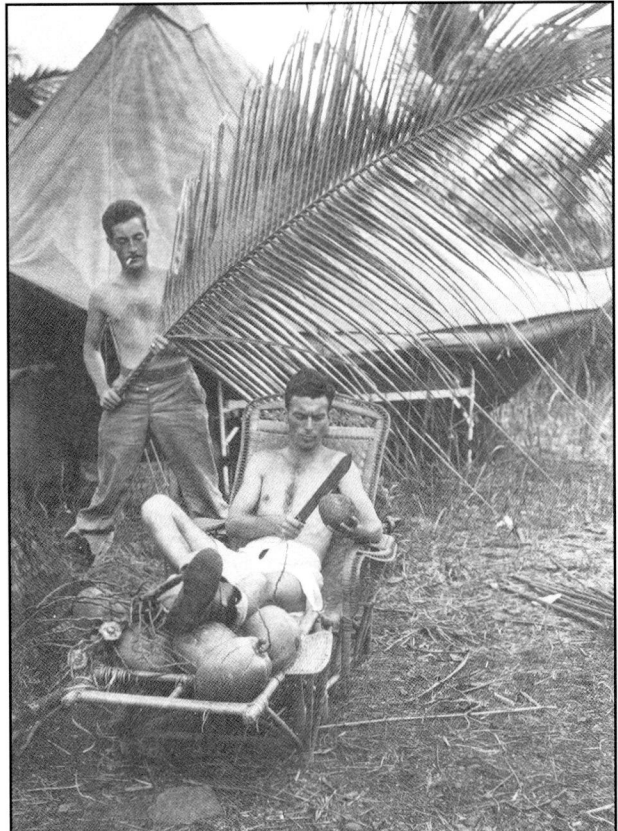
Norb and Dodo Brown

90

own shell ejection box—you can get two bottles in each of these containers. If you raise your seat to the 'top' position, the rest of the bottles with their grass coverings will fit under the seat. The return flight will be Charters Towers to Horn Island (off the eastern tip of Australia), refuel, on to Port Moresby and refuel and then down the coast of New Guinea to Milne Bay which is the eastern most tip. The total distance is some 1500 miles, 500 of which is over the Coral Seas. I had made this trip about three times before. I flew one of the ten airplanes up when the 80th Squadron first came up in early July 1942.

"It is never enjoyable taking a single-engine flight over that much water. Remember there is no air-sea rescue or flying boats to pick you up. Your airplane instrument panel starts to vibrate, engine noise sound rough—what's the weather ahead? At this stage any place in new Guinea could be combat territory, especially the flight from Port Moresby to Milne Bay. My four 30 cals have no amo, the 50s will jam on a few rounds (Do-Do said you still had the cannon). Anyway, all went well. The covers of the 30 cal amo boxes didn't fit tight and some of the straw packing showed up and the crews at Milne Bay noticed and followed me close to my parking spot. Do-Do did share a few bottles, but for the next ten days he didn't fly a mission, he just stayed in his tent and drank. Ed Cragg took over down at Mareeba, but Charlie Fellata was C.O. for only three days between Do-Do and Cragg. Mareeba, Australia is where the 80th changed from P-39s to P-38s.

"Back to the whiskey flight. Charters Towers is only about sixty miles inland from Townsville, but it is about a seven hour train ride. The train stops at every tea room or cattle station along the way and everyone gets off. I reported in to the air base at Charters Towers to present my orders. The base C.O. was a Captain Ludwig from Wausau, Wisconsin. I knew him from college at Stevens Point. About two weeks later he was killed in a hunting accident hunting kangaroos. I wonder if that pile of 30 cal amo was ever found in the brush. Remember we had been up in New Guinea for nearly six months by this time and there had been no booze or beer."

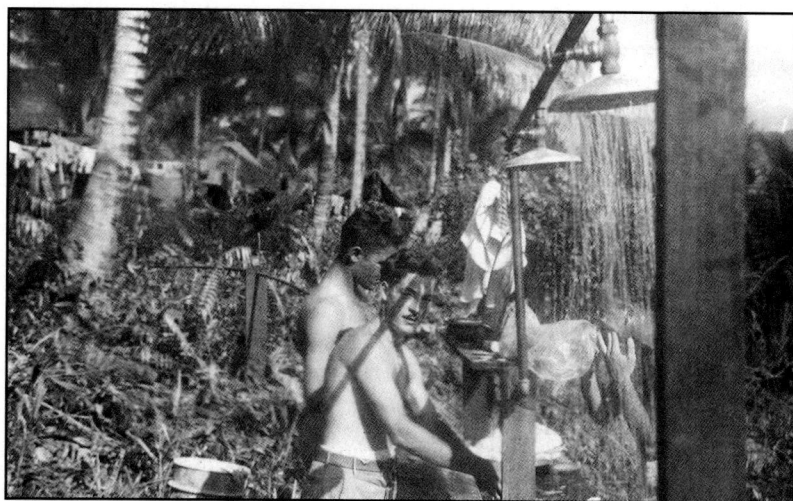

Latrine at Milne Bay. Water was pumped from the creek below up to tanks.

Outside the Alert Tent. L-R: Corky Smith, who became one of top ten Aces in P-38s, George Neater who was killed at Goodenough Island, Norb, Gorden Willett, and Noel Lundy who was shot down on a Wewak mission.

Inside the Alert Tent, playing cards waiting for the phone to ring. Corky Smith with hat on, Norb, Danny Roberts facing camera, Noel Lundy on right, Tom DeJarnette with back to camera. Note the names on the board on the left. It shows the flights for the day. Norb is leading the 'red' flight. The large board behind Danny Roberts lists the planes, their status and history and the crew chiefs' names.

Norb is carrying his parachute from the Alert Tent. Each pilot kept his parachute with him and not in the plane he last flew in. Pilots did not know which plane they would be flying from day to day.

Living area at Milne Bay. The smoke in
the background was from the Jap attack
on January 17, 1943.

The January Bombing of Milne Bay

Japanese bombings of airfields by both sides was a common event, but especially so at Milne Bay, where the pilots had easy access to other Japanese held islands.

"At Milne Bay we had no search lights…the enemy continued to send 2-3 planes every moonlit night…nuisance raids…no damage…we would never hit one of their planes but…it would cause us to go to the slit trenches and stay there until they left the area. With no searchlights you could not see where they were or which direction they were headed…thus the slit trenches…We were exposed for extended periods of time to the malaria bearing mosquitoes. We got down to one third operational strength." -Kirby

On January 17th, 1943, the Japanese surprised the airstrip with a ferocious attack. Those on the ground felt lucky to have survived and those that were on a mission escorting transports to Buna near Dobadura, came back to a bombed out airstrip and had to land on airfields used by the 35th and 36th.

"Another morale breaker happened at Turnbull Drome on January 17. The Japanese managed to get twenty-three bombers, probably Ki-21 'Sally' type, over Milne Bay sometime just after noon before any alarm could be sounded. Coming over the field at about 25,000 feet the bombers dropped their loads and destroyed two B-17s, two P-39s, a B-24 and

93

an Australian Lockheed Hudson. Several other 80th Squadron vehicles and structures were demolished.

Sixteen P-39s of the 35th and 36th Squadrons were off before the drone of the enemy engines died down, but there was no hope that they could reach the bombers' altitude even if they did have enough warning. Records indicate that some P-39s of the 80th were already in the air and managed to engage one formation of Sallys. Lieutenant Jay Robbins made the most of his first combat and damaged two of the Sallys. He also shared an attack on a third bomber with Lieutenant Gerald Rogers and the Japanese went down in flames. Lieutenant Leonidas Mathers damaged a fourth bomber.

Fifth Air Force practice with regard to granting claims did not recognize divided or ground victories, therefore Robbins and Rogers had to come to some decision on the credit for their victory. 80th folklore has it that the matter was decided with the flip of a coin and that Rogers won, giving him his second confirmed victory." (*Attack & Conquer*)

Two people who were on the ground that day were Marion Kirby, a pilot, and Frank Cicerello, a ground radio operator for the 80th.

"They [the 80th pilots leaving for a mission] took off about 9:30 am, circled the field, picked up the transports and off they blundered into the wild blue yonder. We all settled down for a nice peaceful day…when lo and behold…At 12 o'clock someone looked up and the sky had turned black with Jap bombers. As usual, they were flying perfect formation…and dropped their bombs when the lead plane released his pay load…with this method of bombing when you hit, everybody hit. When the lead plane missed, everybody missed…Well, today they were right on target…Our campsite was right off the end of the runway…We ran for the slit trenches while bombs exploded all around us…the earth shook unmercifully…I shook unmercifully, Hager was hollering at the top of his voice…Hager shook unmercifully…This time the lead bomber was right on target. They got everything that was on the ground…B-17s…P-400s…Everything!

A few P-400s came into commission after the escorters had left the area. They took to the air…Jay Robbins was one of them…They caught up with the Jap bombers and destroyed one of them.

After the bombers had cleared the area we brave souls climbed out of the slit trenches… congregated near the grass shack O'club and were discussing the recent event when out of the blue a piece of shrapnel fell at our feet, large enough to eliminate any one of us…While the strip was closed down a B-26 (Martin…the widow maker) came in shot up, could not get his wheels

down. He landed between the bomb craters…When he finally stopped sliding down the metal stripping you could read the name of his plane… 'ShittenGitten.'" –Kirby

Norb says the B-26 was called the 'Flying Prostitute' – no visible means of support. It had very short wings.

"On January 17, 1943, we had our biggest air raid to date. They hit us with 24 bombers

95

and Zeros. There was a mix up on the orders as to whether only the anti-aircraft guns were to be used or if our fighter planes would be scrambled. I counted only two bursts being fired. When the Japs saw no other firing and no enemy interception, the planes dropped so low that I remember standing dumbfounded, and I could see the bomb-bay doors opening and the bombs falling out. When they started hitting the ground, it sounded like some giant's footsteps coming at me. All hell broke loose. As there was no opposition, the Jap planes kept coming in at us time and time again. The raid lasted over two hours or so. It was almost the last of me I thought, but I remember hitting a slit trench near me and fell on top of some other guys. I guess I was so fascinated about the whole event that I kept standing there like a fool and watching the bombs falling.

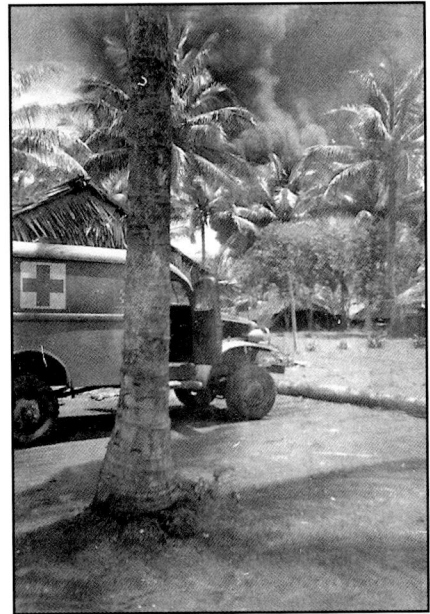

Fuel dump burning in background.

I remember also something landing on top of me or another person falling on me, I never did know which. Whatever it was did not move. One guy was yelling, 'Let me get my

Fuel dump burning in the background

A—in, let me get my A—in!' and I thought how comical it was. Afterwards I remember having a very painful backache.

"The Japs had made direct hits on and destroyed two B-17s, one B-24, one P-39, and two Lockheed Hudsons, over 10,000 gallons of gas. [Also gas trucks and command cars] Ammunition exploding like mad from the ammo dumps nearby that had been hit, and kept exploding for a long time afterwards. Runways were damaged and shrapnel was flying all over the place. When the metal mesh runways were hit, the pieces of the runway became like jagged pieces of shrapnel. They must have been using what we called Daisy Cutters. I remember seeing shrapnel go right through a truck engine, and saw that

What was left of the fuel dump the next day.

the piece of shrapnel had the words USA stamped on it. So I figured the Japs had got all our pre-war scrap metal and gave it back to us as bombs.

"After the raid was over, we heard that one bomber was shot down. We also heard that the anti-aircraft gun crew was told not to fire as the fighter planes would intercept, but that the fighter planes were told that the anti-aircraft would fire and for them not to intercept. Thus confusion added to the events. I guess that is why only two bursts by the guns were heard. It was some experience laying there helpless. We had rifles, but had not yet been issued bullet clips. When we first arrived in New Guinea each man was issued a 45 caliber pistol, but later had to turn them in for use by the infantry. I remember one time I was posted for guard duty at the ammo and gas pump and had to open a case of ammunition in order to see if the rifle was working. As I had used an old army rifle back in Pennsylvania for bear and deer hunting, I was familiar with its operation. I had never been tested at the rifle range during boot camp. Right after Pearl Harbor, the first sergeant asked for any deer hunters from Pennsylvania and we were issued rifles and we were used to protect the east coast from any submarine attacks which they expected but never came. They had dug slit trenches near the airfield and we were sent there. The rifles we used had been packed up in grease since World War I and had to be stripped down completely and cleaned thoroughly, before they could be used and even handled…

"After the air raid, we counted between 150-200 bombs that had dropped on our position. The camp was practically demolished and had to be rebuilt. I remember looking into the bomb craters and thinking that a 21 ton truck would easily fit

One of several B-24s destroyed during the raid.

97

into the hole." –Frank Cicerello (*The 80ᵗʰ Fighter Squadron 'Headhunters' Squadron History*)

P-39 #2499

B-17 #124551. Notice the revetments made from coconut logs.

Swede Hanson in front of the
B-24 #123824

B-17 #4540. Looks like
the man on the right is at
a loss as to what to do.

Bomb craters in the metal runway that forced Norb and the other pilots to land at another runway.

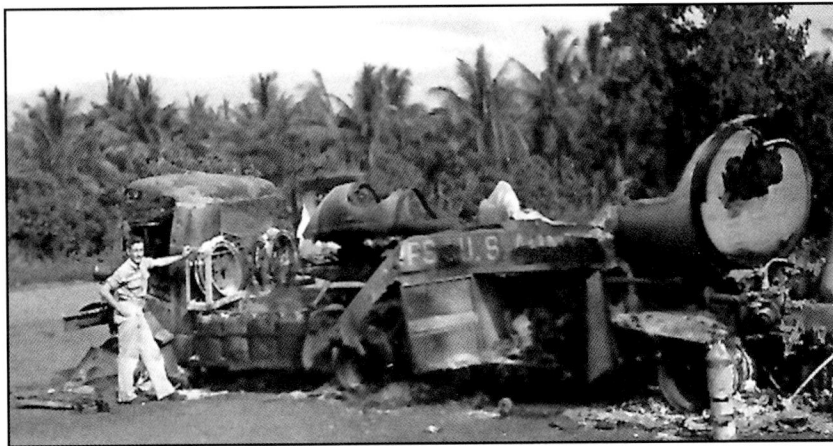

Norb and a refueling truck.

After the raid, the men dug their slit trenches deeper. Norb and Gerry Rodgers. A closer look shows bullet holes in the leaves of the trees.

Norb felt that being strafed was scarier than being bombed. "You couldn't hear the strafing like you could hear the bombs being dropped. You could hear the Jap bombers and see them and if they weren't in your area, you knew you didn't have to jump into the slit trench. The strafing was done when a Jap plane would follow one of our bombers home and then strafe the site. You could hear planes all day long with ours coming home, so you didn't know if a strafing was being done."

Shortly after this attack the 80th, morale low, malaria ridden and exhausted, was sent down to Mareeba to heal up and get the P-38 type aircraft.

"Many in our Squadron were sick with malaria. The food was poor, no fresh meat, no eggs, no fresh vegetables, no beer, no milk. We needed a break. The CO, Coon Dog Connors, was sent out with a very high temp – never to return to the 80th again. Dodo Brown becomes acting CO. Our first tour of duty was about seven months long. We expected six weeks when we went up to combat. This is the time other squadrons stayed in combat before they were relieved." -Norb

After the war the airstrip at Milne Bay was converted into a police training school by the Papuans.

Since they lived on a coconut plantation, coconuts were easy to come by. In the top picture a native climbs a tree to cut down coconuts. They would do this for a cigarette. Right: Norb prepares to cut one open.

101

Tentmates, Red Wilson who did two tours of duty
in New Guinea, Norb, and Danny Roberts who was
killed in November of 1943.

After a long mission. The weariness
is beginning to show.

80th Pilots
Front row l-r: Tom DeJarnette, Jay Robbins, Dailey, Yancey, Leonardas Mathers.
Back row l-r: Al Hailey who broke his back in Norb's plane after Norb left, Bob
Seibenthal, Bennett, Gordon Willett.

orb Ruff's P-38G-15, 43-2212 "Ruff Stuff" around August 1943. The man working on the left prop spinner is Walter "Shorty" Norton. (Via A.G. immons)

(Attack & Conquer)

103

P-39 in a revetment area. Note the belly tank in front of the crate. Belly tanks came in these crates. The belly tanks on the planes had to replaced if a pilot dropped his tanks before entering a battle.

Norb is resting his foot on a 500 pound bomb. The bombs to the right of his leg are 100 pound bombs. Bombs could be carried in place of belly tanks.

The men wore their guns all the time. Note the shoes instaed of Aussie boots. One day there was a huge pile of boxes of boots outside their living area and they helped themselves. The next day there was a large pile of rough wooden boxes used in place of coffins.

Revetment Area
Planes were put in different places and not lined up so it was more difficult for the Japs to strafe them. The pilots were told to "disperse your fighters" and they would taxi them to various revetment spots.

Planes of the 80th had different letters on them. The letters on these planes are 'E', 'F', 'W' and 'Z'. Norb normally flew 'X'. Red Wilson always said, "You could put an 'X' on an outhouse and Ruff would fly it."

This P-38 belonged to the 39th and landed at Milne Bay after a short duty in the Solomon area. The 39th was the first squadron in the Fifth Air Force to get the P-38.

Norb and Clifton Troxell. They had been classmates at Ellington Field, graduated together in the class of 41-I and came over on the Mariposa together. He was assigned to the 35th Squadron, but came over to the 80th often to visit.
Troxell was one of the 8th pilots who had a chance to fly with Lindberg.

Mareeba, Australia

*F*rom late January to early April the 80th was in Australia resting and training in an aircraft that every pilot loved, whether in Europe, Alaska or the Pacific theatre – the P-38 Lightning.

Planes were generally numbered in order of production, but the P-38 came out after the P-39 and P-400. The P-38 was not set up for mass production before the P-39 and P-400 because the pilots could not dive and then get out of the dive. This airplane was approaching the speed of sound on 'compressurablity', which nobody understood at that time. The controls act differently at these speeds in excess of 700 mph. This problem killed a lot of pilots, so production was limited on the P-38.

"Although we may tend to fault Lockheed for taking so long to get the P-38 into meaningful production, any of us who are old enough to recall those fearful times, the confusions, the shortages, the frustrating urgency to do a thousand things at once to fill a thousand pressing needs, will be able to put this, and other 'failures' into proper perspective. Attempting to arm ourselves and defend our freedom, we demanded production miracles of our often poorly funded industries to make up for 20 years of complacency, incompetency, and wishful thinking on the part of our leaders.

Lockheed, as the rest of the US, British and Commonwealth industry, did the best it could with what it had when there wasn't enough of anything, from metal to money to manpower, to go around; and did so according to assigned priorities. In addition to P-38s, Lockheed was building Venturas, Hudsons, and Boeing B-17s in large numbers. Meanwhile, the financing of plant expansion programs in America had to depend upon private money sources until the US Congress at last enacted the Lend-Lease Bill (HR 1776) on 11 March, 1941." (*P-38 Lightning at War*)

The P-38 was a super-charged, dual engine plane that could be taken up to altitudes of 43,000 feet. This allowed the pilots to escort transports and bombers at longer range, since the plane carried more fuel and if one engine went out, the pilot still had another to get back home. With the higher

altitude the pilots could now fly above the Japanese planes, which took them by surprise. It fired 4-50 caliber guns and one 20mm cannon.

"This comfortable old cluck will fly like hell, fight like a wasp upstairs and land like a butterfly. As a fighting ship it's like a big girl and you have to take her upon your lap and manhandle her. It's an extremely honest airplane; it doesn't bite and doesn't do unexpected things."

The P-38 is a leading fighter of World War II. It has a very long range, enabling it to give bomber support deep into enemy territory. It fights equally well at high or low altitudes. The P-38 is also a fighter bomber, capable of carrying 2 tons of bombs in place of the belly tanks.

Its four .50-cal. machine guns and one 20-mm. cannon, all mounted in the nose, produce a concentration of fire power ideal for strafing or aerial combat. The safety factor of two engines has endeared it to fighter pilots who call the second engine their 'round trip ticket.' With one engine knocked out, P-38 pilots in combat have finished the flight and made it home. [Norb once flew over 500 miles on a single engine from Wewak to Port Moresby.]

The P-38 has demonstrated a remarkable adaptability. It has met the enemy on all fronts, coping equally well with the changing needs of different situations.

The P-38 is a big fighter plane. It stands almost ten feet high, spreads out 52 feet, and is over 27 ½ feet long.

When the impression of size ceases to be a novelty, you notice some rather peculiar looking features. The long slender booms tapering into twin ruders are unique in aircraft design.

A closer inspection from the front quarter shows that the P-38 is a midwing airplane, with two liquid-cooled engines and two three-bladed propellers. It has a streamlined center section called a gondola, and stands solidly on a twin-cycle landing gear. There are four .50 cal. machine guns and one 20-mm. cannon in the nose.

Right under the wing between the engines and the gondola, you can see two odd projections. They are shackles for external tank bombs. The plane can carry quite a payload on these shackles." –Lt. Ben Kelsey (*Pilot Training Manual for the P-38*)

Group Headquarters at Mareeba where the pilots went to change over to P-38s.
L-R: Charlie Falletta, Doc. Patrick, Sponenberg (head turned to left.) The ladder goes up to the flight control tower.

In 2000 Norb wrote to Dale Jones about flying the P-38 and some of its potential problems. "Bail out of a P-38. There were many tales about the problem – most untrue. I can't believe the 1st 19 hit the horizontal stabilizer and I never heard of Perry. What outfit did he fly with? Sure it was possible to do this & die – remember *all* airplanes have horizontal stabilizers behind the cockpit and you can hit these in a P-39, P-51, Zero, etc. I've seen Jap pilots hang from these with parachutes partly open. Perry's method according to your letter was to "trimming the aircraft into a shallow dive-etc." First, tell me what *speed* he *starts* this at! What *air speed* does he exit at in this shallow dive? Remember the air speed increases in any dive. If you exit 175 mph or less in level or inverted you miss it. If over 350 you miss it also. No 1 - Don't open chute too quick. I've seen pilots P-38 hanging on one side of the stabilizers with chute partly open hanging from the outside. The plane made many series of lazy 8's before it crash landed. Sure we were instructed on this.

"Mr. Perry is correct regarding torque problems when you lose an engine on take off. When you fly off of a short 3500' runway, carrying amo load for five guns and two large belly tanks full of 100-octane fuel every take off is a hazard. You better have a very good crew chief on this airplane that checked it *before* you get in it. You probably will take off in the dark, single airplanes take off. The Sqdn CO makes one little circle of the field and all 16 airplanes are expected to be in formation – 4 flights of 4. Then on the way to join whatever you will escort today. Any twin engine aircraft has torque problems if one quits on take off. The heavier the load the greater the problem." -Norb

The first Jap kill with a P-38 by the 39th Fighter Squadron was disputed, rather humorously, by General Kenney.

"On November 26, 1942, five P-38s took off and headed across the mountains to Lae. Captain Bob Faurot intended to plant his bomb on the ground installations, but he overshot and the bomb exploded in the water just off the end of the runway, which ran right down to the beach. There was a boiling explosion, and a solid tower of water rose into the air.

Simultaneously, a Zero was taking off to intercept the attacking Lightnings. The Japanese fighter flew straight across Faurot's bomb, and the blast caught the plane and simply flicked it over into the sea. Faurot had other pilots to supply eyewitness confirmation, the Zero was in the air, and he claimed credit for the kill.

But not without argument. General Kenney went to see Faurot and ask him if he had the nerve to call that the first P-38 kill in the Fifth Air Force. Faurot grinned and asked if he was going to get the Air Medal. Kenney said, 'Hell no…I want you to shoot them down, not splash water on them!'" (*P-38 Lightning At War*)

Bob Farout, a former All-American football player, was with 80th while they straffed Japs at the Buna landing. He was one of two pilots of the 39th Squadron lost in the Bismarck Sea Battle.

When the 80th received the P-38 it caused some hard feelings from the 35 and 36th[th] Squadrons who thought they should have received them first. Some of these hard feelings still exist with the veterans of the 35th and 36th Squadrons and the 80th.

"The P-38 Question: The 39th Fighter Squadron was the lucky unit to introduce the P-38 into combat in the Fifth Air Force. It was a simple flip of a coin that decided the 39th would get the Lockheed fighter. From the very beginning the 39th did well with the P-38 – except for the maddening teething troubles such as leaking cooling systems and ground crews who were totally unfamiliar with the type. On the first two full combat missions flown by the 39th twenty Japanese aircraft were listed as confirmed destroyed for no losses, albeit General Kenney tried to pump up the score as much as possible to give the young pilots a booming start.

In January 1943 the 9th Fighter Squadron joined the 39th as the second P-38 squadron in the Fifth Air Force. Tom Lynch was one of the sparkplugs in the 39th and the 9th got some impressive talent in the form of Dick Bong, who was to become the top American ace of the war, and Lieutenant Gerald Johnson, who would rise to command the entire 49th Fighter Group later in the war. Other rising stars of aerial combat were included in both squadrons.

For the third squadron to receive the P-38 one of the 8th Fighter Group would be selected to give each group in the SWPA one unit. Again, the lucky squadron would be selected by the flip of the coin and the 35th won.

Tony Trotta was one of those in the 35th who was elated at the prospect of getting the P-38:

'Thur. Jan. 21st, 409th Day of War. Up at 9 A.M. Washed. Heard we're leaving – just the 35th to go back to Australia for P-38s. Boy, that is good news. Received clothing issue. Ate dinner & went to work.'

However, his entry for January 26 has a different tone: "Our movement is called off! We got 'screwed.' The 80th put up a stink and they're leaving now instead of us. If anyone in the outfit died the boys couldn't be any more mournful than they are. The best outfit in the group and we got 'screwed!'

The truth is somewhat different although a bit difficult to accurately determine. A number of stories sprang up about the real reason for the switch of squadrons to receive the P-38. First of all, the 80th was in no position to influence the decision. Phil Greasley had moved up to a higher headquarters and although he probably would have wanted to get P-38s for the 80th, he was in no position of authority to alter the decision.

Captain Ed Cragg had taken command of the 80th by the beginning of 1943, but he was a brand new commander and didn't have any real influence on the matter. There was no pro-80th lobby that would get the unit any preference over the 35th.

The decision was made on the basis of serviceability. While the 35th Squadron had a good record and maintained a high degree of readiness, the 80th was riddled with malaria and Denque Fever [and had been in combat for seven months in a row]. Whitehead was not about to take a combat ready unit out of the line for transition to a new aircraft type while he kept a marginal unit in action: The 80th could use the transition time to reduce its illness rate.

According to Morris, the 80th was rewarded for its high malaria rate while the 35th was penalized for its effectiveness. It was a new twist on the old saw about three ways to do things: the right way, the wrong way and the Army way!" (*Attack & Conquer*)

"Two pilots who came into the 80th during February and March of 1943 would have prominent roles in justifying the decision to get the squadron operational on the P-38. One

111

of these pilots was Lieutenant Ken Ladd who was described as 'one of the nicest guys you could ever meet' by Yale Saffro, who would be his crew chief later in the year. Ladd was an exceptional pilot who scored consistently with the 80th and later took command of the 36th Squadron in 1944 and was killed in action over Balikpapan.

Lieutenant Cy Homer joined the 80th in March and was assigned to Norb Ruff's flight.

Ruff noticed that Homer had a bad leg and asked him about it. Homer replied he had injured it while racing motorcycles.

Ruff wiped his brow and wondered what they were sending out of flight school as pilots now. Two years before an aviation cadet had to be in perfect physical condition. After the first combat mission flown with Homer in the flight Ruff had his answer; he was the best, or at least the second best, pilot that Ruff had ever known including Dick Bong when he flew with the 80th later in the war. Norb Ruff quietly made sure the Lt. Homer was nearby when the flight was ever in a combat mission.

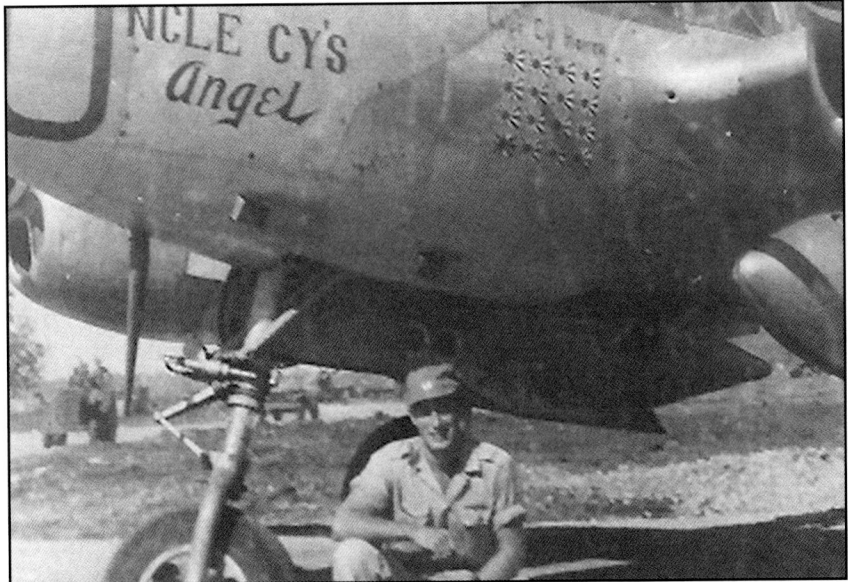

The 80th moved down to Mareeba at the end of January and prepared to convert to the P-38. P-39s were listed on squadron rosters until March, at which time they were presumably exchanged for more P-38s. 80th pilots were sent down to other bases in Australia for transition training while others who had been trained on the P-38 became operationally ready. [They were on rest leave.] Don McGee came to the 80th from the 36th Squadron as did George Welch. Carl Taylor came from the 8th Group Headquarters to assume duty as 80th Executive Officer in March and the Squadron was becoming combat ready again." (*Ibid*)

Both of these pictures show Norb with his new plane.

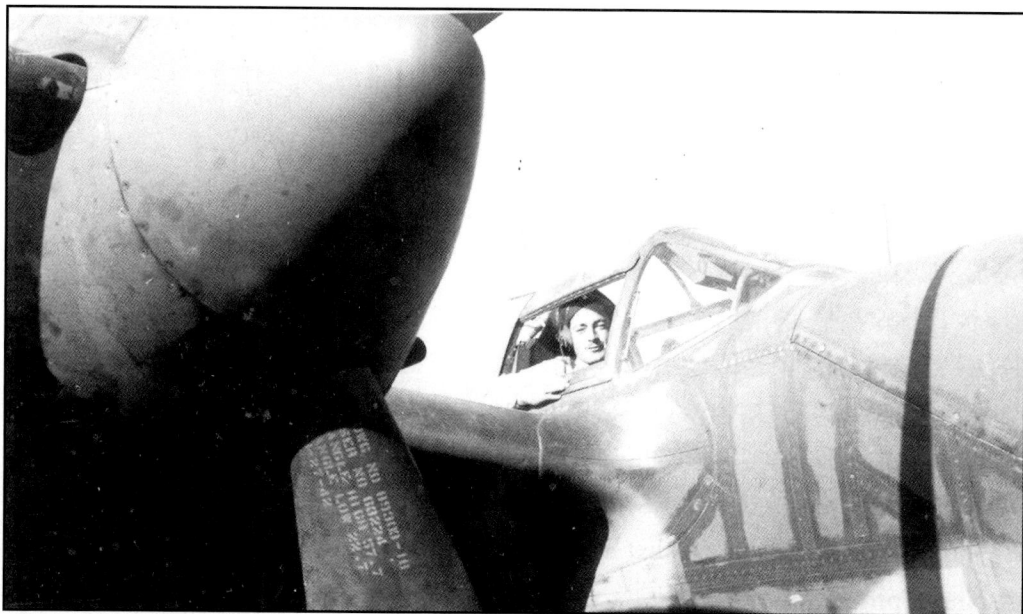

The First 80th General

"There is one thing about the 80th Fighter (and loving) Squadron of which I am very proud. The last account I had which was several years ago we had produced in excess of 45 GENERAL Officers. I am certain that it must be approaching 50 by now?...A little quiz…Who do you think was the first one in the squadron to wear the star?

It goes back to early 1943…let me start earlier than that with a little background…The 80th acted as a replacement squadron in the early part of the war. The 35th and 36th were the first American squadrons to go to New Guinea with the 80th remaining at Petrie, Australia furnishing the sister squadrons with replacements. The 39th and 40th (35th Group) replaced them. Then the 41st Squadron of the 35th Group and the 80th of the 8th Group went north in the middle of July 1942. [New Guinea.] Then the good guys arrive on the scene. The Panama contingency arrive (all wearing white hats). There was only one thing in error…they were composed of 41-I, they primarily were classmates and the squadron had many members of the same class. (We graduated from flying school five days following Pearl Harbor and we were used to bring the combat units up to strength, in other words, we were the expendables.)

Ok, with so many expendables, they found no reason for promotion. They would not promote one man without promoting the group so they took the easy way out by promoting none. We would have classmates arrive from the states only to be returned because they had too much rank for the theatre (heresay). Naturally, we were getting peed off. When we left Milne Bay in early February, '43 to go down and pick up our P-38s they were not all ready, naturally, so they gave half of the squadron leave while the other half checked out [in the P-38s]. (Incidentally we had been operating at below 50% strength due to malaria. I was in the group that went down first. Rumors had been flowing freely that there might be a chance that someone might get a promotion…slim, but a chance! So while in Sydney I took the opportunity to prepare myself for the event…I went to the

Marion Kirby

PX (years before they ever heard of BXs) and purchased First Lt bars, and just to make certain that I covered the correct rank, I added the Captain's Bars, Major's Leaves, the Lt. Col's Leaves; the Chicken Colonel's Eagles and of course, The General's Star.

We return to Mareeba, Australia (a little town just inland from Cairns). Mareeba looked like a movie set…false fronts on all of the buildings, unpaved main streets, hitching racks in front of each building and ant hills higher than any building surrounding the town. Upon arrival by train, (previous century manufacture) we entered the depot and called the camp requesting transportation. About an hour later a ten-wheeler arrived. There were three of us; Raymond Daly, Noel Lundy and myself. To kill the time while awaiting transportation we each donned our new rank. Daly became a Lt. Col, Lundy was a new Full Bull Col., and naturally I pinned on the Star, the first to do so in the history of the squadron!!!

The truck arrived, Lundy and Daly get in the back and I ride shot-gun in the cab. We arrived at the gate…the first time we had ever had a guard post at one of the gates. The guard comes half-assing out to the truck. He checks the backend first…Lo and behold…a Lt. Col and a Bull Col…He damned near knocked himself out with a brace so still that 'The Corps' would have been proud. That was not enough…He checked the cab and there was a Brigadier General…Holy Manure…I immediately gave him 'at ease' before he fainted. He told us to pass on and went immediately to the telephone to alert the camp that we were being invaded by a whole mess of brass.

We get to the camp area, unload (had to carry the B-4 bag myself, no batman). We hear that there is a new bunch of pilots in camp and that Capt. Danny Roberts has them in his tent briefing them. I immediately picked up a tree limb (it was a eucalyptus tree limb) to act as my swagger stick. Stroking my leg several times as I walked, I entered Danny's tent. Danny's eyes popped out and the group popped, too, so stiff that the breathing had ceased. I immediately gave them 'at ease'…and started my little spiel…Gentlemen, I am certain that Capt. Roberts is briefing you in regard to the combat that is in store for you…I might add that I guess the first thing that impresses you is my age…well, to tell you the truth, it is rough up there in New Guinea and those few of you that survive will be promoted fast…in fact, damn fast. Thank you, Capt. Roberts." Each time I have related this story someone would always ask, 'What if they would have caught you and court-martialed you…' Well, they would probably have sent me to the island of New Guinea and ordered me into combat…and that is where we were heading anyway." –Marion Kirby

Norb flying a P-38 from Mareeba to Port Moresby

115

Tom Baldwin, Danny Roberts, Norb and George Halveston on the crash boat out of Milne Bay. The boat was run by an Aussie captain and when not used to find downed pilots, it was occassionally used by the men for a break.

Bill 'Horrible' Hager a ground officer, Norb, and Sponenberg on rest leave.

Norb at Bondai Beach near Brisbane.

Swimming at Bondai Beach

Three-Mile – Port Moresby

$\mathcal{N}$ot much had changed at Port Moresby since the 80th left for Milne Bay, except now they were flying the P-38 Lightning, now painted the 80th's color scheme: bright green spinners with silver and green striped rudders. The Japanese would soon learn to hate those colors.

"Weevil-infested toast, powdered eggs, salt pork, Australian jam, coffee, and chlorine-laced water once again passed for breakfast at Three Mile Drome on the morning of September 4, 1943. The pilots of the 8th Fighter Group might have felt they deserved better fare, at what could be the last meal for any one of them. Here they were, at a primitive, muddy airstrip in the malaria-ridden jungle of New Guinea, in the pre-dawn darkness about to fly a dangerous combat mission, sure to be outnumbered by Japanese Zeros. Why complain about lousy food?" (Taken from *AcePilots Main Page*, Major Jay T. Robbins – 8th Ftr. Group/80th Ftr. Squadron)

In late March and early April, when the 80th was done checking out in their new P-38s, they were not sent back to Milne Bay but to Port Moresby again. This time they would be at Three-Mile

Aerodrome. Before the war this was the air field for the city. It was from here that Amelia Earhart flew before going to Lae, New Guinea, on her last flight before she disappeared.

This was the original airdrome at Port Moresby and

had 3000' of runway. "We used this field for most of my 50 missions in P-38s. We landed (and took off) going in the opposite direction (toward the camera)." Norb's plane sat to the right of the picture.

"This was the city airport before the war. By 1942, in July, there was this one, then Wards Drome, which was a dummy drome with fake airplanes, etc., 7 Mile, which was the big bomber base and the best field, 12 Mile, 14 Mile and another way up the coast called 30 Mile which wasn't used by us.

"The story I heard at 30 Mile. The greatest French Ace of WWI was 'Borqua.' He became a missionary and was sent to New Guinea to this location and died a few years later of malaria. Whenever the French Fleet was in the area, they would put a wreath on his grave. Nick Patrick, our Flight Surgeon went up to 30 Mile and supposedly found his grave."

On April 8th, the 80th had a new CO. Captain Edward "Porky" Cragg replaced Capt. Falletta, who had been CO for only two days.

"Cragg was an aggressive leader who got into the thick of every fight and who sometimes came back with holes in his P-38 and even himself. He would lead the 80th Fighter Squadron to some difficult battles and impressive victories throughout the remainder of 1943." (*Hard Driving Headhunters, Fighter Pilots in Aerial Combat*)

It was Cragg who gave the 80th their new name, The Headhunters, in honor of the headhunters from New Guinea who helped rescue pilots. Crewchief Yale Saffro was commissioned to create the Headhunters logo. Saffro had been an artist for Walt Disney before the war. This logo is still used today by the 80th.

Cragg was shot down on December 26th, 1943 along with the Operations Officer Freddie Taylor. Taylor made it back, Cragg did not. After Cragg's death, Jay Robbins became CO and did an excellent job. Later Robbins was sent to Group Headquarters.

120

'Headhunters' logo designed by Yale Saffro. This was actually the second design.

The first design, also created by Saffro depicts Donald Duck pouring urine on the Rising Sun. It was dropped because the pilots thought it would not be approved by the government.

With the advent of the maneuverability of the P-38, the 80th started racking up victories against the Japanese planes, which showed what can happen when the pilots finally had good planes.

May 21, 1943: "The P-38s of the 80th Fighter Squadron took off to act as top cover for C-47s en route to Wau. Immediately after takeoff the 12 Lightnings were ordered to intercept enemy aircraft over Salamaua. One P-38 was forced to abort the mission, but the remaining 11 were flying below broken overcast at 23,000 feet when 20 Hamps, Zekes, and Oscars were sighted slightly above and to the left of the formation. Belly tanks were dropped and the attack was made by turning into the enemy.

The Japanese fighters were in no definite formation but in groups of three at various altitudes. This made it impossible for the Lightnings to maintain formation, so attacks were made by elements. Captain Ed Cragg made the first pass on a Hamp-type aircraft, and his first burst took more than half the fighter's wing off. It went down in an uncontrollable spin…Six of the Japanese fighters were downed by the men of the 80th in that fight, and all P-38s returned safely." (*Pacific Sweep*) Norb was on this mission.

In June the 80th saw many new faces join the squadron and many familiar ones leave. A new Operations Officer, George Welch, was moved from the 36th to the 80th. Welch was flying a P-40 during the Japanese bombing of Pearl Harbor and shot down four Jap planes. He was featured in the movie, "Torro, Torro, Torro." After Pearl Harbor, he was sent on a War Bond tour for a year. Then a year to the day of Pearl Harbor, he shot down three more planes. By the end of the war he had seventeen planes to his credit. After the war he got a job with North American as their chief test pilot, flying the F-100 Super Sabre for them. He was killed in 1954 while test-piloting this plane.

Other pilots who came in around this time were Ed DeGrafenreid, Paul Murphey, Myers, "Screwy Louie" Scribner, Robert Feehan and Jennings Myers. The last two men died in combat.

In July General Kenney decided that a new Fighter Group was needed and formed the 475th Fighter Group which would be made up of three squadrons, the 431st, 432nd and 433rd. Each existing squadron of the Fifth Fighter Command had to give up some pilots. The 80th lost Ed Czarnecki, Noel Lundy, Danny Roberts, Zach Dean, James Ince, Marion Kirby and Campbell Wilson to the new 475th Group. Happily for Norb, Lt. Robbins was not one of those transferred out.

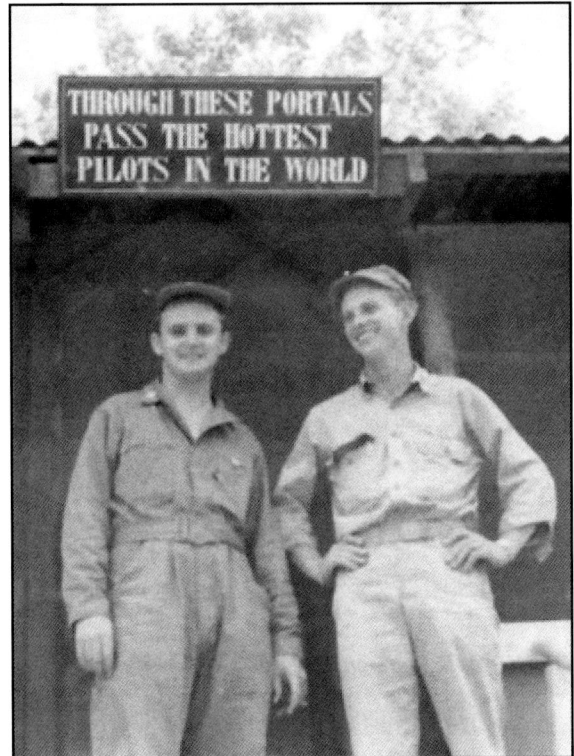

Ed Cragg and George Welch

Louis "Screwy Louie" Scribner

John Jones

122

"Now the word gets out that thirty nurses are coming up to Port Moresby and we are going to have a hospital. Each squadron fighter unit, as well as the bomber units, now have to build an officers' club to entertain the nurses. Every off duty pilot is needed. Our Lt. Woods, a ground officer, 'found' all kinds of material. I think he called it a

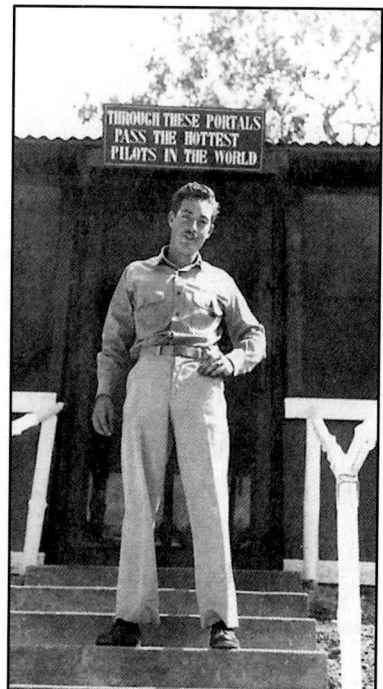

midnight requisition.

"About this time Jay Robbins has been with us long enough to get his first rest leave. Naturally he heads for the hospital down 2500 miles south to Melbourne to see his girlfriend, except she is on a boat heading for Port Moresby, one of the thirty volunteer nurses enroute.

"The officers club at 3-Mile gets built. The sign over the door is hung and the outside latrine gets a fence around it. Other squadrons have their clubs finished, and the nurses are entertained at four or five other ones before they spent an evening at the 80ths. I was on a late mission and when I came back, found a pair of pressed kaki pants and came to the club after shaving. Here were many tables set up with one nurse to three or four pilots. The first words I heard from one nurse was, "I don't know why you boys don't like it here—we think it's just grand!" I left early—most of these women were not prom queens from high school and never got this kind of attention before. I left early and never got involved with the nurses."

It was during his time at 3-Mile, flying his P-38 "Ruff Stuff" that Norb shot down four enemy aircraft. Although he claimed seven Japanese shot down, he was given credit for only four. All were fighters, except for one dive bomber. His first was an Oscar shot down while escorting bombers to Madang, New Guinea. Two of the planes were shot down in one day.

"The first time I shot down a Jap plane, I felt we were just shooting down planes. It was quite a shock to see the pilot suddenly coming out of his plane with his parachute open. It really hit me that this was more than a plane – there was a man inside!"

In May, 1943, Ed Cragg recommended Norb for promotion to the rank of Captain. He was promoted on June 16, 1943

"The 11 & 14 June 43 missions – Reasons. By this year we were flying P-38s. Each airplane carried 2 belly tanks which you can drop before combat. We were sent to Goodenough Island on detached service later – 16 airplanes & pilots with some crew chiefs expecting a large Jap reinforcement to come into Lae & Buna area. The U.S. now is going to try and take back Lae, Salumaua, etc. We will drop troops airborne into Nadjab area. The Japs have large bases in New Britain & Rabaul so to prepare for our time at Goodenough we need belly tanks closer than Pt. Moresby. So we flew empty tanks down to Milne Bay which was closer – dropped them off and flew back. Milne Bay also had plenty of 100 octane gas. As you can tell from Cleve's Form 5 we were only there about 16 days. Long enough to lose one real good boy, Neater. Our home base was still 3 Mile at Pt. Moresby. Later in Oct. we would again stage out of Dobodura near Buna for the U.S. landings at Finchhafen which we covered. This is on one of your maps up above Lae. At the time we flew belly tanks down to Milne Bay the Aust. P-40 sqdns were again based there. One other Aust. Sqdn with Spit Fire 5's was over on Goodenough with us. I had gotten to know some of these boys pretty good since I trained with them when I was in 7th Sqdn of the 49th in P-40s down at Brisbane in Feb, March 42. Real good boys with more guts & courage than average!" (Norb in a letter to Dale Jones)

In August of 1943, the Japanese-held area of Wewak was put in the sights of the Fifth Fighter Air Force. The Japanese had a large base there and taking it out sent the Japanese reeling.

"Wewak is located about 400 miles over the highest parts of the Owen Stanley Mountains from Port Moresby. P-38 escorts had to be in the air for almost two hours before they arrived over the target. If an aerial battle resulted they could expect to run at full power for another fifteen to thirty minutes before the long run home. If the pilot had to correct his navigation [due to weather] another block of time up to twenty to thirty minutes was involved. The missions to Wewak from Port Moresby tested the endurance of both P-38 and pilot." (*Attack & Conquer*)

"Being in the air for five hours is a long time to be in one position. You couldn't move around and stretch and your backside would get sore. You could swear the crew chief who was the last one in the plane before the pilot got in, had left his false teeth on top of your parachute, which was already in the cockpit." –Norb

"August 20, 1943: Earl W. Smith was flying my wing. I was leading the Squadron. He motioned a single plane below. I said go ahead and covered him with the remaining planes. We also had transports on the ground to cover. He made a quick pass, downed the Nip and was back in formation in a matter of two minutes. He was all smiles. Earl was a very happy excitable guy. I got a Nip on one of these first missions. We finished the mission, came back home and landed all except Earl. He decided to put on a little air show over a transport in Port Moresby harbor next to our strip on 3 Mile. He hooked a

Taken at 3 Mile in Mid-1943
Back row l-r: Ince, Borowski, Daly, Ruff, Neater, Homer, CPM Wilson, Seibenthal.
Front row l-r: Hope, Thomkins, Sineath, Freeman, Krisher

wing in the water and that's where he ended up. The Sqdn record could have called it a *test* hop."
-Norb

"August 23, 1943: Leonidas Mathers: Leon was married – born in Mathersville, Mississippi, about the class of 41-I or H. He came to the 80th with the Panama group with Cragg, Kirby, Lundy, etc. He was an excellent poker player. Evenings in the squadron for lack of anything else to do – there was always two poker games going on. One low, one high stakes. Toward the end of the month the game – high stakes one – would end up usually with two guys, one C.K. Taylor and Leon. Usually Leon Mathers would send home the collective winnings like $3-5000.00/month. C.K. wasn't the best fighter pilot either – he had a hard time completing a mission – some type of airplane trouble.

"Now the day before Leon went in we were together on a combat mission and both he and I had written up our airplanes for problems after we completed the mission. Mine were minor. Leon said his engine would cut out at altitude. The next day we were 'off' of flying. I was writing letters. C.K. & Leon played poker all afternoon. Leon again got the money. About 4:00 pm phone rang – both planes were ready for testing. We drove down to the strip together in a jeep. I check out my plane – all okay, landed and was standing on the wing. I could see Mathers approaching on down wind leg out over the bay on single engine. He was low, the other prop just idling. There is an island in the bay. He flew low in behind the island and never came out. I still don't know if he feathered the wrong prop or if both engines just quit. He did set it down in the water, drowned. I told Cragg what I had seen. He asked me to go out with the crash boat the next morning with native skin divers. At this time we thought he was still in the plane. We could bring up small pieces of aluminum, but the major portion was in too deep of water to reach. He floated in the next day with his chute still on. Anyway, the Squadron could report the death rather than 'missing' in action, if you don't have a body, especially if he's married. [Mathers was from Matherville, Mississippi.]

"Well this isn't quite the end, yet. C.K. later transferred out of the 80th – lived through. Mathers wife was living someplace in the Chicago area, I believe. C.K. looked her up and married her. Guess you could call this the 'last hand.'" -Norb

The Comfort Station

The picture to the right shows Cleve Jones, Farley Sineath and Dick Hartmann at the three-hole comfort station at 3 Mile. The covers for the

holes cannot be seen. They were spring-loaded to the down (cover) position. When men sat, the covers were against their back, and when they stood up, the covers automatically dropped back into place. Every morning, an orderly, an enlisted man, poured gasoline into the latrine, then tossed a match into the hole. This burned out the waste and attempted to keep down flies and disease.

Occasionally representatives from various companies in the United States would visit war zones. Some were legitimate, checking on aircraft parts, trying to find out what was or was not working or how to improve their product.

One time a man came from AC Sparkplug Company.   He was a rather large person who liked his food. He made a habit of getting up early, eating with the first group of men, then going back to bed. Then he would get up later and eat breakfast with a later group. This was when pilots were allowed one egg a week and other meager rations. The men really began to hate him, because besides eating their food, he didn't seem to do anything to help the war cause. He was not in any danger, was making big money and did not have to worry about the draft.

One morning, the orderly poured gasoline down the hole, but didn't have any matches, so he went back to his tent to get some. Meanwhile, the representative needed to use the facilities. So loaded with his magazines, he sat and decided to light up a cigar. He struck the match, lit the cigar and dropped it into the latrine. The match hit the gasoline vapor and gaboom, he ended up with a ring of burns shaped like the latrine hole on his backside. Dr. Patrick, the flight surgeon had quite a job to do. Justice was served.

Neither Farley Sineath nor Cleve Jones made it through the war. In July, 1943 Sineath, from Columbia, South Carolina, dropped out of formation during a mission. "I led the squadron that mission. I think we were escorting transports that day. Kirby had that flight of four. Nobody saw Sineath drop out of formation and no radio message. It will always be a mystery – no combat that day. We never got any information later on Sineath. He may have had an oxygen problem" –Norb (See Chapter 5 for Cleve Jones' story. Jones was from Salt Lake City, Utah)

George Neater at the alert tent.

"George Neater was a 1st Lt. with the 80th in P-38s while we were on detached service from Port Moresby to Goodenough Island. This chain of islands is off a north coast of New Guinea, just north of Milne Bay. The date was July 4, 1943. As I remember he was flying Griffin's wing-while in a two-ship formation. Neater broke the rule of always flying a little above your element leader. They were buzzing the strip and

127

he got a little below Griffin and took a palm tree before hitting a truck. George Neater came into the 80th in July 1942 with the large group from Panama. A real nice, quiet gentleman and a good officer born in Iowa. Flew a lot of missions in P-39s." –Norb (Neater was from Council Bluffs, Iowa.)

John Guttel, right, in front of Norb's P-39, was one of the few Jewish pilots.

Guttel was part of one of the most costly missions flown by the 80th on August 21, 1943; one that today still affects Norb. Norb and his three flight members, 2nd Lt. Robert E. Feehan, 1st Lt. John Guttel, and 1st Lt. Elwood G. Krisher were escorting bombers to Wewak with

John Guttel in front of Norb's plane prior to the switch to P-38s

the squadron of 16 planes, four flights of four planes. Escorting B-25 bombers was the most dangerous type of mission. The fighters had to protect the bombers and expected attack from Zeroes at any time. The pilots flew automatically—their concentration could not be on their plane, but what was coming over their shoulders. Zeros could rapidly come down from above and behind them, so their eyes constantly searched the skies for the enemy planes. Guttel was leading the second element of the flight, and Norb was flight leader. As Norb looked over his right shoulder for the enemy, he would check his instruments and this time saw that his oil gauge was set on zero. With no oil pressure his engine froze and momentarily flipped him on his back. In order to stop resistance he hit the feather switch to turn the prop to the feather position.

Normally when a pilot had engine failure and needed to return to base, his wingman would return with him in case they met the enemy or if the damaged plane crashed his location could be noted by the other pilot. Because they were protecting bombers and they knew they were going into battle, Norb dropped out of the flight to return the four hundred miles over the Owen Stanley Range alone. The 2nd element, Guttel, an experienced pilot with 110 or more missions, took his place. The squadron now had three flights of four and one flight of three planes. Had his wingman returned with him, the squadron would have been short two planes instead of one going into battle. Norb made it home; Feehan, Guttel and Krisher did not. None of the other pilots who returned from this mission knew what had happened to them. Feehan was from Trenton, New Jersey; Guttel from Boston, Massachusetts; and Krisher from Bonesu, New York.

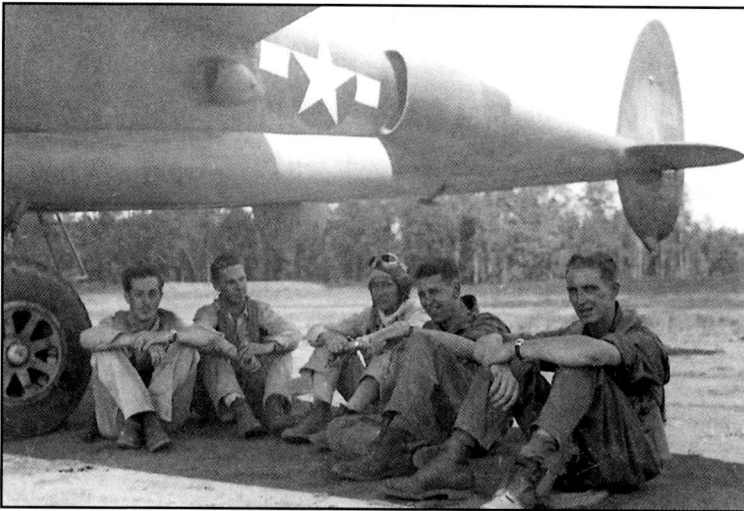

Norb, Raymond Daly and Seaborn Childs at Dobodura. At press time of the first edition, the men are the right were not identified. Further information reveals that they could be 2nd Lt. Norman Shea next to Childs and Flight Officer Willis Evers. Both were lost on November 2, 1943 on a Rabaul mission.

The photo to the left was taken September 22, 1943 at Dobodura. "We flew one flight of 16 P-38s covering the landing at Finschafen in the morning, then came back to Dobodura, refueled and at alert at which time this photo was taken. Note the three pilots on the left have their mae wests on. The other two may have not been 80th pilots as they don't have mae west's on and are not wearing khakis. They could have been from another squadron or 80th replacements. That afternoon the 80th flew the second mission over the landing area. We were assigned close cover—500 feet over the entire landing area. LST's (large landing craft) were backed up tight to shore. Over radio control, X was on Fighter Pilot, was aboard a destroyer, call sign "Duck Butt." Shortly after we got there, he called and said an unidentified aircraft was at 30,000 feet out about thirty minutes approaching the area. A little later he again called, "Another flight at 20,000 feet," then later - "Another flight at 15,000 feet, all about 15 minutes out." This is the first time the 80th covered (with the Navy) an American landing in this area. We had fighters stacked up from 500 feet to 40,000 feet. Control should have turned some of us loose to intercept—no way—we stayed right over the area all the time. The Navy was firing up through us. Jap bombers are coming through from above, with radio silence from control. Some pilot called "Duck Butt, how are you doing?" He answered and you could hear the Navy guns firing, "pop, pop, pop." He said, "I'm okay but "shit oh dear, what commotion." I don't think we claimed any planes shot down, nor did we lose any. Another P-38 squadron had one shot down—a pilot named Cloud. He was picked up out of the ocean. Later his sister became Siebenthal's wife." –Norb

"On the morning flight over Finschafen, my wingman was Jess Gidley, a new replacement and a good pilot. Alone, wheels down, Jap dive bomber flew over. Two people in the plane – one behind the other. I think all 16 of us got a chance to shoot at it. When I got my turn the gas was streaming out behind the airplane like a white cloud. Then Gidley got his chance and put the torch to it. Both people were not alive when I flew over it. The airplane was flying straight and level. This was Gidley's first victory. He was lost after I came back [to the states]." -Norb

129

"January 23, 1944: Jess E. Gidley (80th). P-38J (42-67152). 1st Lt. Gidley was from Richmond, CA and was one of the old hands of the 80th. He had a number of destroyed and probable claims and may have been trying hard on this mission to Wewak, New Guinea to get another victory. Cy Homer witnessed what he believed to be Gidley's P-38 collide with a Japanese fighter and fall into the jungle near Wewak." (*Attack & Conquer*)

"One pilot you will see mentioned in "*Attack & Conquer*" was one of the first in combat in P-39s. Don & I were not in the same flying schools, but joined the 49th Group and we went overseas together. When I went to the 80th, he went to the 36th. His name is Don McGee. We were very close friends. When the 80th received P-38s he joined the 80th and left the 36th. He has enough stories to fill a book. First flight in P-40, he bailed out. Second flight he ran out of runway, went off end of field, turned over on the back and was stuck in the aircraft. He got shot down by our anti-aircraft guns at Pt. Moresby. Earlier on a combat flight he landed his airplane in a dummy airdrome at Pt. Moresby. Came home and went back overseas in P-51s in Europe. Retired from Air

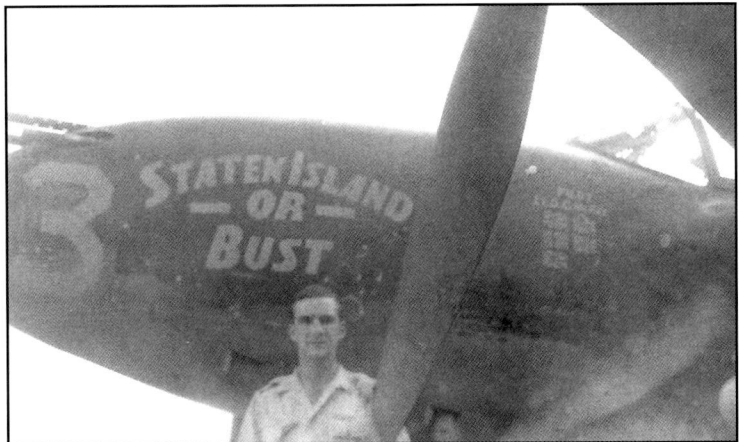
Don McGee

Force, went back to school and became a lawyer. Two sons were both Air Force pilots. He really had a good guardian angel. He had "Staten Island or Bust" on the nose of his airplane." -Norb

Don and Norb came over on the Mariposa together. Don ended up in the 36th before joining the 80th. Norb was one of the few who was able to overcome the animosity between the two groups.

"Norb Ruff was about the best friend I had in the 80th. I think he was the best friend of everyone there. From the time I joined in March '43 in Mareeba, I believe he met about every new pilot on the first day of his arrival. He made himself their friend, 'father' and mentor to all of them. He even welcomed me, a guy brought in from the 36th, whose commanders and everyone in the outfit (by association with them) they were to be treated at least, with disdain by all members of the 80th.

Norb and I knew each other this time, so I think I received a little more humane treatment. I know Norb spoke for me. He picked me up as I arrived and tried to place me in his tent. There was one bunk unoccupied there. His attempt was vetoed by his bunkmates who felt they were overcrowded already. I had to search further with no luck. I finally had to draw a small two-man tent from supply, a cot, blankets, mosquito net and find someone to help me set it up. After a while and a couple of flights in the P-38s, the 80th was moved to Port Moresby…to 3 Mile Strip. We settled in with a new commander, Ed Cragg.

Not being familiar with who had been flight leaders in Milne Bay, where the 80th had suffered a big hit from malaria, Cragg solved his organization problem by posting three choices on the bulletin board, with the notice to the pilots for each to list his name under the flight leader he chose to fly with…Robbins, Ruff, McGee. In a couple of days all of the pilots were listed and came out as above. I wondered what was wrong with me? So I tried to fly most of my missions with Ruff. For the rest of my time in the squadron I was shuffled around a lot, seldom leading flights until I was promoted to Captain. (Note: There were so many of us from flying school class of 41-I that they would not promote one without promoting all, so they promoted none.) [This was one of the reasons for the animosity from the 80th. Men were being brought in from the 35th and 36th to the 80th who were higher-ranking than the men in the 80th, so men in the 80th could not get promoted.]

"I dug out a picture of Norb and me. In it I was serenading Norb on the occasion of his returning to the States at long last, a trip most of us hoped for, in vain, for many months. It was futile for many of us to expect to take the trip while McArthur's order that nobody was going home until he started getting replacements. Things had not really started to heat up in New Guinea, and Ruff had been saying he was sick of carrying all of that .50 caliber stuff without having any opportunity to spend some of it. The word going around had it that he was holding his frustration by shooting up the Japs at Hansa Bay on his unproductive missions to the Wewak area. Doc Patrick, who was having a running fight against the higher authorities to have Mac's rescinded or at least modified so that some of the pilots who had been in combat too long might be sent back to the states. Apparently Ruff's side trips added strength to Patrick's arguments and Ruff was sent home.

Not too long after this, Sack Freeman, who was with me at Rabaul reported to Doc Patrick that on our return, stopping at Kiriwina, I had a vomiting session there. Shortly after returning to my tent at Kila, Sack and Doc appeared and told me I was going home, and if I wanted to argue about it he could offer me three choices…be grounded from combat, transfer to higher headquarters or go home. I had been in the theater twenty-two and a half months, flown a hundred and fifty-four missions, had been shot down once by our own people, shot up on my first mission and crash landed a P-39 safely on Fisherman's Reef." –Don McGee

[Note from Kirby: "Fibber McGee (Donald) is a lawyer now, probably retired, is a DOUBLE ACE. He shot down I think six planes and crashed five of ours. After he came back to the states, he then was shipped to France and put in a tour over there. He is the one that said about bringing the enemy down the runway and letting the ack ack pick them off your tail"]

Victories

Chippewa Herald Telegram, September 15, 1943: "Ruff Downs Two Japs in Day: Bloomer Pilot Bags Third Foe Over New Guinea: Captain of 24 Sees Much Fighting in South Pacific: Capt. Norbert C. Ruff, Army Air Force flier from Bloomer, Wis., chalked up two more enemy fighter planes to his credit today, according to an Associated Press dispatch from New Guinea. This totals three known Jap planes which the 24-year old Bloomer boy has sent crashing to earth in fighting over the South Pacific islands.

The Associated Press dispatch received by the Herald Telegram today follows: 'Somewhere in New Guinea. Sept. 15 (AP) – Capt. Norbert C. Ruff, of Bloomer, Wis. today shot down two enemy fighters in a raid on airdromes at Dagua and But. The Americans engaged 10 or 20 Japanese fighters in elements from 5,000 to 7,000 feet looking for low-flying strafing planes.'

Capt. Ruff shot down his first enemy plane on July 27.

They wore their flights suits until they practically wore out.

132

The war and nearly eighteeen months overseas were beginning to take their toll.

An Associated Press dispatch of that date said he knocked the enemy fighter out of the skies while flying a P-38 Lightning fighter in which he was escorting U.S. bombers over Madang, New Guinea.

In a letter to his sister-in-law, Mrs. Arvilla Ruff of this city, the captain referred to this victory. He said he had then completed sixty successful missions and had escaped several hot engagements without a scratch.

His squadron has more enemy planes to its credit than either of the other two units in his group, a communication received through other sources said, also. Censorship bars have been let down somewhat and he was able to say more about operations than previously. Among his duties on the South Pacific front he acted as assistant operations officer, test pilot, senior flight commander, and oxygen and weather officer. Capt. Ruff is the oldest man (in experience) in his squadron."

The official record read: "GO No. 233, Hq Fifth Air Force, APO 925, 15 October, 1943: Norbert C. Ruff, 0430945, Captain, 80th Fighter Squadron, 8th Fighter Group, is officially credited with the destruction of two enemy fighter type aircraft in aerial combat in the vicinity of Dagua, New Guinea, at 1030/K on 13 September 1943. While flying in a formation of fifteen P-38s in a fighter sweep preceding a B-24 strike, this officer observed fifteen enemy fighters. He led a flight of three P-38s to attack. In the ensuing engagement one enemy aircraft was destroyed and

Trying to relax at the Officer's Club.

133

the pilot was seen to bail out. Another Zero was seen to crash into the ground after receiving a burst of 200 rounds."

Two days later Norb took out another enemy plane. "Norbert C. Ruff, 0430945, Captain, 80th Fighter Squadron, 8th Fighter Group, is officially credited with the destruction of one enemy fighter type aircraft in aerial combat near Boram Strip, Wewak, New Guinea, at 1000/K on 15 September 1943.

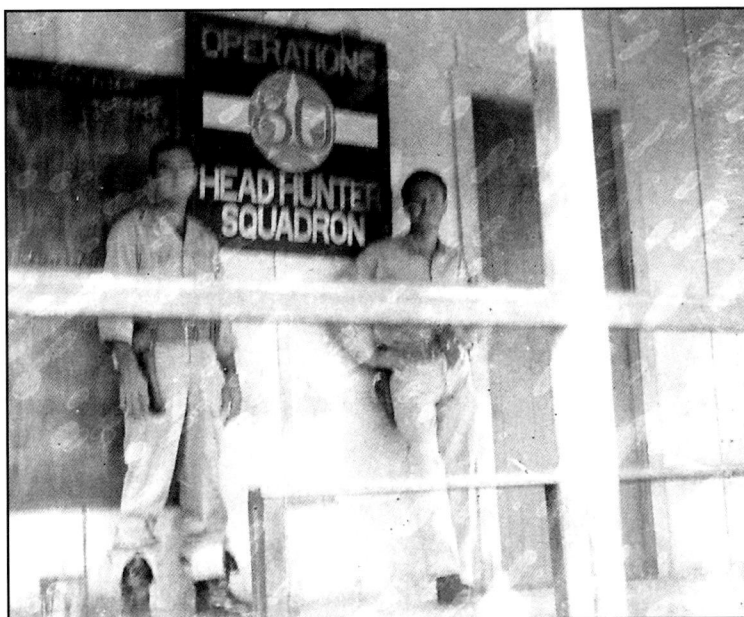
Don McGee and Norb in from of 80th Operations Headquarters.

While on a fighter sweep ahead of bombers, fifteen P-38s encountered approximately twenty-five to thirty enemy fighters. In the ensuing engagement Captain Ruff, after firing a long burst, closed in from two hundred and fifty yards to about sixty feet causing the airplane to explode."

Associated Press report in the *Chippewa Herald Telegram*: "Somewhere in New Guinea, (AP): Captain Norbert Ruff of Bloomer, Wis., accounted personally for one enemy fighter during another smashing victory of the Fifth Air Force pilots over the Japanese at Wewak, New Guinea. Forty-eight enemy fighters were shot from the sky in brilliant combat and at least 10 bombers were destroyed on the ground. Capt. Ruff's squadron, known as the 'Head Hunters' has more than 100 enemy planes to its credit."

Attack & Conquer gave a more detailed account of the September 13th and 15th missions.

"Cy Homer was back in Norb Ruff's flight during a sweep over Wewak during a B-24 strike on September 13. Red Flight had already found a number of Japanese fighters in the air and Homer could see the P-38s diving to the attack. Homer dropped his tanks as soon as he saw Ruff get rid of his and followed him down through at least two different Japanese formations.

One of Ruff's attacks was effective and the Japanese pilot of the Oscar took to his parachute. Homer flew by close enough to see the helpless enemy dangling there, but decided to leave him alone since other Oscars were attacking and two of them were behind Ruff.

134

Homer was above Ruff at this time and came down quickly to pull up very close to the rear Oscar and fired a burst. The Oscar rolled over and went down and this pilot was able to escape by parachute, also. Ruff dodged the other Oscar and in the general whirl of the battle that forced Homer and him down to about 5,000 feet managed to claim another Oscar.

The two P-38s climbed once again and patrolled the B-24s for about ten minutes before they made for Marilinan to refuel. Ruff was justified in his assessment of Homer's skill as a pilot and went home alive within the next few weeks, thanks in part to Homer's ability as a fighter pilot.

One of the great days that the 80th had in September was on the fifteenth of that month during another sweep of the Wewak area to cover a B-24 strike. Captain James Wilson led the 80th formation of sixteen P-38s through perfect weather and caught up with the B-24s at 15,000 feet near the target. Wilson was at 18,000 feet and could see the top cover about 4,000 feet higher.

There were two huge columns of clouds about ten miles apart between which the American formation passed like a majestic parade. About twenty miles from the target, the 80th pulled out ahead of the bombers and ran into the enemy. First one Oscar appeared, bright and shining in natural metal and angry red hinomarus. Then there were others, popping up from the undercast. Wilson dropped his tanks and led the 80th down to the attack.

Don McGee was leading the second flight and caught one Tony over the Boram Strip, sending it down in flames. Someone else in the flight shot large pieces off another Tony and claimed it as a probable (this may have been Corky Smith's claim). McGee later saw about eight Oscars make halfhearted attacks on the front of the B-24 formation and assumed that the Japanese were not especially eager this day.

Other flights had good hunting as well. Clifton Troxell was down from 8th Headquarters and got two claims for Oscars. Norb Ruff got his last claim when he shot down

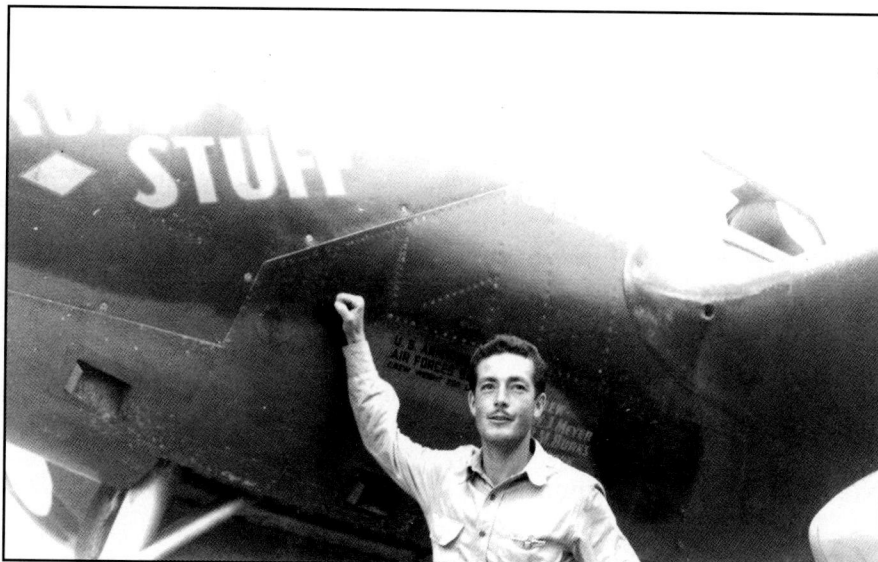

what he believed to be a Hamp. Ruff had lost at least three former tentmates in combat and must have felt like a fugitive from the law of averages before he went home." (*Attack & Conquer*)

Norb's last combat mission was on September 26, 1943. "On September 26 a fighter sweep preceded an attack by B-24s and later B-25s on Wewak. The 80th Fighter Squadron sent a force of 16 P-38s up ahead of the bombers and finding no opposition, they orbited at 16,000 feet for rendezvous. As the P-38s approached the strip at Wewak, two or three enemy fighters were sighted very low off the water. Immediately after this sighting ten Tonys were sighted at 15,000 feet. The P-38s dropped their belly tanks and gave combat. Most of the enemy fighters were more inclined to either half roll or go straight down rather than attempt head-on passes. No doubt these pilots had learned something of the tremendous firepower that emanated from the nose of the Lightnings. The mutual support tactics of the American pilots worked well, and three of the Tonys were downed in the process." (*Pacific Sweep*)

"After 18 months with the 80th, I was the last pilot still with the 80th, still in combat after Lowood when the Squadron came up to full strength of 40 pilots the first time. Some were sent to join the 475th Group, some came home early. Oct '43, after a 30 day leave at home, I was C.O. of a Squadron at Santa Rosa, Calif. We would get a group of new 2nd Lts out of flying school and give them 100 hours of combat training, aerial gunnery, skip bombing, night flying, etc. in P-38s before they went overseas." -Norb

Some of the original pilots of the 80th were Phil Greasley, Whip Austin, Bill Greenfield, Joe McNay, Bill Frank, Gentry Plunkett, Harley Brown, Pinky Hunter and Todd Dabney. These came from the 35th and 36th when the 80th was formed.

Finally, in October 1943, after being overseas for twenty-two months, Norb received his leave orders. For the first time since entering cadet school in early 1941 Norb was going home to his family. His last combat mission was September 26th. On October 8th he left Brisbane on an LB 30, a B-24 converted tanker and by October 10th had arrived in San Francisco having made stops in New Caledonia, Fiji Island, Canton Islands and Hawaii.

After he left, Murphy inherited Norb's letter 'X' and renamed it "Sweet Sue.' Haley was flying Norb's plane when an engine quit. He broke his back when the plane crashed on take-off.

Leadership

"An essential element of leadership is that one has to want to do it. Remember that this is not a game (combat)...this is death. A leader has to have something inside him that makes him forget death and remember victory" -Col Walker M. "Bud" Mahurin, WWII Ace, 20.75 Kills (*You've Got the Lead, Flight Lead Handbook*)

If what Col. Mahurin said is true, then every single pilot who strapped himself into whatever plane he was flying that day was a leader, whether he was designated as one or not. Many in the 80th felt that the leadership in New Guinea was poor or non existent. Not one command personnel from the 8th Fighter Group ever flew one combat mission while Norb was with the 80th. Consequently, there was no respect for group officers. They just sent the new pilots to the squadrons, let them figure out what to do, then when they came back, reviewed their gun camera film to figure out what worked and what did not.

Pilots were required to fly four hours a month to receive 50% more in pilot's pay. Most from group headquarters would take a plane and fly it the required time, without going into combat. While there were some officers from the 8th Group headquarters that flew combat, none of them ever flew with the 80th. The

following story is a good reason why it was probably better they did not go into combat with the pilots who knew what they were doing.

"I remember only one time that a group officer showed up at our strip at Milne Bay. This was Col. Storm. He came over to get a little solo flying time. He taxied out. The brakes failed, he went off the side of the runway, broke off the nose gear and bent the prop."

Several pilots, many of them Aces in WWII were interviewed regarding leadership and discipline for the manual *You've Got the Lead, Flight Lead Handbook*. Many of these men flew with Norb - Corky Smith, Marion Kirby, Don McGee, and Paul Murphey, Jr.

"Discipline: Since the first aerial engagement, the importance of discipline has been stressed as absolutely essential in combat. Take time to read about the leading aces, enemy or ally, of previous wars. The one thing they all stress is discipline. -Gen. Charles J. Cunningham, Commander, Twelfth Air Force

Discipline must start with you, the flight leader. You have to possess self-discipline. Norb Ruff felt that a leader with self-discipline commands respect. He felt a leader shouldn't be the one to go out drinking with the boys every night and expect to command respect in the morning. Finally, he said there is a time and a place for this activity, but the true leader must discipline himself before he starts disciplining others.

Flight discipline applies to much more than regulation adherence. It applies to mission accomplishment, flight leader and wingman contracts, and flight obligations. In terms of mission accomplishment, read the following war story from an interview with Norb Ruff, WWII pilot in the Pacific:

'On this particular day our job was to escort 16 B-24s on a bombing mission to the Guddang area…We had 16 P-38s and were out of Port Moresby…I was the leader that day…En route to the target we passed within visual range of Japanese Zeros escorting bombers…We knew they were going to bomb Port Moresby…Our job was to cover the B-24s and I sure wanted to jump them...The Japanese didn't break their escort formation either…Coming home we had to escort some shot up B-24s but we did manage to mix it up a bit…The job that day was escort. That's what we're talking about in discipline…'"

In the letter to Mr. Blake in 1985, Norb reflects on those that came back. "I guess I wish more pilots had lived through the recent years to read these fine articles. We have lost a lot of them in their 50's and early 60's, all with sudden heart attacks – no warning. Here's a few – Tom Baldwin, Stan Borowski, Miles Bourdow, Seaborn Chiles, Ed 'Yardbird' DeGraffenreid, Tom DeJarnette, Cy Homer, Don Hanover, Robert Nevels, Jim Selzer, Darrell Swalha (Lockheed rep.). I am sure there are more. When you realize how few of us lived to come home at all you don't end up with many readers in 1985 – 42 years later. McGee is

Norb's last tent before going home. His tentmate was Harrison Freeman.

138

now reporting a heart condition also – suppose it's due to all that lazy, relaxed living on government rolls we enjoyed those years? At each reunion one of the pilots makes a public thank you to all the ground officers and especially the crew chiefs for keeping us in the air. We

Norb and Doc Patrick
The picture to the right was taken on the flight line. Doc Patrick would be around when planes landed to handle injuries. He felt bad that he couldn't do anything about all the cases of malaria. As the war went on he kept more and more to himself.

surely owe them our lives. The Yale Saffro's (who also did the artwork on our planes), the Slim Gardners, the Bill Meyers who became my crew chief as a corporal and later became line chief and Master Sergeant in the 80th under Robbins. When I came home Murphey inherited him and Murphey lived to come home. The Phil Debolts who was Siebenthal's crew chief. Phil wanted to become a pilot but they didn't let him come home even though I tried. At Jay Robbins' retirement ceremony in 1974 at Scott Field, Phil rushed up to me. I hadn't seen him since 1943. First thing he said, "Ruff what does the 'C' stand for? I told him Casper. He said, 'I never knew so we called our son Norbert Charles. He's 26 years old.' Then there's Ruff-House Bradley who was the last man and first man we saw on returning from combat. He ran the crash truck and the red & green lights on the end of the runway. Even though he stuttered, we knew the 38 side arm he always carried would keep the strip clear when we landed. He even ran off McArthur's command car on 12 Mile one time with him in it. Then you think of Flight Surgeon Nick Patrick. What a hellova life it must have been. No one to talk his business to, very little he could do. He worked hard to get through medical school – no G.I. benefits at that time. It was real hard on Nick when a pilot didn't come back. Toward the end he spent less and less time with the pilots – stayed by himself. He's the one that met my airplane after a Wewak mission. 'Ruff you're going home – you've put in 125 missions – and the last one left of the original Petrie group.' Then

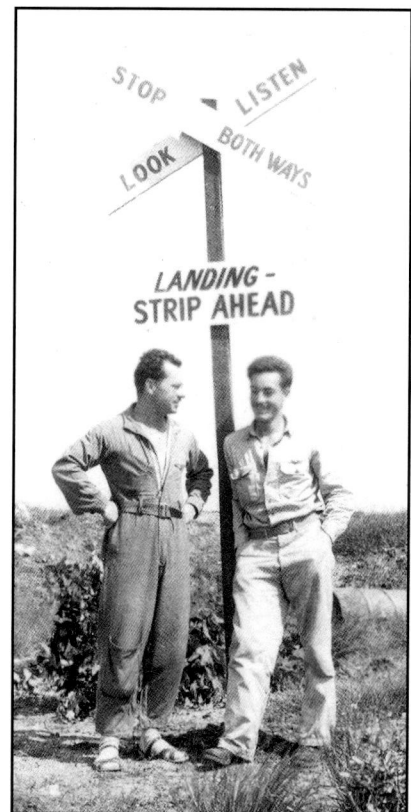

139

there were the Lts: Salty Peters, armament; Ab. Baracas, communications; Bill Pruss, engineering; Bill Hager, ordinance; Ron Mallock, adjutant; James Richtor, G-2; Matt Buchele, headquarters. All these people did an excellent job and it was *years* long."

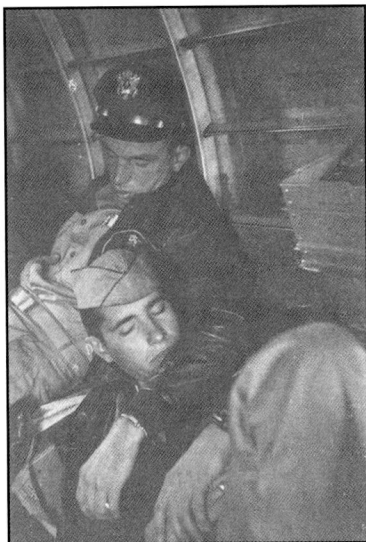

Coming back from rest leave in Australia on a DC3. Gordon Willett is the one in the front.

Griffen with Japanese prisoners.

Decoration ceremony at Three Mile

Caption on back of picture read: "Some pilots going to Goodenough Island.

Cook house for the 80th at 3 Mile. Officers had one end and crews had the other.

Taken in front of cook house. Ed Cragg is driving. Cleve Jones is directly behind him, Harrison Freeman is to the left of Jones. The man in the back was a cook.

Crashed P-38 at Three Mile.

Robert Adams, the "Pomeroy Decoy"
Came from Pomeroy, Washington. He
strafed with Norb numerous times at
Lae and Salamua when coming back
from Wewak when they did not want
to waste their unused ammo.

Lieutenant Sandifer (in undershirt)
on return after crash landing and
MIA in 1943. Corky Smith is to
the right of Sandifer and Cy Homer
is to his left. Norb is kneeling in
front of Homer.

At alert shack at Three Mile Aerodrome. L-R: Johnny
Jones, Norb, Cragg, Robbins

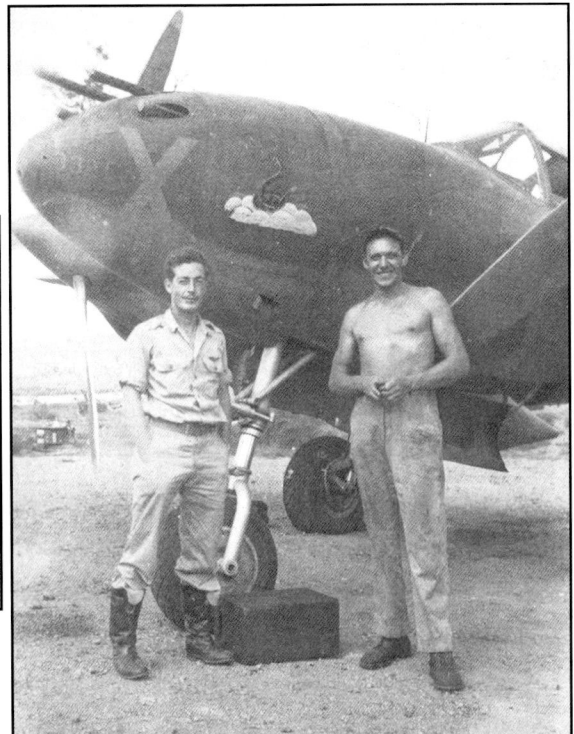

Norb and Bill Meyers, his crew chief.

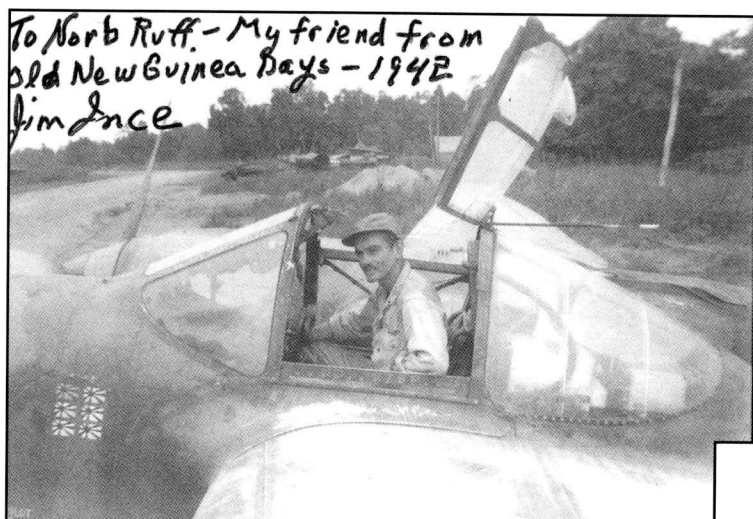
To Norb Ruff - My friend from
Old New Guinea Days - 1942
Jim Ince

Mark Kasper

On crash boat at Port Moresby. The men used the boat when they
had a rare day off and went to Fisherman's Island. Fisherman's
Island is where Don McGee landed his plane.

P-38. Note the wear pattern on the right side of the cockpit. This is from the pilots and crews climbing in and out of the plane. The round items on either side of the plane are the superchargers.
(*P-38 Lightning in World War II Color*)

Jay Robbins. He named his plane Jandina, which stood for Jay and Ina, his wife. He had 21 kills at this time.

Two views of Salamaua The picture above shows the long narrow point of land that came out from shore. It was about 1/4 to 1/2 mile long and very narrow - only about 20-50 feet wide. The larger part at the end was filled with Jap guns. Norb strafed the camp area on the left side of the point when coming back from other missions.

The picture below shows the airfield, which was located to the right of the peninsula above. It was a single runway airstrip used heavily in the early part of the war. The first Allied airplane landed there on September 13, 1943 after the Australian 5 Division occupied it the day before. Today there are still old Jap gun enplacements and tunnels located in the area.

145

14-Mile was another Aerodrome the 80th flew from. The first large dip on the left was known as Saddle Mountain.

"Ruff Stuff" at 3-Mile

Corky Smith. He ended up with eleven kills, making him the fourth
highest Ace in the 80th for WWII

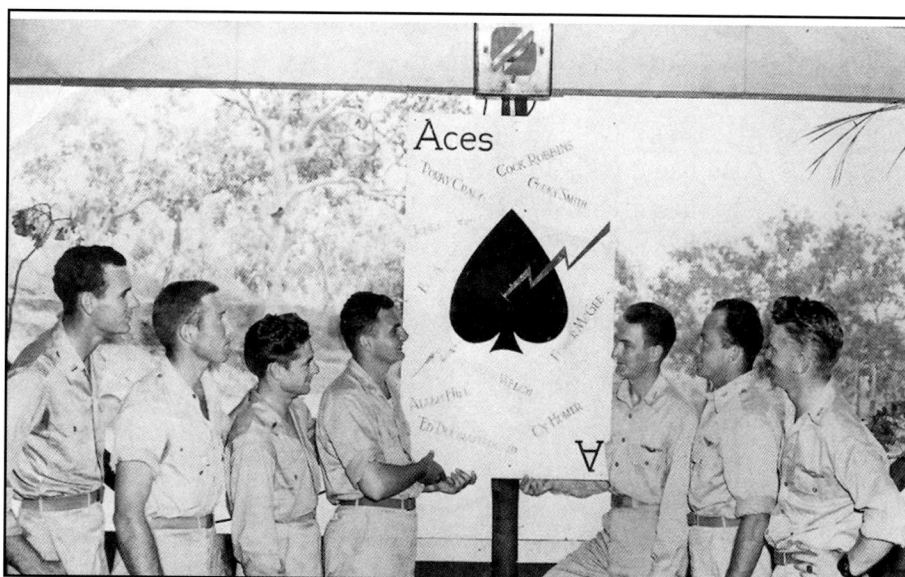

This publicity photo picture was taken for a newspaper (unknown). The article mentions
that these pilots were with a bombing unit, but they were all pilots of the 80th Fighter
Squadron. It was taken before the end of the war since most of these men had more kills
than listed in the article. There is a complete list of confirmed kills near the end of this
chapter. "New Guinea...Yank pilots who are making air history in New Guinea, have
their names inscribed on a giant ace of spades, speared with lightning. The ace pilots
of an advance bombing unit of the Fifth Air Force are, From Left to Right: Capt. Jay.
T. Robbins, of Coolidge, Texas, who has 14 planes to his credit; Lt. Cyril F. Homer, of
Sacrameneto, Calif., with six planes downed, Second Lt. Edwin L. DeGraffenreid of
Shreveport, LA., also with six planes to his credit; Major Edward Cragg, of Greenwhich,
Conn., who has blasted 14 Zeros; Capt. John L. Jones, of Patterson, N.J. who has shot
down nine planes; Lt.Cornelius M. Smith, Jr., of Brooklyn, N.Y., who has destroyed five
planes and Lt. Allen E. Hill of Sterling, Ill., who has shot down six planes."

80th Statistics
Confirmed Aerial Victories

J.T. Robbins (21)   Also had 1 with 36th F.S. while assigned to 8th F.G. Hdqtrs.

E. Cragg (15)

C.F. Homer (15)

C.M. Smith (11)

K.G. Ladd (10)   Also had 2 with 36th F.S.

G. S. Welch (9)   Also had 4 with 47th F.S. (Pearl Harbor) and 3 with 36th F.S.

A.E. Hill (8)   Also had 1 with 36th F.S.

J.L. Jones (8)

B.W. Adams (6)   Also had 1 with 6th N.F.S.

E.L. DeGraffenried (6)

P.C. Murphey (6)

R.H. Adams (5)

J.L. Myers (5)

C.B. Ray (5)

L. Scribner (5)

H.J. Freeman (4)

D.C. Hanover (4)

V.C. Jenner (4)

L.S. Mathers (4)

D.T. Roberts (4)   Also had 3 with 432nd F.S. and 7 with 433rd. F.S.

N.C. Ruff (4)

L.B. Blair (3)

R.I. Bong (3)   Also had 37 with other F.S.

J.E. Gidley (3)

E.C. Krishner (3)

C.E. Taylor (3)

J.R. Wilson (3)

W.A. Brown (2)
C.L. Cobb (2)
J.C. Corallo, Jr. (2)
R.E. Daly (2)
H.B. Donaldson (2)
W.F. Evers (2)
A.B. Hailey (2)   Also had 4 with the 432nd F.S.
J.C. Ince (2)   Also had 3 with 36th F.S.
D.C. McGee (2)   Also had 1 with the 363th F.S.
G.T. Rogers (2)
R.M. Roth (2)
J.K. Stanifer (2)
C.H. Troxell (2)   Also had 3 with 35th F.S. and 1 with headquarters
N. Zinni (2)
W.A. Caldwell (1)
W.H. Fotheringham (1)
D. H. Furgason (1)
J.G. Griffon (1)
R. P. Hanson (1)
G. T. Helveston (1)
L.G. Henkes (1)
G.R. Hope (1)
M.T. Kasper (1)
K.B. Lloyd (1)
N.R. Lundy (1)   Also had 2 with 432nd F.S.
R.L. Peters (1)
B.S. Reed (1)
H.J. Sheehan (1)
E.W. Smith (1)
R.F. Souhrada (1)
F.D. Tomkins (1)   Also had 3 with 432nd F.S.

Total of 224 planes

First Squadron Victory: Gerald T. Rogers; Last Squadron Victory: Louis Scribner

Distinguished unit citations:
For action over Papua, July 23, 1942 to January 23, 1943
For action over New Guinea, August 20, 1943 to September 15, 1943
For action over New Britain, October 24, 1943 to November 7, 1943

The 80th Squadron Fought On

The 80th continued their fighting until the end of the war, using bases from Nadzab, Biak, and Owi.

"For the remainder of the war, the majority of the 80th's activities consisted of light and medium bomber escort and ground support attacks. From its first combat base in New Guinea the squadron was stationed in the Netherlands East Indies, then moved to Mindinoa from where they launched attacks throughout Borneo and the Celebes Islands. During this time, the legendary aviator Charles Lindbergh flew with the 'Headhunters' as an instructor, earning several kills. From Christmas 1943 to Christmas 1944, the 80th was busy providing aerial support for the landings in the Philippines. The squadron moved to Okinawa on 29 August, 1944 and flew its first mission against the Japanese mainland on the following day. On 12 August, 1945, the 'Headhunters' flew their final combat mission of World War II, in which the squadron commander was shot down." (*The 80th Fighter Squadron 'Headhunters' Squadron History*)

"This was also the time that Col. Charles Lindbergh came into our lives. He had been living with the 475th for several weeks. Finally he came over to Owi and stayed with us for a few days. We would all gather around Cock's [Jay Robbins] at night to ask questions and to just listen to him. That was really something for a bunch of young fighter pilots to experience. He taught and showed us how to literally wean our engines. Our gallon per hour consumption was cut from about 40 per hour down to 20 per hour. You simply pulled the mixture controls back and leaned out the fuel mixtures. The throttle settings were also a little smaller but the air speed loss, which was about 20, did not effect our ability to stay with the bombers. Getting to meet and shake hands with this man was something." - Paul C. Murphey

Charles Lindbergh was not the only famous pilot to fly with the 80th. In April, 1944, Dick Bong joined the 80th for their air battle over Hollandia. Because Bong had so many kills to his credit, he was given his choice of squadrons to fly with. At one point he chose the 80th. On April 12, flying with the 80th, Major Bong took down his 26th, 27th and 28th Jap planes. These kills took him over Eddie Rickenbacker's WWI record making Bong the new 'Ace-of-Aces.' Unfortunately, the 80th was not credited for Bong's kills.

On August 19th, 1945, the 80th's final flight was to help in the final scene of the Japanese battle for Pacific domination. They were chosen to escort the Japanese delegation to the signing ceremony ending Japanese hostilities.

"The 8th Air Group consisted of the 35th, 36th and 80th Fighter Squadrons, stationed at Ie

Shima Field. During the entire escort operation, only the pilots of the 8th group were to fly. All other aircraft were to stand down. The no fly edict had teeth. Any aircraft, friend or foe, flying near the truce mission was to be destroyed. Maj. Jack Breeden of the 80th Squadron, was selected to lead his P-38s on this most unusual flight. Breeden and his squadron were to fly north, intercept and escort these previous foes, now non-combatants. Breeden's pilots were particularly concerned about the unused Kamikazes, who had recently bloodied the skies and US fleet in the battle for Okinawa. These pilots all were pledged to death before dishonor. No greater dishonor could there be than surrender, indeed unconditional, irrevocable surrender, and loss of national pride.

"Major Breeden's squadron consisted of four flights of P-38s, each configured with long range belly tanks and full 50 caliber loads. The aircraft were unpainted, but each sported nose art by one of Esquire magazine's understudy artists. At long range, these vibrant markings were unnoticeable, but in close formation they provided an interesting contrast to the Pacific blues. Major Breeden led his squadron into the air, turning to parallel the Okinawan

coast. The P-38 pilots climbed to comfortable cruise altitude, spread, checked their guns, and settled in for the flight north.

"At about ten o'clock, Captain Onishi's mission cleared the peninsula of southern Kyushu. Regular communications with Moca had been established earlier. Now, the calls of Bataan 1 were being monitored by ABC and WBC radio, then rebroadcast to the world as voices of the surrender aircraft's pilot. Major Breeden's squadron spotted the Betty's, and turned to cut them off. He commanded 'I'm your escort plane, follow me.' When relayed to Onishi, he looked up, and saw the squadron of P-38s at his one o'clock position, slightly high. Too many aircraft. The American pilots dove in from both sides, then pulled up, streaking past the peace mission. The Japanese crews sat agape, watching the swirling fighters flash by, sunlight glinting from their aircraft, stunned by the display, by their numbers, enthralled by their nose art. Onishi called to the escort, 'Please identify yourself.' The escort aircraft wiggled its rudders, slid into position, then called 'Maintain your bearing.' The escort south had begun.

The flight escorts and Bettys pointed directly toward the Ryuku Islands. Major Breeden arranged his squadron of four flights of four aircraft around and above the Bettys. One flight was deployed to each side of the Bettys and slightly aft. The other two flights stacked high and aft, monitoring the entire procession. The flight southward was through generally clear skies. They avoided islands or land masses except when required for navigation. Large thunderstorm cells and puffy white clouds were scattered along their route. After two hours, the northern islands of the Okinawa group came into sight.

The Bettys and their P-38 escorts began a slow descent abeam Tokunoshima while approaching their enroute stop. The early afternoon sun cast short shadows from the mountains to their east. Above Ie Shima, Major Breeden's P-38s broke off their descent, turning the escort over to the next squadron." (*The 80th Fighter Squadron "Headhunters" Squadron History*)

Today, the 80th is the only WWII Squadron still in existence. In 1971 the 80th was close to being deactivated.

"In 1971, while stationed at Kunsan, AB, ROK, the 80th Tactical Fighter Squadron was in the process of being deactivated. Fortunately, former 'Headhunter' Lt. Gen. Jay T. Robbins, who was Vice Commander of TAC at the time, caught the action and rescued us at the last minute. Instead, we were re-equipped with new F-4s, and were re-staffed with new personnel, primarily from the 391st Tactical Fighter Squadron. The 391st Tactical Fighter Squadron's insignia was a tiger's head on an inverted triangular green background. Below the patch, on a rocker, was the motto 'AUDENTES FORTUNA JUVAT' which translates from Latin: "Fortune Favors the Bold.' As the new 'Headhunters' were removing their patches, they would grasp the triangular patch by the upper left hand corner to tear them

Caption read: "Head-Hunters. Lt. Delbert H. Furgason hunts Jap heads, so he carries a Boong head-hunter of New Guinea for his insignia. Two Boongs approve."

152

off. All would tear off except the word, 'JUVAT.' It caught on immediately. The harder the higher echelons attempted to stamp it out, the more entrenched it became (to the point of covering the Wing Commander's flight suit with 'JUVAT' patches each time he hung a flight suit on the line to dry!)

"The two smaller-sized round patches with the 'Headhunters' and '80th Tac Ftr Sq' rockers entered use in the early 1980s. They were brought about by new Air Force regulations requiring unit designations to be on every squadron patch. Fortunately, after several years of patience and hard work by Yale Saffro, and several pounds (literally) of paperwork, we were finally able to convince the Air Force Heraldry Division that the original 'Headhunter' patch design shouldn't be changed. Our unit patch is now the only official patch in the Air Force without any unit designation markings.

Today, we are once again called the 80th Fighter Squadron (and stationed under a direct descendant of our original 8th Pursuit Group), we once again proudly bear the name given to us by Capt. Edward 'Porky' Cragg in 1943, and we once again wear patches very similar to the original 'Headhunter' patch designed by Yale Saffro." (*Ibid*)

The Headhunters Reunite

Several years ago, Marion Kirby, using his own resources and many hours of his time, started locating their old comrades along with those people who had served with the 80th. This started reunions which are held every eighteen months in various cities. Stories were told, friendships re-established, and new ones formed with younger members of the 80th.

When he was putting together the first reunion in 1970, Kirby made a little error in locating a rather "important" member of the group. "I was trying to invite General George C. Kenny, our commanding General in the SWPA. I found a *Mrs.* George C. Kenney in New York City. I wrote her, and extended an invitation and added to the invitation, 'What a wonderful person the LATE General was and how much I admired him.' In a very few days I received an air mail letter. 'Where in the hell did you get, THE LATE GENERAL STUFF? I asked Mrs. Kenney and she assured me that it was just a RUMOR. I do not know who started the rumor, but I will bet I can drink him under the table…and if I can not, I will pay for the drinks. Gen. GCK'"

One of the things done at the reunions is the singing old songs. Some of the men wrote their own songs in honor of pilots, battles and whatever came to mind. The Juvat Choir cut a CD entitled, *The Juvat Boys Choir Headhunters*, which is available for purchase on the copyright page.

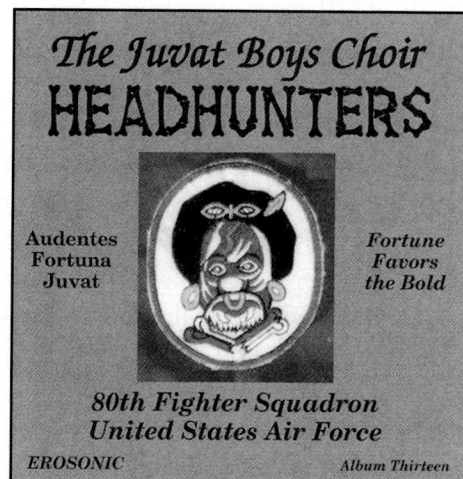

The Juvat Boys Choir
HEADHUNTERS

Audentes
Fortuna
Juvat

Fortune
Favors
the Bold

80th Fighter Squadron
United States Air Force

EROSONIC   Album Thirteen

New Guinea Waterfall

This was a song that Mark, Norb's son, remembers Norb
teaching Mark and his sisters.
The original song was *Korean Waterfall*, but Norb changed the words.

Beside a New Guinea waterfall one bright and sunny day
Beside a shattered P-38 jet a young pursuiter lay
His parachute hung from a nearby tree, he was not yet quite dead
So listen to the very last words the young pursuiter said

I'm going to a better land where everything is bright
Where whiskey flows from telephone poles, play poker every night
We haven't got a thing to do but sit around and sing
And all our crews are women, Oh death!, where is thy sting?"

Oh death where is they sting
Oh death where is they sting
The bells of hell will ring-a-ling-a-ling…
For you, but not for me.

Death Rains Down

Michael "Spades" Waite, Andy "Stinger" Scott, James "Taz" Merchant and David "Fuge"
Epperson. In memory of Lt. Gen. Jay T. Robbins

(Well it) started way back in '42, at a place called Mitchell Field
We were headin' off to fight a war didn't know what it would yield
We were green and we were new to the game but we were ready for a fight
We knew some of us weren't comin' back, we said that's all right
      We flew out of Moresby, strafin' Zeros on the way
      We flew at Hollandia, killing Nippons in the fray
      We are the Headhunters, with a history strong and proud
      We'll see you around, when death rains down

(There) was a man named "Porky" Cragg, led a squadron to its fame
We had friends who brought us back to the fight and they gave us our name
They were saviors in the jungle, their name denoting fear
The Nippons are gonna get their ass kicked cause the Headhunters are here.
      We flew over Wewak, strafin' Zeros on the way
      We flew in the Lightning, killing Nippons in the fray
      We are the Headhunters, with a history strong an proud
      We'll see you around, when death rains down.

(Well) "Porky" Cragg flew his last flight in a sad twist of fate
Jay T. Robbins was next in line, he was our saving grace

154

He taught the Headhunters how to fight, 22 kills of his own
And even now he looks down upon us, we are his second home.
>   We flew out of Nadzab, strafin' Zeros on the way
>   We flew in the Lightning, killing Nippons in the fray
>   We are the Headhunters, with a history strong and proud
>   We'll see you around, when death rains down

His name was "Cock" Robbins, 22 kills on the way
He flew in the Lightning, killing Nippons in the fray
He is a Headhunter, with a history strong and proud
We'll see him around, when death rains down
We'll see him around, in a lonesome cloud.

Twin-Tailed Lightning
1982 Robbie Robbins
Robbie is the son of Jay T. Robbins and was a member of the 80th in Korea
Song is sung to the tune of *Running Bear*

In the jungles of New Guinea, the Headhunters carved their name
They were brave and they were fearless; downing Zeros was their game.
From the beaches of Port Moresby, it was three miles to their 'drome
"Twas a dirt strip carved in a hillside; this is the place they called their home.

Chorus:
Twin tailed Lightning was their warplane
As they roamed Pacific skies
Searching out the sons of Nippon
Sending them to their demise.

They were known not as a number; but as a name denoting fear
A tiny native was their log, making history for all to hear
With names like Homer, Norb Ruff and Murphey, Cragg and Robbins and Kirby, too
They swept the sky clean of the Jap menace
And came back victors when they flew. Chorus

They flew out from their airdrome in their Lightning climbing high
Looking up to find some Zeros; gonna blow them from the sky
All the odds were against them; all they had were their planes
And some friends down in the jungle, who made sure they'd fly again. Chorus

Making aces was their standard, two-hundred kills, even more
With fifty cal and twenty mic-mic, they always ran up their meatball score
About the odds they never worried, from treetop level they'd cut 'em down
And when they landed from their melees, they would drink and f--- around!! Chorus (twice)

We've Been Everywhere
Original song *"I've Been Everywhere"* by Geoff Mack. Parody lyrics
Dick Jonas & Jim Ritter

Well I'm sittin' in the bar, out at Kunsan-by-the-sea
When a trash hauler saunters in and parks his ass right next to me
He checks my goatskin shoulder and he asks me, "What is that?"
I say, "That's my squadron patch; I'm a Headhunter – a Juvat!"
He says, "You're a Juvat? I think I've heard of you;
Say, where in the hell have you all been, and what did you all do?!"

    JBC Chorus
We been everywhere, Man; we been everywhere
We cross the mountains bare, Ma; we breathed the flak-filled air
Of Zekes we've had our share, Man, we been everywhere

Been to Mitchell Field, Brisbane, Lowood, Moresby
Dorodura, Nazdab, Morotai, Owi
Dulag, Tacloban, Mindinao, Leyte
Townsville, Oodnadetta, Kokoda, Wadbi
Borneo, Meomoot, Bogadjim, Madang
Wewak, Fiji, Marilinann, Kavieng
        JBC Chorus (…MiGs…)

We been to Gaegu, Kwangju, Fuchu, Kunsan
Inchon, Osan, Pusan, Suwon
P-Y Do, Cheju do, Guam, Okinawa
Hachinohe, Morioka, Sendai, Wakkanai
Tachikawa, Itazuke, Niigata, Pohang
Kagoshime, Hiroshima, Ie Shima, Hot dang!
        JBC Chorus (…SAMs…)

We been to Hanoi, Haiphong, Phuc Yen, Yen Bai
Lan Son, Hoa Lac, Phu Tho, Son Tay
Hoa Binh, Ham Dinh, Thai Binh, Bac Ninh
Thai Nguyen, Gia Lam, Viet Tri, Do Don
Thud Ridge, MiG Ridge, Northeast Railroad
In town, cross town, up town down town
        JBC Chorus (…DAKs…)

We been to Seoul, Kimpo, Honolulu, Wake, Midway
Hong Kong, Bangkok, Bagulo, Manila Bay
Hualien, Tainan, Taitung, Keelung
Chiayi, Hsin chu, Koashsiung, Ping Tung
Saigon, Singapore, Tokyo, Taipei, Angeles City, all night, all day. JVC Chorus (…death…)

Third reunion in San Diego. Some of those identified are; Back row: Stevens, Norb, unknown, Jay Robbins, Unkonwn, Unknown. Front row: Unknown, General Kenney (head turned), unknown, Glen Hope, Unknown.

Jay Robbins, Marion Kirby, Norb

Several generations of Headhunters
Jay Reidel, Norb, Capt. David "Duece" Paulus, Marion Kirby and Pete "Rosie" Roblus

Reunion 2002
Back row: Kirby, Unknown, Norb, Unknown
Front row: Unknown, Unknown, Jim Ince, Unknown, Unknown. The reason Norb does not know the names of some of these men is that they served after Norb left.

2005 Reunion
Earl Conrad, Jim Ince, Norb, Glen Hope and John "Whitey" Freberg.

Jay Reidel is an alumni of the 80th Fighter Squadron. In 1979 he was assigned to the 80th Tactical Fighter Squadron as operations officer at Kunsan, Korea. After four months, he became the Commander of the 80th. He had over 4000 flight hours. Today he is President of the 80th Headhunters Alumni and belonged to The Juvat Boys Choir.

Top Ten P-38 Ace Pilots of WWII

Some of these pilots had kills with other planes. For example Robbins and Roberts each had one more kill than listed below.

Maj. Richard I. Bong	49th FG, 5th FC	40 kills
Maj. Thomas B. McGuire, Jr.	475th FG	38 kills
Col. Charles H. MacDonald	475th FG	27 kills
Major Jay T. Robbins	8th FG	21 kills
Lt. Col. Gerald R. Johnson	49th FG	20 kills
Maj. Thomas J. Lynch	35th FG/ 5 FC	17 kills
Lt. Col. Bill Harris	18th FG	16 kills
Maj. Edward Cragg	8th FG	15 kills
Capt. Cyril F. Homer	8th FG	15 kills
Maj. Daniel T. Roberts	8th/475th FGs	13 kills
Lt. Col. Robert B. Westbrook	347th FG	13 kills
Michael Brezas	MTO/15th AF	12 kills
Capt. Kenneth G. Ladd	8th FG	12 kills
William Sloan	ETO/MTO	12 kills
Capt. Francis J. Lent	475th FG	11 kills
Maj. William Leverett	MTO/14th FG	11 kills
Maj. John S. Loisel	475th FG	11 kills
Capt. Murray J. Shubin	347th FG	11 kills
Capt. Cornelius M. Smith	8th FG	11 kills
1st Lt. Kenneth C. Sparks	35th FG	11 kills

Chapter Five
Remembering Comrades

Lt. General Jay Thorpe Robbins

Jay Robbins has been mentioned many times in this book. He and his wife, Ina, were life-long friends of Norb and his wife, Eileen. Their life paths crossed many times. The following was written after Jay's death in 2001.

"Lieutenant General Jay Robbins, a long-time resident of San Antonio, died Saturday, 3 March, at the age of 81. He was born on September 16, 1919 in Coolidge, Texas and graduated from Coolidge High School in 1936. General Robbins received a Bachelor of Science degree from Texas A&M University in 1940, and commissioned as a second lieutenant through the Reserved Officers Training Corps (ROTC). In July 1941, he entered active duty with the Army Air Corps at Randolph Field. He received his pilot wings in July 1942. In September 1942 General Robbins was assigned to the 80th Fighter Squadron (Headhunters) in the Southwest Pacific Area. In January 1944,

he became the commander of the squadron and in September 1944, he became deputy commander of the 8th Fighter Group. He flew 607 combat hours in 181 combat missions in P-39 and P-38 aircraft and scored 22 aerial victories, all against Japanese fighter-type aircraft. He twice destroyed four enemy fighters during single missions and was awarded the Distinguished Service Cross for each of these battles. He was the leading fighter ace from the State of Texas in all wars.

General Robbins was assigned as Commander of the 434 Army Air Forces Base Unit at Santa Rosa Field, CA, from February to November 1945. While there, he handled air defense preparations for the first meeting of the United Nations in San Francisco, CA.

He next served as squadron operations officer with the 412th Fighter Group at March Field, CA, the first organization in the Air Force equipped with F-80 jet fighter aircraft. He joined the newly established Air Defense Command (ADC) at Ent AFB, CO, in January 1952. His innovative ideas led to the establishment of the emergency broadcast system still in use today.

General Robbins was Deputy Commander and later Commander of the 20th Tactical Fighter Wing at RAF Wethersfield in England from July 1957 to August 1961. In July 1962, he graduated from the National War College, Washington D.C., and went to Norton AFB, CA, where he became the USAF Director of Aerospace Safety. During his tenure, the USAF established two consecutive record years in low world-wide accident rates.

General Robbins became Commander of the 313th Air Division in Okinawa, Japan in 1965. In March 1967, he was named Chief of Staff, Pacific Air Forces (PACAF), with headquarters at Hickam AFB, Hawaii. From July 1968 to February 1970, General Robbins was Commander of the 12th Air Force, based at Bergstrom AFB, TX. In February 1970, he was named Vice Commander, Tactical Air Command at Langley AFB, VA, and in August 1972, he was appointed as Vice Commander of the Military Airlift Command at Scott, AFB, IL. He retired from active duty in September 1974.

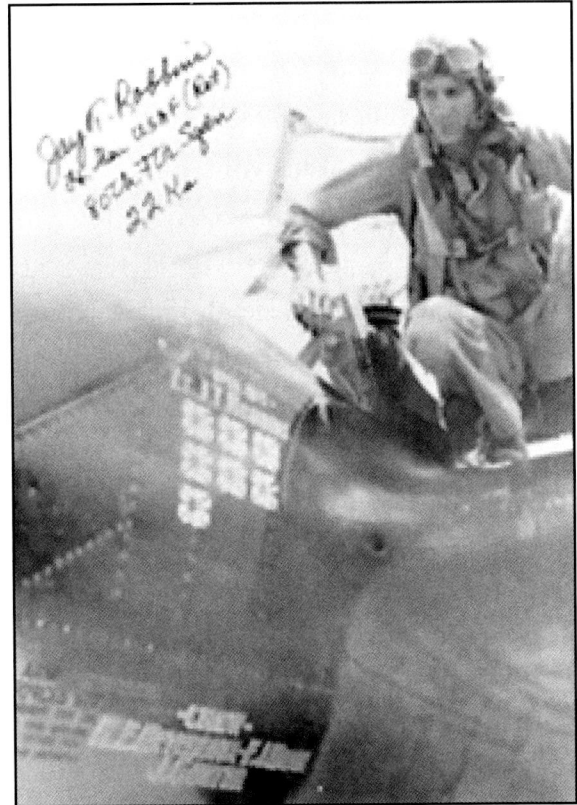

General Robbins was a command pilot with over 7,000 flying hours; most of which was in fighter aircraft. His military decorations and awards included the Distinguished Service Cross with oak

One of the planes Jay crashed. The name was Jandina II.

leaf cluster, Distinguished Service Medal with two oak leaf clusters, Silver Star with oak leaf cluster, Legion of Merit with oak leaf cluster, Distinguished Flying Cross with three oak leaf clusters, Air Medal with six oak leaf clusters, the Air Force Commendation Medal with oak leaf cluster, and the Presidential Unit Citation Award with two oak leaf clusters.

Jay and Carl Bong, one of Dick Bong's brothers. This is when the P-38 was at the Poplar, Wisconsin High School before it was restored and put in the Bong Memorial. On this day Norb and Jay had lunch at the Bong homestead in Poplar.

General Robbins was an active member of the Retired Officers Association, American Fighter Aces Association, P-38 National Association, Order of the Daidalians, and the 80th Fighter Squadron Association. He was a member of the Board of Directors of the Retired Officers Association from 1979 to 1985, and a Board of Director, National Bank of Fort Sam Houston from 1976 to 1992.

In 1993, General Robbins was selected to be one of the original inductees into the Texas A&M Corps of Cadets Hall of Honor. A model of his WWII P-38 is prominently displayed on the northwest corner of the parade field on Lackland AFB, and his F-100 aircraft from RAF Wethersfield is located in front of the Air National Guard headquarters building on Kelly AFB.

General Jay T. Robbins met and married the former Ina Louise Priest of Winchendon, MA, during World War II, when she was serving in Australia as an Army nurse. Both sons, Ronald and Robert were also career Air Force pilots. In addition to his wife and sons, General Robbins is survived by his brother, Jack D. Robbins of San Antonio, and his three grandchildren, Jay, Glynnis and Patrick."

"Jay and Ina had their first born son, Ronald, while at March Field. A few years later second son, Robert arrived. Both became Air Force, twenty-year pilots. Ron still flies for Northwest Airline after the Army tour of duty.

Jay and Ina were based in many locations in the U.S. as well as Okinawa, Turkey and Washington,

Norb and Jay with their muskies.

D.C. While Lyndon Johnson (fellow Texan) was president they were invited to spend a night at the White House. Years later in 1959, I was working in England and Europe. Jay and Ina were at Weathersfield, England. I spent a night with them and visited with another old pilot friend from back in Santa Rosa, Dan Sharpe.

Jay died in San Antonio, March 3, 2001. Ina came up later that summer and spent a week with us. She died later the next fall. At the ceremony in 1992, when the P-38 (full-scale) replica was dedicated at Lackland AFB, Jay invited me and a few ex-combat pilots down to San Antonio. Lackland is where most Air Force enlisted people receive their weeks of military training before being assigned to regular units. Here they learn to salute, march in parades and say 'Yes, Sir.'

When Jay retired in September, 1974, he was CO of the Military Airlift Command at Scott AFB, Illinois. He again invited a few of his many friends to spend his last three days of service with him and attend the reviewing ceremony. He had thirty-three years of military service. Eileen and I both had quarters at the base for those three days. We were as close as brothers. He, Ina and the boys would spend a week with us whenever they changed commands." -Norb

Captain Daniel T. Roberts
The "Gentle Ace"

2nd Lieutenant Daniel (Danny) T. Roberts came into Norb's life in Australia in May, 1942. They quickly became close friends and tent mates at Port Moresby. It seemed everyone liked Danny Roberts, and in a time when many personalities were thrown together in volatile combat situations, it is highly unusual that no one had anything bad to say about the man. Danny was a soft-spoken man who, before the war, was going to become a minister. He did not smoke, drink or swear.

"One pilot of the 80th, who nearly spent the war in utter obscurity, was to become a great legend of the Pacific air war. Daniel Roberts was a young Second Lieutenant. He has been described as being almost too nice to have been a successfully aggressive

164

fighter pilot. He never drank, smoked or uttered a strong curse in anyone's direction, and that gentleness of spirit may have persuaded someone in charge that the young pilot would do better as a base commander at a spot in the middle of the Australian desert called Doodnadatta. This horrible place had nothing more than camels and aborigines to recommend it and Robert was on the verge of despairing his strong desire to meet the Japanese in combat. [Norb says he called them "devils."]

Danny is the one in white.

Somehow an influential General happened to be passing through the base on his way to Darwin and Roberts thought that he had nothing to lose by telling his story. The General was sympathetic and Roberts was relieved shortly thereafter and was reassigned to the 80th by the middle of July, 1942

Roberts was assigned to a tent with Lieutenant Norbert Ruff, in some ways the complete opposite of the mild pilot just reprieved from oblivion. Ruff was a slender young man with a trim mustache and complete military bearing. His conversation was brusque and clipped with a rich whiskey voice. He and Roberts hit it off from the beginning and nobody was more grieved than Ruff when Roberts was lost late in 1942" (*Attack & Conquer*)

In 1968, Bob Anderson wrote an article about him called *The Gentle Ace*. After the article came out, Norb and Bob corresponded.

"November 3, 1969: Dear Bob Anderson: I have just finished reading your wonderful article "The Gentle Ace" on Danny Roberts. You can well imagine it brought back wonderful and some not so wonderful memories. My name is Norbert Ruff – flew 75 missions in P-39's & P-400's plus 50 missions in P-38's. I was in the original group which formed the 80th Sqdn and was the last of the 'original' group still flying combat with the 80th. I returned from N.G. about the time Danny was killed. Dan was from Springer, New Mexico and was one of the best people that ever lived. We were tent mates and quite close for many months. Dan did not drink, did not swear – the nearest was 'dad-nabbit' and when he used this, people moved!" -Norb

"November 5, 1969: Dear Norbert: Thank you for your kind remarks concerning my story about Danny Roberts. My very real regret was and is that I did not know Danny Roberts, for as I said in my story he was gone before I arrived at Dobodura where the 433rd was then stationed.

Your letter confirms and adds strength to my original feelings concerning Roberts and the fact that someone should write his story. Everyone with whom I have talked or written correspondence has referred to Danny with great affection and feeling. Some of it has bordered on reverence, and you must admit there were few commanding officers or flying mates who could attain that respect, by everyone, enlisted personnel as well as officer cadre, and yet Danny Roberts did it and without the usual vices practiced by all of us such as swearing, smoking and boozing.

The CO of the 433rd, now Colonel Warren R. Lewis, followed in Danny's footsteps and was my CO for almost the entire time I was overseas. He came to the 475th Ftr. Grp. Reunion at Colorado Springs a few weeks ago, and when he was checking out the big 11 x 14 enlargements of what was then his squadron, he came across the one photo of Danny I had acquired from his Dad. Louie stood there for a moment then said,

'Danny, Danny!! There was one of the finest men I've ever known!'

He got a big kick out of seeing the approximate 150 photos on display, but the last one he looked at was the one of Danny.

I don't ever recall hearing a name spoken with such obvious affection as that of Roberts. Marion Kirby said, 'I loved him like a brother.' Colonel John Loisel said, 'There's Danny (referring to the photo). What a man he was!' General Franklin Nichols saw the photo and remarked, 'That's Danny Roberts. God what a fighter he was!' John Babel said, 'I've never known a man like him.' And there were many more comments made.

Usually when referring to a former CO or flying mate, one is inclined to hear an occasional barb or cutting remark, but not once have I heard such comment. Nothing but praise for this man. So you can see that while I wrote about him, and much was edited out about his gentle nature. I really had to tell it second hand.

Incidentally, we heard much later that the Japanese buried him at Alexishafen where he and his wingman Dale Myers went down, a most unusual thing for the Japanese to do. As far as I know, he still lies there."

"The Gentle Ace"
By Bob Anderson

"I was not one of those destined to know and to treasure the friendship of Captain Daniel T. Roberts. By the time the lumbering C-47 flew over the Owen Stanley Mountains of

166

New Guinea, from 5th Air Force Headquarters at Port Moresby to Dobodura and had deposited me there, a new and eager fighter pilot, Captain Roberts was dead.

With the passage of the years since those desperate times in 1942 and 1943, when the 5th Air Force struggled for dominance over the Japanese, the lyrical sounding name, Danny Roberts, has been all but forgotten except by the former fighter pilots of the 80th, 432rd and 433rd squadrons.

Danny enlisted in the Air Corps as an aviation cadet at Santa Fe, N.M. He was assigned to the

Danny and Norb at Milne Bay

Ryan School of Aeronautics at San Diego, Calif., where he flew PT-22s, then to Randolph Field, Tex. for basic and finally to Brooks Field, Tex., where he graduated September 26 with the famous class of 41-I [According to Norb this should be 41C.]

He was assigned immediately to Mitchell Field, N.Y., where he served with various squadrons until reassigned to Hamilton Field, Calif. On Jan. 15, 1942, he departed the United States for duty in New Guinea with the 80th Fighter Squadron of the famous 'Head Hunters,' the 8th Fighter Group. [He was not assigned to the 80th until July.]

Respected Enemy

In the 80th he soon made a name for himself by displaying remarkable calmness in combat. He developed an immediate ability to visualize an entire area of a dogfight. Because he was flying Bell P-400s, he also developed a healthy respect for the enemy and a talent for running for his life when required to do so. Certainly no one in the 80th saw anything unusual in this. The odds for surviving the enemy Zeros while fighting them in P-400s, was practically nil, so Roberts and everyone else who flew the outgunned aircraft learned evasive tactics promptly – or died.

On Aug. 26, 1942, in the company of Captain William Brown, 1st Lt. George Helverston, 2nd Lt. Gerald Rogers and two other pilots, Danny Roberts blasted two Zeros from the skies over Buna Mission. After the many humiliating fights against the enemy, it was an especially satisfying mission. For Danny, this was the beginning of an illustrious victory record.

Six Bell P-400s clattered over the top of the Owen Stanley Mountains weaving between cloud formations, then dived across the Hyrographer Mountain Range for a fast fighter sweep across the dismal lowlands at Buna Mission on the northern coast of New Guinea.

167

Although the Bell-400s slipped down the side of the mountains at low level to avoid being observed, the Japanese were alerted and ten Mitsubishi Zeros were scrambling. The six American pilots dropped external belly tanks, pushed throttles and RPMs to maximum and sped for the Japanese strip at Buna.

At 1,500 feet, Capt. Brown led the P-400s in a dive at the scrambling Zeros. Just seconds separated the start of the combat, but the advantage still lay with the Americans.

An airborne Zero banked into a climbing turn immediately after takeoff and fired at Roberts' P-400 without any hits. In return, Roberts carefully sighted and squeezed the gun button. The cannon chugged and thumped, and the .50 caliber machine guns stuttered. A furrow of dust fluffed along the dirt strip beneath the approaching Zero as the slugs from Danny's guns rushed to meet it. The hail of bullets plunged home. The Zero shuddered, veered to the right and dived into the ground with a thunderous explosion.

Each P-400 had succeeded in making a pass. In the ensuing melee, as dust billowed across the field behind each Zero as it took off, the Bells wheeled about and started back for another strike. For once the P-400s had all the advantages and were calling the shots.

Roberts fired at a Zero head on. The enemy plane broke away to the right and crashed and burned on the beach. Roberts fired one more burst at another Zero. It stalled away out of control.

The sky was beginning to assume a hostile atmosphere as more and more Japanese planes piled into the air. The P-400s turned for the safety of the cloud covered Owen Stanleys and home at Port Moresby.

It was to be eight months before the quiet Danny Roberts would be in a position to score again, but in the meantime his qualities for leadership had made themselves known within the 80th Fighter Squadron. He had advanced in rank to Captain, and he had moved from flying the 'tail end Charlie' slot to flight leader. He had led the 80th on numerous missions. In addition, the 80th was now equipped with Lockheed Lightning fighters and was more than a match for the best of the Japanese planes."

Danny was moved to the newly formed 475th Fighter Group, the 432nd Fighter Squadron, then the 433rd Fighter Squadron, where he became the CO on October 4, 1943. "If the men of the 432nd were sorry to see him go, the pilots of the 433rd were just as curious to see if he was as good as Captain John Loisel of the 432nd said he was. The pilots of the 433rd needn't have worried. He was."

For the next month he led the 433rd, covering bombers, fighting over Rabaul until his last mission.

"Mission #3-91. Nov. 9, 1943. 12 P-38s. Mission: Low cover for four squadrons of

B-25s to Alexishafen. Time of attack: 1020. Altitude: minimum.

The 433rd was flying low cover for the 38th Bomb Group over Alexishafen. The Japanese occupied it and were willing to fight for the skies over it.

Mitchell bombers were coming away from Alexishafen after a very successful run when 15 to 20 Tonys, Zekes, Oscars and Hamps ran headlong into the 433rd over Sek harbor at between 2,000 and 6,000 feet.

The squadron was in perfect formation behind Danny Roberts. He made four quick passes at a hamp, low over the water and the enemy plane exploded into a fireball and crashed.

The sky had cleared of enemy fighters long enough for Roberts to single out a Zeke that was racing back towards the temporary safety of the strip at Alexishafen. Roberts' wingman, Lt. Dale Meyers, swung in behind Roberts to offer protection and also to be in position for a shot in case Roberts missed. Lt. William Grady slipped into the number three position.

Just as the Japanese plane reached the strip, it banked sharply to the right. Danny Roberts swung his P-38H to the right as did Lt. Dale Meyers, but Meyers was unable to turn quickly enough. His plane plunged into Roberts' speeding Lightning.

Fire blossomed in the air and the remnants of both aircraft plunged earthward spewing parts and debris. The airplanes plunged into the jungle near the strip from an altitude of 200 feet. Neither pilot got out.

The dogfight ended. The squadron gathered for the flight back to Dobadura. Here and there stragglers tacked onto elements that became flights. It was quiet on the way home once it had been established that Roberts and Meyers were gone. A numbness spread through the pilots – shock and grief.

In the years since the war, Danny's name is spoken with affection and respect. How long did he command the 433rd to earn this accolade? Just 37 days! As time is measured this is nothing, yet in those 37 days the gentle Danny Roberts stamped an indelible mark on the hearts and in the minds of all he met.

In the end, even the enemy respected Capt. Daniel T. Roberts. Many months after his death when our squadron was moved to Biak Island thousands of miles from that small spot of land where Danny fell. Australian troops advanced into the abandoned base. There they found two graves, each marked by a crude cross. In one rested the remains of Danny Roberts and in the other, Lt. Dale Meyers.

I regret I did not have the privilege of knowing Danny Roberts, the gentle ace. He was a giant among men."

Captain Danny Roberts' Victory Record

Aug. 26, 1942	2 Zekes	Buna Mission	80th Ftr Sqd
April 11, 1943	2 Vals	So. Of Oro Bay	80th Ftr Sqd
Aug. 21, 1943	2 Hamps	Near Dagua	432nd Ftr Sqd
Sept. 7, 1943	1 Oscar	Morobe Harbor	432nd Ftr Sqd
Oct. 17, 1943	2 Zekes	Morobe Harbor	432nd Ftr Sqd
Oct. 23, 1943	2 Zekes	Rabaul	433rd Ftr Sqd
Oct. 24, 1943	1 Zeke	Rabaul	433rd Ftr Sqd
Oct. 29, 1943	1 Zeke	Bet. Lakauni &	
		Matupi Island	433rd Ftr Sqd
Nob. 9, 1943	1 Hamp	Alexishafen	433rd Ftr Sqd

Squadron Combat Record for 37 Days of Roberts' Command: 55 enemy aircraft destroyed in 37 days with loss of three pilots. 10 days of perfect maintenance. Not one turn back of any aircraft which had taken off on a mission."

"His crew chief for these 37 days was Ted Hanks who I have had many letters from over the years. He also attended an 80th reunion. The 80th had a painting made of Danny and a P-38. Hanks took this painting to the governor of New Mexico and it hangs in his office at the capitol." -Norb

Cleve had been in Australia promoting the Morman Church before the war.

Cleve Jones

In 2000, Dale Jones, youngest brother of Cleve Jones wrote to Norb requesting information about his brother and his death during WWII. Cleve was 17 years older than Dale and one of five boys and one girl born to the Jones family. Cleve was killed July 23, 1943 in New Guinea.

November 7, 2000

Dear Dale,

It was good talking with you last Saturday P.M. I have gone thru my WWII negatives and found a few of Cleve. Reprints will take 4-5 days and I will forward these later. Considering these were taken 57 years ago, and the film developed under very crude conditions in my tent—not bad!

...On the phone we did not get a chance to talk about the

8th Fighter Group book – "Attack & Conquer" written by John Stanaway and Lawrence Hickey published in 1995. One of the pictures I took of Cleve is on page 101. On page 30 – photo taken at Petrie, Australia, Cleve is the 7th man. Book was available at "Borders". Page 312 gives a short note on the loss of Cleve. As I remember he was on fire on the right hand belly tank. Normally in combat you released these external tanks before the fight started, sometimes these tanks would hang up and not drop off. I'm sure he tried to release them. These fights spread out over quite an area and altitude as you can imagine. I was given credit for one "Oscar" that day. We were escorting B-24's to Bogadjim (near Wewak) and I ended up alone after downing the Oscar and started looking for friends. Many airplanes, P-38's & Oscars & Tony's west of me and below me and I headed for the area. Saw Cleve on fire and talked with him—kept telling him to "get out." He answered ok, said he was going to set it down in the river, which he did. When he touched the water the plane became one big ball of flame."

"November 24, 2000
Dear Norb,

By the way here's a little sidelight. Tevis Ferguson, who was killed 15 July 1942 on a training flight at Petrie, had married shortly before he went overseas. My oldest brother Wes (who is now deceased) worked in the San Francisco area with Tevis' wife, Sybil. Wes and Sybil became acquainted because Tevis and Cleve were in the same outfit. After Tevis was killed, they got better acquainted and married in 1944. They had eight daughters of their own before they finally adopted a boy. Sybil is still living and resides in the Los Angeles area near my brother Bill. She and her family are an integral part of our family and we all get together every time we go to California." –Dale Jones

November 27, 2000
Dear Dale,

You have Cleve's 201 file but you feel it is not complete. Naturally it is a history of his time in Air Corp with copies of all orders which sent him wherever he went. I'll go through mine and see if his orders are on any of mine. Cleve and I were in the same tents, etc. at Lowood, Port Moresby both places and at Mareeba.

I don't recall Cleve having malaria, but down at Milne Bay we had almost all of our pilots down with malaria from November thru January '43. The CO, "Coon Dog" Connors, was relieved with malaria. I remember flying ten days in a row because of sick pilots. Regarding storage of personal baggage in Australia – this was standard practice. Wool clothing (dress uniforms, pants) etc. would rot away in 2-3 weeks up in New Guinea, leather shoes would be green inside & out with mold. All due to high moisture & heat. I had good clothes stored at a large clothing store in Sydney. When

171

down on leave I'd check out what I needed, bring them back for cleaning & storage. I had all my issued winter flying gear (sheep skin) & boots stored in a foot locker down there, also in storage at this store. The jungle climate would actually eat that stuff up in a few weeks.

Cleve at Mareeba when the 80th switched to P-38s.

Regarding TDY & travel – Charters Towers is 60 miles inland from Townsville. To get there by train (Townsville-Charters Towers) took a full day. The train stops at every little cattle station. There was no train north of Townsville. So to get Mareeba to Charters Towers you had to fly or catch a ride down to Townsville by plane. When we arrived at Mareeba there were no planes there. We had to go get them so we went to different places where they were assembled or repaired. So Cleve, 22 March, 1943 went from Mareeba to Charters Towers to pick up a P-38 and bring it back to Mareeba. He could only ferry one – it was a short flight, he may have made more than one trip. I don't remember being on this one. Distance not over 100 air miles.

One time I was sent to Charters Towers to pick up a repaired wrecked P-39 when we were at Milne Bay that was a flight to Horn Island (tip of Aust.) across 500 miles of Coral Sea to Pt. Moresby, refuel, then on to Milne Bay same day.

Form #5 is the term for the log book. Gives date, type of aircraft, time, length of flight. Starts right from flying school, includes Sqdn & when you leave one squadron it goes with you. In combat it gives combat missions, number and a short message, "Escort B-24's Bogadjim" etc.

Cleve's missions should have started July 42 thru July 43 in two types of aircraft in his form #5.

Be sure to say hello to Tevis' wife, Sybil for me. I thought about her & Tevis' family many times. Those were hard years for all.

Dale, I don't want to imply that Cleve made a mistake by not bailing out and that he would be alive today. It was a no win situation had he bailed out and landed okay or landed his airplane okay. Now he is in enemy territory by over 500 miles. The natives here are friendly to whoever holds the territory. He is on the other side of the Owen Stanley Range of mts, 10,000 feet high. There has not been, nor will be any land or air-sea rescue from this area. The Japs did not take pilots as prisoner of war. Not one of all the pilots I knew in 9 squadrons that were shot down lived to be returned after the war. We know of 3 in the 80th that were beheaded, many more still missing? As I told you earlier I lost 3 one day. Enough for now. Regards, Norb Ruff.

June 24, 2001

Dear Dale,

Rec'd yours of the 19th yesterday and I will try to answer your questions. I, too, enjoy gardening. We have ripe tomatoes now on plants I started Jan 15th. I started from seed 28 other varieties of later tomatoes on April 15.

In the book "Attack & Conquer" Stanway made *many* errors: Page 311 – George Austin died in a mid-air collision with a pilot named Sponenberg (he lived) at Petrie with the 80th. He was operations officer – like second in command. The date of July 2 is correct. I flew in the broken formation for the funeral.

Page 312 – George Neater – he was flying Griffin wing, got too low, hit a palm tree (not a truck) – Goodenough Island.

Cleve Jones – He did not land in a *dry* stream bed. It's a wide river with plenty of water. I think he felt he could put out the tank fire by going down in the river. I have always felt he couldn't release a tank. Sometimes they would hang up. The fight started about 20,000 ft. He was low when I saw & talked with him. Maybe 2-3,000 feet.

Page 313 – Leon Mathers – The day before we were both on a mission. On landing he wrote up his airplane and said one engine cut out at altitude. I wrote mine up because I had to pump down my landing gear. This day August 23 late in the afternoon, the flight line called both of us and said our ships were ready for test flight. We went down together in the same jeep. My flight was short – take off-pull up gear & lower a couple times-all okay. I land and taxied to my revetment area, talked to my crew chief and watched a P-38 on single engine keep getting lower. He flew in behind an island in Pt. Moresby Bay and never came out. He landed in the ocean. Was found floating with his parachute still on the next afternoon. He made no attempt to bail out, but maybe released his safety belt too quick on landing.

Page 24 – Lower rt hand photo. These pilots were all 80th. Left to rt: Whip Austin, Phil Greasley, Pinky Hunter. Photo was taken in N.Y. probably & before the 80th was formed. See page 29 for the 1st 80th pilots which came from the 35th & 36th Sqdns.
Now for your questions:

CZ – Combat Zone – CM – Combat Mission

I have marked our map about where I think Cleve attempted to land in the river. About 10 miles west of Bogadjim and about ten miles from the mouth of the river.

Cleve was a very quiet individual and kept to himself. Most pilots did a lot of drinking on leave (no drinking in combat) in Aust. Cleve and I never went down on leave together. On days off we would take the crash boat out to a little island out of Pt. Moresby and swim. He never got in trouble doing low level flying around the bases etc. Also flew his missions – just one real good pilot and a brother to be proud of. Don't remember him having a beer or a drink – maybe a coke. Best Regards, Norb Ruff.

General Jerry Dix

Letter from Gerry Dix: July 4, 2001

Dear Norbert,

   I read your letter a number of times and gone over some of the memories I had of the 80th in New Guinea.

   After about 60 missions – P-400s there, I was eligible to return to the US because of my injuries on the Langley deal. I was assigned to the Philadelphia Air Defense Wing – we had a gunner school at Milville, NJ and were flying P-47s. I left there in June as the Ops Officer of the 355th Ftr Group and I flew a number of orientation flights with Gabreski, Zeriphi and others of the 56th Group. I was in the advanced echelon – the 355th arrived in Sept. and I flew about 70 missions with them in P-47 and later in P-51s. On D-Day 1, as Ops Officer, planned the mission and took off at 2:30 am for a seven-hour area coverage of the landing. Then flew again on a mission at 5:00 pm and returned to base about 9:00 pm with a hole in the canopy and a burned out radio caused by a bullet from a formation of Stukas. Our group got fifteen which was half of the thirty Germans shot down that day.

   On D+2 I led a group mission to Southern France to shoot up train engines. On my firing pass I hit some high cables, caught fire, lost power and crashed landed in a vineyard. As I threw my gear in the burning plane, a detachment of Germans came up and took me prisoner. After eleven months I returned to the states.

   After a short time as a Plans Officer, I went to Williams Field, checked out in P-80s, then on to March [Field] where I took over the 71st Squadron. After my adjutant and engineering officers were killed in crashes, I was fired by Gen Bacus, Commander of the 12th Air Force.

   After that I went to Turner Field at Albany, GA as Ops Officer for the 20th Ftr Group. There volunteered for assignment to Greece as a member of a staff of American officers advising the Greeks on air power in their fight against communists. The only time we and our allies were in such a fight.

   I returned home in '49 and went to Denver as air advisor to the Colorado Air Guard. When they were called to duty in the Korean War, I went with them as Deputy Wing Commander. When they left for Europe as the 50th Ftr Group, I went to Alexandra as Commander of the Air Base Group and later was Commander of the 366th Ftr Group (P-51's then F-80's).

In '58 I went to Japan as Dep. Wg. Comdr of the 67 Tac Rcm Wg at Itamic (?) Air Base. When the Wg moved to Yahoda, I became Dept for Operations with RB-29s, B-57's, F-80's, B-66's, C-118, 51's at Kadema, and Two Race Tec Sqdns one of which had a hot line to Washington.

After three years in Japan I returned to the US and was Base Comdr of Shaw AFB. After four years I went to Hurlburt as Dep. of the Special Warfare Ctr under Gil Pritchard. My last year there was as Commander of the 1st Air Command Wg and I retired from there to take the job of Exec. Of the Sumter, S.C. Chamber of Commerce. In 1970 I joined the National Bank of S.C. as Personnel Director and Property Manager. Retired from there in 1984 when I was 67 years old. My next birthday in Oct. (01) I will be 84." My Friendship, Jerry Dix.

Charlie Bateson

Charlie Bateson was killed on October 8, 1943 shortly after Norb went home. He was part of the 80th and well-known to Norb.

"A few years ago Kirby told me that Corky Smith, while on active duty at the Pentagon, saw photos of a pilot being beheaded and he identified Charlie as this pilot. It has always bothered me that of all the pilots in New G. that I knew so well, that were shot down, *not one* was returned as a prisoner of war. Not only pilots from the 80th, the 39th, 35th, 36th, 475 Groups three squadrons, also the 40th and 41st Sqdns. Many were classmates in flying schools.

"Bateson was a good fighter pilot, very serious, kind of a loner, did his job, not boisterous as most fighter pilots, good sized, well built and extremely quiet. He was only with the 8 PRS [Photo Recon.

Howard Peterson, Don McGee, Norb, Charlie Bateson and Ken Ladd who was killed on October 14, 1944. He was the CO of the 36th Squadron.

175

Squadron] about two weeks. He came into the 80th later than the Panama Group (which would have been July 1942), but had been with them earlier, got sick, was in a San Francisco hospital and then followed into the 80th the summer of '42. Naturally we

A 'Photo Joe' was like other P-38s except it did not carry any guns or ammo. They took pictures at high altitudes and many were being shot down by the Japs. The 80th rode shotgun on these reconnaissance flights.

were at 12 & 14 Mile in P-39s, then to Milne Bay, then to Mareeba Aust. on the change to P-38s, back to 3 Mile at Moresby. He joined the 8PRS on September 21, 1943, which is about the time I remember. I came home in Oct. '43." (Letter to Bob Rocker, August 26, 1996) [PRS is Photo Recon Squadron]

Robert E. Ludtke, who was flying with Bateson when he was killed, wrote about the incident in a letter to Bob Rocker.

"This is in reference to your letter dated 8-11-96 concerning the Alexishaven mission flown by the 8th Recon Squadron in which Lt. Bateson was lost. The following narrative contains information which I can recall.

On the afternoon of October 8, 1943 Fifth Air Force called and requested a mission be flown to Alexishaven to check on Japanese airplanes that were on the ground there. Myself in a photo ship and Lts. Bateson and Holton in P-38 escort departed Port Moresby around 1:00 pm. By that time the clouds had built up over the land area and an overcast with a few breaks restricted our altitude to about 18,000 feet. The closed cover became more dense as we approached the target and that altitude was a little low to continue over an enemy installation. As I recall we had no radio contact with each other after departure. I can't remember if we were having radio problems. I would guess that we were approximately 50 miles from the target and I had visual contact with the escort above and behind shortly before I made an 180 degree turn to return to home base. I did not hear a transmission reportedly made by Bateson about bandits at five o'clock. At that time I observed two Zero type Japanese aircraft through a break in the clouds. They were in close formation with camouflage paint scheme with a basic color of bronze or brown. They appeared to be turning to do a split S. I broadcast on the radio 'Bandits at twelve o'clock high' and fire-walled the throttles to make a hasty departure since I was unarmed. [Photo planes are not armed.] I did not witness any aerial combat or see any of the two fighter pilots until Holton returned to Port Moresby alone.

I hope the above will provide a few more details of this fateful mission. It has been many years ago and I have spent the last two days looking at scrapbooks trying to resurrect the details, but things are a little hazy. I was unaware of the fate of Lt. Bateson. I did take a couple of search missions on my own when returning from others at low altitude in the vicinity of the encounter to see if I could spot a parachute or wreckage with negative results."

Chapter Six
Late 1943-1946
The Jet Years

*A*fter nearly three and a half years, Norb was finally on his way home. When he landed at Hamilton Field in San Francisco he hitched a flight to Denver, then caught a plane to Minneapolis. Being weary and still rather shell-shocked from his long time in New Guinea, Norb was in no hurry to get home, so he got a hotel room, slept, ate some good food for once and had a few drinks. He slept for ten hours each night for the next three nights. After feeling a little more rested, he took a bus to Bloomer, where, instead of taking Norb into town to the bus stop, dropped him off at his mother's house.

Norb already missed flying and his friends. "One day you would save a friend's butt, the next day he would save yours. You knew from day to day what you were going to be doing. It felt permanent. Now I was only home one hour and people started visiting. The mayor came and left some dressed pheasants. Within two hours Al Takenoff came over with a case of beer." It seemed everyone wanted to welcome him back and hear his stories.

And the citizens did welcome him back as a hero. Local papers wrote his exploits. Each news article added just a little more to explain his experiences overseas. While the pride the town felt in Norb was great, it by no means overshadowed the pride they felt in all their servicemen and women. Dennis Mickesh, who was only a young lad when the war broke out, recalls his father discussing the servicemen and the letters the Advance printed. He also recalls his father picking up the mail and shouting with joy when Norb shot down a plane.

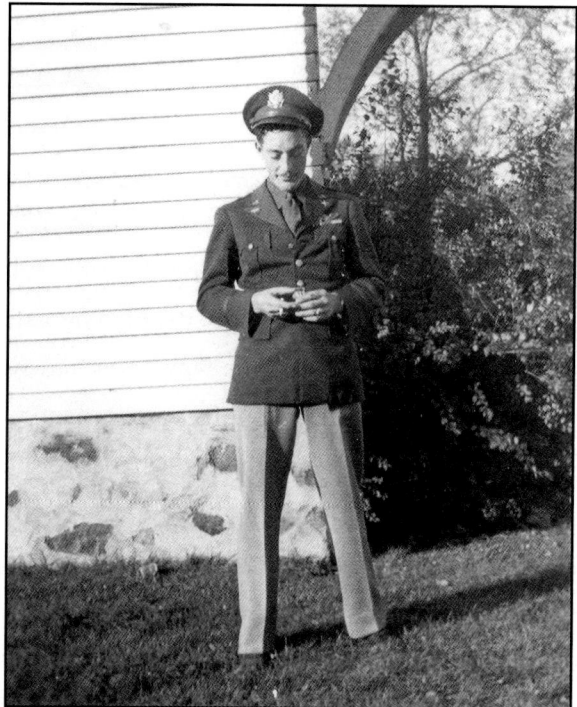

Chippewa Herald Telegram: October 4, 1943: "Captain Ruff on Way Home After 107 Missions: Capt. Norbert Ruff, flying ace of Bloomer, has been awarded the Bronze Oak Leaf Cluster to the Air Medal for completing 107 missions against the Japanese, it was announced from Allied headquarters in the Southwest Pacific today. Last Wednesday Capt. Ruff was the guest of fellow pilots somewhere in New Guinea at a farewell party, according

Norb receiving the Air Medal from Deputy Base Commander Major Waltman at the Santa Rosa Army Air Field on January 13, 1946. The man behind Waltman is Bill Leverette who shot down five planes in Africa during one mission. The man at the far end of the row is Kirby, the man to Norb's right is Danny Sharpe.

to a radio transmission from Robert J. Doyle, Milwaukee Journal war correspondent. The 24-year-old captain is one of the last fighter pilots remaining in the area who went over in January, 1942. He has been granted a leave and is now on his way home.

Ruff has an air medal with oak leaf cluster citations added and a Distinguished Flying Cross with one cluster.

He is credited with shooting down four Jap planes. He accepted his chance to go home when his superior officers decided he had earned a leave of absence in the United States. He expects to be on his way soon and will spend part of his leave at Bloomer with his mother, Mrs. Helena Ruff, before receiving a new assignment.

Cited frequently in this newspaper for his feats against the Japs in the Southwest Pacific, Capt. Ruff has become one of the well known heroes of Chippewa County in the present conflict. He learned to fly fighter planes in Australia-first in a P-40, then a P-39. He arrived in New Guinea, ready for action in July 1942. Two days after landing he took part in a strafing mission against the Japs who were landing at Buna.

'We didn't get much action against enemy planes in those days,' he said. In October he was part of the escort with transport planes which flew the first infantrymen of the 32nd division over the mountains. Ruff was based at Milne Bay for several months, and then learned to fly the twin fuselage P-38's. He went back to New Guinea where his unit saw fast action. His command shot down more than 100 Jap planes.

Ruff got his first Jap fighter on Aug. 23 near Madang while on his way to help a fellow pilot who had six Zeros on his tail. Ruff moved in and shot off a wing of one of them. On Sept. 13 he shot down two more fighters near Wewak, deep in enemy-held territory.

Ruff was leading his flight when four Zeros dropped their belly tanks and came at the first flight of his command. His unit took out eight or ten Japs heading for the bombers they were escorting. 'I got a head-on pass at my first plane as he was doing a slow roll. I was firing at him and he dove down through a hole in the overcast. (The squadron was flying high over the bombers.) I followed him down and let go another blast at him before he crashed into a mountain. A few minutes later I got another Jap in my sights and the pilot bailed out,' he related to Doyle.

Two days later he got his fourth Jap, but had a close call. He dove through a formation of Jap planes and ended low and alone with the Japs coming at him three at a time while he tried to climb back. A bullet exploded in his plane's tail, but he knocked down one fighter before returning to base. Capt. Ruff is expected to be in Chippewa Falls also when he returns, to visit Mrs. Arville Ruff."

Bloomer Advance: October 19, 1943: "Will Honor Local Boy With Banquet: Tickets Now On Sale at Various Places, But Better Buy Early: This coming Monday evening (October 25) Bloomer and community will honor one of its illustrious sons, Capt. Norbert Ruff, with a banquet at the St. Paul's Catholic Church.

Capt. Ruff a Noted Flyer: Norbert, who returned home last week on furlough from the South Pacific, where he has served for over a year in the air corps, has been in most of the major engagements in that area, and has four Zeros to his credit.

His squadron has been cited for its great achievements, and this Bloomer lad has had many close brushes with death, but came through without a scratch.

The banquet, served by the Christian Mothers of St. Paul's Catholic Church, has been set for 6:45 Monday evening and tickets may be obtained at the following places: Kitch Pharmacy, Bloomer Brewery, Babbitt's Tire Service, Les Woodruff, Bloomer Agency, Ed Gehring, Joe Ruff. The tickets are $1.10 and due to the fact that the reservations will soon be sold out, we urge you to secure yours early.

Complimentary Tickets: All soldiers (Bloomer or in the Bloomer area) who are home on furlough (or their mothers) will be admitted free and may call at the Kitch Pharmacy for their complimentary tickets. Gold Star mothers will also be given complimentary tickets."

Bloomer Advance: October 19, 1943: Capt. Ruff, Famed Pilot, Arrives Home: Bloomer Boy is Credited with Shooting Down Four Jap Planes: We were all set for a story on Capt. Norbert Ruff this week, but the Bloomer boy who's blazed a name for himself in the sky, was too busy trying to forget combat memories and went duck hunting Saturday afternoon, so our interesting view will have to wait.

Norbert came home Thursday night on a brief furlough to visit his mother, Mrs. Helena

Ruff, this marking his first visit back home since he entered the service in 1941, and tho' he's the same lad, he's a bit more mature, inclined to be a bit serious beyond his years. But piloting a fighter plane, and having four Zeros to his credit, he's gone through an experience that does not fall to the lot of many men.

Norb and his brother, Dick, after hunting.

Though this is unofficial, we are told that out of the thirty-five boys who received their wings the day Norbert graduated from an air field in Texas, only two survive.

Capt. Ruff, on duty in the South Pacific, has been in the thick of fighting for months, and contrary to some versions, gives the Jap credit for being a dangerous foe in the skies, and that the Zero plane, probably not as substantially-built as the P-38 that Norbert is flying, is an evasive target, manned by skilled pilots.

In combat, Capt. Ruff is credited by the Associated Press for shooting down four Zeros and ranked as an outstanding pilot, and his squadron has written a glowing epic in the skies.

Not only Bloomer and community, but all America is proud of the great achievements of this young man – a lad defying death in the war-tinted clouds in the South Pacific.

And a safe landing at the finish, Norbert."

Chippewa Herald Telegram: October 26, 1943: Bloomer Joins in Paying Tribute to Captain Ruff: Homecoming Banquet Staged for Pilot Who Downs Four Japs: Bloomer and vicinity paid tribute to Capt. Norbert Ruff last night. A crowd of neighbors and friends filled St. Paul's School auditorium to capacity at a homecoming banquet in honor of the quiet and unassuming young man who has returned home for a visit from distant New Guinea, where as a member of the Fifth Air Force, he shot down four Japanese planes.

Capt. Ruff was the principal speaker of the evening. He recounted his experiences in New Guinea and Australia and answered a number of questions.

'War isn't all blood and battle,' he said. 'It develops a friendly companionship, a close spirit of confidence and trust in a squadron that's hard to beat.

Lead Primitive Lives: This is particularly true in New Guinea, where the boys are thrown so closely together and are surrounded by the most primitive sort of native life, the captain said. There are no 'outside interests' there, no night clubs, no movies, nothing to do but eat and sleep and fly and fight. As a consequence, the members of a squadron grow as close to each other as human beings can, he said.

'I miss the boys of the squadron,' he declared.

Capt. Ruff paid an earnest tribute to the members of the squadron who 'keep them flying.' Of 300 men in an outfit, he said, only about thirty are fighter pilots, the others keep the planes in condition. 'And it is important, ' he pointed out, 'it means a lot to know that your plane will take you there and take you home, that you will not be forced down somewhere in the jungle because someone slipped up on the job, back at the base.'

Lands Among Natives: In response to a question, Capt. Ruff told of his own experience in a forced jungle landing. Because of propeller trouble, he was forced down in a small clearing near a beach. Because the landing area was so tight, he ripped his tires to pieces in bringing the plane to a stop. After making his peace with the natives with some gestures with his 'forty-five' he was able to signal his buddies who were looking for him. They flew in the necessary repairs and with native help, he put on new wheels, fixed the 'prop,' enlarged the cleared area enough to take off and finally got away. But it took him two weeks to do it.

Norb and his family at the banquet. His sister, Norma; brother Dick, and his mother, Helen.

In response to still another question, the captain said the Japs are tough fighters although the present crop of pilots are not as good as the earlier ones. And their fighter planes, the Zeros, are good planes, but Jap planes lack fire power and are easier to knock out of the sky than American planes. At first, American fighter pilots had their troubles, he went on, but that was before the 'bugs' had all been eliminated from the planes. Now they feel they are winning and will continue to win.

Tried to Kill Rescuers: 'The Japs seem to believe they are right. In any event they fight hard. They are no cowards,' he said. He told of one incident where Americans tried to take five Japs off the floating wing of a submerged enemy plane. As the Americans approached, they discovered that the Nips had rigged a machine gun on the plane wing. Two of the Nips were killed while the Americans

183

shot away the machine gun, another was killed when he tried to use his pistol and a fourth was killed when he drew a knife after he had been taken aboard the American boat. The fifth was taken prisoner.

Americans in New Guinea get a 'big bang' listening to 'Radio Tokyo' every evening. Capt. Ruff said. The broadcaster sounds like an American but the broadcasts are just funny. Radio Tokyo usually reverses the figures of American and Jap losses while identifying the spots where the fights took place. Since the American pilots know how many Nip planes they have knocked down, they are intrigued to say the least, to hear Tokyo making claims of the exact opposite with a little thrown in for good measure.

The captain wondered whether some of the Nips in New Guinea didn't really believe they were on an island of the western American coast. And many of them, he declared, are convinced that Japanese troops are now fighting in California and that Japanese victory is only a matter of time.

Natives are Interesting: The speaker recounted numerous interesting experiences with the natives. They learned readily how to 'thumb a ride,' he said, and nowadays it is quite usual to meet them standing with thumbs up almost anywhere along the trails that pass for roads on the island. Nor do they care much where they go, they just like to go along for the ride.

Capt. Ruff said the primitive conditions in which the Americans find themselves make the boys over there realize more than ever what life in America really means.

'They are all anxious to get this war over with and come home,' he said and he believed they would come home better citizens and with a higher appreciation of their country because of their experiences.

Capt. Ruff believes that as a result of the pressures of war, aviation has taken great strides and that it is impossible now to imagine what will happen in the next quarter of century.

'We may one of these days spend a two-weeks vacation making a trip around the world,' he said citing how he himself covered the 10,000 miles from Brisbane to Minneapolis in three days and two nights of flying time.

B.J. Kostner acted as toastmaster at the homecoming banquet. Rev. Father Haas, pastor of St. Paul's Church, and R.M. DeWitt, superintendent of schools, spoke briefly, eulogizing Capt. Ruff and other Bloomer boys now in the service. A number of other service men were guests and were introduced to the audience.

Speaks here today: Kiwanians and their friends of Chippewa Falls kept Captain Ruff busy for over an hour this noon answering questions about his experiences. Rather than give a talk, Capt. Ruff very graciously consented to let members and their guests fire questions at him and he kept his audience highly interested throughout the entire time."

Bloomer Advance: October 26, 1943: "Man Who Has Flown On 125 Missions, Yearns for Action: Capt. Norbert Ruff Was Last Man in His Squadron That Fought Japs in New Guinea – Zeros are Good, But Our Planes Are Better.   Nosing his P-38 Lightning into a murky sky on his 125th mission Capt. Norbert Ruff added another flight to his record in the New Guinea area which has been filled with adventure – the kind that ages a man before his time.

Norbert, at 24, is a veteran, a pilot who has fought with the best Japan had to offer, and came off the field with the distinction of never been shot down or wounded.

'Call it lucky if you want to,' said Capt. Ruff to the writer, 'but if you're lucky enough to come back from a flight, give some credit to the flying experience you have had and the rest to the lads that are flying with you.

Norbert, 5 ft. 11, a bundle of 160 pounds of steel, has still the catchy smile when he talks to you, even grim war couldn't wipe off that grin.

Got Wings in 1941: It was at Houston, Texas, where Capt. Ruff was given his coveted wings when he completed training, and it wasn't long before he was sent to Australia, this early in 1942, and since that time he has lived on borrowed time, fighting in the skies almost daily, adding glory to that branch of the service that is now slowly crushing the Japs, a gathering momentum that shall sweep on to victory.

Our Ships the Best: Yes, the Jap Zero is a good plane, but not on the par with the type America is now putting on the runways. A Zero, first only partially armored, was quick as an owl in the sky, but Japan quickly learned that America's fighters, though probably a bit slower on wing turns, had too much punch, and the Zero of today had added weight to make them tougher targets.

'Visibility Sixty Miles: Just how far can you see, say at 15,000 feet?' we asked. 'Well, that's rather hard to answer,' said Ruff, 'but I'd say that on a clear day you could see sixty miles.

Sunny Days Mean Trouble: And sunny days isn't the right type of weather for fighting. Ruff said Zeros, hid in cloud formations, would dart in 'from the sun,' only by flying in mass formations could they overcome this sun blindness.

Not So Eager Now: The sons of Nippon aren't so 'itchy' for a fight now, and, in direct contrast to the earlier days of aerial warfare, do not engage in individual combats, fighting only in packs.

Average Life Is One Year: Just how long can a pilot expect to live after he's in a fighter squadron? 'In New Guinea, I'd say that the average life of a pilot is about a year,' said

Ruff, this, of course, did not include the casualties, and fliers who had been sent home who were on the verge of a breakdown.' [Norb's note on this today: "I lied about the average life expectancy of a pilot. In the area were many parents of flying sons in the Air Forces. Both my college roommates, Bud Jenneman and Herb Trankle, were from Bloomer, but not in combat. The average life was about three to four months."]

Oxygen Masks Uncomfortable: And wearing an oxygen mask is not comfortable equipment, said this young flier. Pilots who are in the pink of health, and who have not been worn down by combat duty, do not need oxygen masks until the higher levels are reached, but anything from 12,000 feet and on they are usually worn by all fliers.

Chilly at 20,000 Feet: In tropical New Guinea (pilots wear only jersey and shorts) one doesn't notice the cold until the indicator points to 20,000 feet or better. All ships are equipped with heaters, but Norbert said that while it helped a lot, the heaters did not keep them warm.

Jap Pilots Young Fellows: The average age of the Jap fliers are about the same as that of American pilots, but they are not given the intensive training we give our fliers, 'but they're smart in the air, and once they challenge you I'd say they lack nothing in aggressiveness,' said Capt. Ruff.

Gets Hot Reception: Ruff's first sight of Jap planes was a few days after he had arrived when a group of 28 bombers came over and bombed them, but they did only minor damage.

Got First Zero in July: Norbert's first Zero was sighted when his squadron was near a Jap base. 'He was flying at about 4,000 feet and never suspected I was on his tail until I gave him a machine gun spurt that shot off his wing. I followed his rolling plane until I saw him crash,' said Ruff.

He shot down two more Zeros in August and bagged his 4th one in September. Only one of the Jap pilots baled out, but Ruff didn't say what happened to him.

Has 900 Hours in Air: Capt. Ruff was non-committal when we wanted to know if he had shot down more than four Zeros, but he's been in the air a total of 900 hours, and has been on 125 flight missions, so he's been in on a lot of killings.

Fight Starts at 20,000 Feet: Squadrons usually engage the enemy at heights of 18,000 to 20,000 feet, and before the scrap is over they may be down to 4,000 feet, as they can maintain their terrific speed by diving at their foe. And you pick out the Jap you are after when the fight starts, staying with him until you've either downed him or he's streaking for home. And there's two very necessary things for a flier to remember: first, have the altitude when you sight a Zero, then maneuver your plane so you get on his tail. And it takes practice and a quick eye for shooting when you race at a speed in excess of 600 miles per hour, often head-on at a Zero, and who must either face the music or go into a power dive.

Was Made Captain in June: Capt. Ruff was given his rating as Captain in June, this year, and was serving as flight commander. Though he did not reveal the number of buddies who had made the supreme sacrifice, he is the lone remaining member of his squadron that flew with him when he first came to New Guinea.

Flying Sub-Conscious Effort: Piloting your plane becomes secondary nature with you, said Ruff, after you have been up a few times, and once you're in the air you're constantly on the alert for the enemy. And operating your ship and shooting at the same time must be developed by continuous practice and it is an art you've either got to get good at or you don't stay in the game.

Japs Wear Parachutes: And the Jap flier has been stripped of some of his glamour, for now we learn that they are all equipped with parachutes, thus discounting the story they sacrificed the chute to make their loads lighter.

'Do Japs carry side arms?' we asked. 'That I cannot answer,' said Ruff. 'Some of them do, but I do not know if it is standard equipment. Our pilots all wear sidearms.'

Getting Back Home: And it'd not be hard to get lost in that jungle country. Often out on missions that mean up to 600 air miles, a pilot (if separated from his squadron) must be able to fly unerringly to his base. 'You can either fly by compass, but a lot of us pick out landmarks that give us a good idea where you are,' said Ruff.

In flight they are constantly in communication with one another over their two-way radio, but he didn't reveal the distance of his set.

Zeros Plainly Marked: No, the Jap doesn't try to hide the markings of his plane, said Ruff. Every Jap ship is emblazed with the big red circle, but this is the only camouflage they do not attempt.

Saluted Gen. MacArthur: At some undisclosed camp in New Guinea Capt. Ruff had seen Gen. MacArthur and saluted him, but didn't get to have a conversation with the army leader.

A Cautious Witness: 'Must we kill off every Jap, or will they yell quits?' we inquired. 'That question I cannot answer,' replied Ruff.

Radio Is Only Contact: No, they don't get daily papers over there in New Guinea, the only exception being the ones sent from their home towns. At night they listen to short wave broadcasts, and during their few leisure hours play such American games as football, baseball and basketball and naturally they play cards. Letters from home ranks as No. 1 cure for homesickness, and Ruff said they were more precious than gold.

Put In Long Hours: And just what are the hours of an American pilot in the combat

187

zone? 'You've got to be with your ship an hour or so before dawn,' said Capt. Ruff, 'and if you're out on a mission, you'll not be back at your base until late afternoon, or just before dark.'

In New Guinea they were quartered in tents, dirt floors, and slept in screen-covered beds as Ruff said they had more bugs in New Guinea than in any other place on earth. 'Some were an inch long, and a lot of them were transparent,' added Capt. Ruff.

Ten Men to Plane: It takes a ground crew of ten men to keep one plane in operation, men that are highly trained for this type of work. Each crew is assigned to one certain ship, and the pilot, upon returning to his base, makes a report if his ship isn't functioning right.

Grounded For Two Weeks: Capt. Ruff once stayed two weeks with a group of friendly natives in New Guinea when a faulty oil line acted up. And in this jungle country setting down a P-38 isn't an easy trick, but Ruff picked out a cleared patch in the wilderness, within sight of the ocean, being met with a reception committee of menacing natives with spears. [This part of this article is incorrect. At the time Norb went down, he was not flying P-38's. His squadron did not receive them until the following year.]

But he convinced them he wasn't looking for trouble, and the following day signaled to American fliers who were out searching for him, using his parachute. He was also able to signal what parts he needed, and several days later they arrived by chute, but it took him two weeks before he was able to get his ship back into the air again.

Problem in Transportation: A lot of natives in new Guinea had never seen an automobile before the war, and some pointed at the wheels and wanted to know what they were for. Shipping, too, is difficult in that land. In different states in Australia railroads are not of similar gauge, so a freight car must be unloaded when a different gauge is reached.

From December to the middle of February they had a wind the natives call a 'guba,' very much like a hurricane. They have two seasons in New Guinea: rainy – and more rain. But it doesn't interfere with farming because there isn't any.

'Yes, the natives were very friendly to us,' said Ruff. 'But they're just as friendly with the Japs, too, so we haven't any advantage there.'

And it didn't take him long to get home! His base in New Guinea is some 12,000 miles from Bloomer, but he made it by plane in five days, flying into San Francisco then home by train.

Yep, he's anxious to get back into action, and is due to leave Nov. 1st. Now he's headed for China – if they'll give him that assignment, for he wants to be in there shooting when the Nippon flag is bowed in defeat.

A grand guy – a great fighter, but that's what our air force is made from, men that are men 100% clean through. And you're coming back, Capt. Ruff, and when that happy day arrives we'll be one of the thousands to welcome you back at your Chippewa home, and when we shall again live in a free land, made so by men like you."

After the hoopla died down, Norb spent the next thirty days relaxing, eating his mother's good food, hunting with his brother, Dick and wondering where his next orders would take him.

After his leave, Norb headed back to California where, within three days he received orders to go to San Diego North Island. In time, before he left the service in 1946, he would work at fifteen different bases in California. Whenever someone was sent from one field to another, he had to check out; turn in flying gear, gun, go to every department on the field to get signatures showing he was not indebted to that department and that he had turned his gear in. This was known as "Clearing the Base." When arriving at the new base with new orders, the process was reversed; checking into each department, receiving new gear and sometimes getting a physical.

North Island was the largest Navy Base at San Diego. Since the Army Air Force did not have a base to fly from, they used the Naval Base. Flying from a Naval base was different for Norb and other Army pilots. The Army Air Corps used numbers on their runways. With the Navy, a pilot looked at the control tower for their bearings.

When Norb first went overseas, he had never had any training in combat. Later, P-38 pilots were trained with over 100 hours before leaving the states. Norb was sent to one of these squadrons to train men in combat tactics in P-38s. He also checked them out in the planes.

Norb's second duty was as west coast defense. If radar picked up anything from the west, pilots were scrambled and went up to intercept. After six months or so he was reassigned to Ota Mesa, putting him even closer to Mexico. There he also trained pilots in P-38s and participated in the West Coast Defense Command. At this time the WCDC was not needed and some bases were being consolidated. Norb's group was moved to Santa Rosa, and he served as Squadron Commander, again training brand new Second Lieutenants in P-38s.

The instructors in Norb's squadron had served in all theatres of war – Germany, Africa, South Pacific. They all had different ways of fighting and every new

Waders Jay and Norb made from inner tubes for duck hunting. Jan. 6, 1946

pilot had to learn each technique since it was not known where he would be fighting. What worked in Japan did not work in Germany because of the different types of enemy planes.

"Now I am at Santa Rosa, California and CO of a Squadron of P-38 trainees. About New Year's Day, 1944 a group of us go down to the East/West Football game at San Francisco only fifty miles south. After the game we went up to the bar on top of the Mark Hopkins Hotel. This bar was powered and rotated around.

"Here was a black, curly-haired, slim guy with a letter jacket on with his back toward me. Jay had just returned from New Guinea. During our long conversation he asked where I was stationed. I told him and he said, 'I'll try to make it.' Now he is a major and I'm still a captain, so he ranks me. Thirty days later he arrives in Santa Rosa. Ina and Jay were married the year before. She is still in service in New Guinea and Australia and doesn't join him until late 1944.

"On our days off Jay and I do a lot of duck, pheasant, goose and dove hunting together both in Santa Rosa area and over in the Sacramento valley. We had become friends with Henry Sullivan and his family – one of the city's friendly citizens. Harvey, Elizabeth and their two young sons, Jim and John, had us out to their home for dinner many times. Harvey had access to many of the local hunting spots and as well as to the Grace Bros. cabin in the valley. The Grace family owned the local brewery. This cabin was over the mountain range inland in California in the middle of grain, tame rice growing farms – excellent duck, pheasant and goose hunting. We remained friends of the Sullivans all their lives – both Harvey and Elizabeth have passed away. We visited them a few years ago after attending a Squadron reunion on

Jay and Norb getting ready to go duck hunting.

the West Coast. In 1962 Jay and I spent a night with the Sullivans. I was on my way to Australia to start up a unit we built for a company in Sydney. Jay was now a General and in charge of the 4th Air Force at which time covered the west coast of the U.S. The military airport at Santa Rosa was given to the city as the municipal airport and Jay was assigned to escort Mrs. Hap Arnold to the dedication ceremony at the field. General Arnold was head of the Air Force during WWII and had already passed on."

Periodically the instructors would get called back to their original theatre. Norb was called back to the South Pacific as a flight commander.

Norb, Jim Sullivan, Jay and John Sullivan.

"Back to 1944. There was to be a new jet fighter cadre organized to run test on the first jet fighter, the Bell P-59. It would be one pilot – ex-combat – from each of the five P-38 training bases on the west coast. It would be at a separate, small field. I liked to fly and put my name in.

"The same day I got my orders to join this unit, I also got my orders to go back to the 5th Air Force and become CO of one of the old squadrons. Col. Atkins told me to take my pick, and I elected the jet cadre. As far and I knew I could have been trained in jets and then sent back over. Had I decided to stay in service it would have been a quick promotion to major to go back overseas. I had to fly these jets! We did this at a little secluded airfield in Oildale, California not far from Fresno. Jay stayed at Santa Rose and Ina returned from the Pacific and joined him.

"The first fighter jet, the Bell P-59 was built in Buffalo, New York. This is the same company that built the P-39, P-400 and P-63. This cadre was composed of five pilots, all captains with one major, all returned combat veterans from different overseas areas of operations and forty enlisted men all Tech's and Master Sergeants with nine to twenty years service, plus two ground officers in charge of aircraft maintenance.

"We would pick up the jets at the factory. It took twelve stops to refuel to get them from Buffalo back to Oildale. We would have to reach 40,000 feet to have enough fuel to make the next stop. At sea level, fuel consumption was fourteen gallons per minute, at 40,000 feet the consumption was four gallons per minute. In 45 minutes you would use up nearly all of the 900 gallons aboard. Now these designated airports were the only ones that had the JP-1 fuel needed for these jets. To land at any other airport meant the fuel had to be trucked in. Naturally some flights were delayed because of weather. The weather reporting was good up to 20,000, but above that was a guess. Naturally this short range was one of the reasons not many P-59s were built." (Only about 50 were built.)

When the pilots picked up the planes in New York, a representative at Oildale told the five pilots how to start the plane and gave them a tech manual to read. Then they went up on their own. They sat over the gas burner, which made the cockpit burning hot. The pilots were wringing wet and when they got out of their cockpit, their suits were soaking wet.

Norb was one of the first five pilots to fly these jets On April 5th, 1945. His last flight with P-59 was on December 16, 1945. On special days like Air Force Day or Memorial Day there was a list of bases the pilots could fly for shows. This was to benefit the civilians to "show them what their tax dollars were going to."

The first jet was a top secret plane in 1942 and a wooden prop was put on the nose to make it look like it was a propeller-driven plane. Whether true or not, this next story makes an interesting tale. On one of the test flights out of Edwards, then known as Muroc, pilots out of Van Nuys Airport, checking out in P-38s, saw the jet. No one would believe them when they said they saw a plane with no props flying. The story was passed around, so the test pilot of the P-59 dressed up in a gorilla mask, wore a derby hat and had a cigar stuck in his mouth. The next time he flew past the P-38 pilots he waved at them. Of course now no one would believe the pilots when they said they saw a plane with no prop flown by a gorilla, with a derby hat and a cigar. Norb cannot confirm this story, but does know that when the plane was shipped overseas, it was covered with canvas and the fake propellers pushing out the canvas making it look like the plane was propeller-driven.

"Lockheed was building the F-80, the second jet fighter approved for the Army Air Force, and we would soon be given these after about a year. During that year, besides doing various tests, we would be called to different fighter bases to demonstrate the P-59 jet. These bases would have 'open house' for the local civilians to attend the show as well. I chose to do the one on Air Force day at Santa Rosa where I had formerly been based. This was a very enjoyable day as you can imagine. At that time we would do a single airplane show. A little more than a year later we would do as many as eight airplanes together, shows such as the last Cleveland Air Races done in 1946 with the F-80s.

"On April 10, 1945 Dorothy Hanson, a home town girl from Bloomer and I married at Fresno California. We had known each other in high school, but never dated. Both she and two sisters were teachers. One sister married a Navy man and lived in San Diego. Dorothy lived with them and worked at Consolidated Aircraft Company during the war. After returning from combat, I was first stationed at North Island Navy Base at San Diego in a P-38 training unit which later moved to Santa Rosa. This is where Dorothy and I met again following high school.

Norb with his niece Ragna Rae Heim, at San Diego. She is the daughter of Lucille Hanson Heim, Norb's first wife, Dorothy's, sister.

"Now the cadre is moved first to Chico, California over in the Sacramento Valley and then to Santa Rosa, California and then to March Field inland from Los Angeles. Before leaving P-59s this cadre of men had an excellent safety record, not one accident or any pilot injury. The ground crew of Techs and Master Sergeants are due their share of the credit.

"Here [March Field] we get F-80s, the second Air Force jet built by Lockheed. Dick Bong had been killed doing army acceptance flying at the plant on August 6ʰ, 1945, the same day the first atomic bomb was dropped on Hiroshima. He was the sixth pilot to be killed in an F-80. Milo Burcham, chief test pilot of Lockheed was the first to be killed in an F-80."

Between July and August of 1945, after several crashes occurred, including, Bong's, all the machines were grounded. There were several defects in the planes, which had to be fixed, but had nothing to do with Bong's crash. All F-80s were grounded.

Jay Thorpe with his F-80 at March Field in June of 1946

Since the first flight of the plane, there were fifteen accidents. Six pilots were killed, eight were destroyed, four had major damage and three minor damage. After investigations and accelerated

F-80 at the Cleveland Air Races in September of 1946. This was the last time the races were held.

service trials, on September 1 the F-80 was in the air again. Norb made his first flight in P-80A (F-80)" on January 21, 1946. His last flight was on September 24, 1946.

At this time the pilots were still using regular cloth helmets and several pilots were killed because of this. "A jet airplane on take off is slower getting up to speed than a prop job. It just sits there at first with full throttle. Pilots banged their heads against the inside of the airplane when they hit rough air at high speeds. We were first issued the leather tank helmets in F-80s because of this. These were too heavy at 4-5 'g's' and you couldn't hold your head up. So, a lighter, stronger helmet was developed for jet pilots."

Another problem the pilots had was learning the differences in landing the jets. In prop planes like the P-38, the propellers would put drag on the plane and help slow it down with the engine at idle as in landing. Without the propellers for drag, many inexperienced jet pilots overshot the field and would have to go around again and make a new approach on landing.

Norb at the Cleveland Air Races in September of 1946. In 1947 they were held in Detroit. The F-80 was painted with eight coats of paint.

194

"Shortly after the bomb was dropped, [at Hiroshima] the 1st Fighter Group returned to the States after many years of combat in the European and African areas. This was the first fighter group to receive F-80s and was assigned to March Field. The cadre was absorbed into the Group and I was assigned to the 27th Squadron where I spent most of 1946 checking out the pilots in the new jet. Most of this was done at Muroc (now called Edwards Air Force Base) because of the long runway.

"The 1st Fighter Group had been flying P-51s most recently, but had P-38s earlier. Now that WWII is over, many of the noted pilots who wanted to stay in service transferred into this new jet group. Rex Barber, who shot down Jap Admiral Yamamoto; Jay Robbins with 23 victories, joined the 27th Squadron. Rex became CO and Robbins was Operations Officer. Robbin Olds, a noted ace from Europe, whose father was a General, also joined. Olds became a second ace later in Korea and also became a General. While at March Field he married the actress, Ella Rains. Tex Hill, former China Flying Tiger, was Base CO.

"While at March Field, Jay and Ina Robbins and Dorothy and I rented a house together at Lake Elesinor. We split the grocery bill, drove one car to the field and left one for the wives. Jay and I even got in some duck hunting on Lake Elesinor which was a shallow lake. This picture shows Jay and Norb in their homemade waders. They used old automobile inner tubes to fashion them, since you could not buy waders during the war.

"After the Cleveland Air Races show in the fall of 1946, I found I did not care for the peacetime Air Force. There was not much new at the test center at Edwards as far as new fighter development. My flying days were numbered and a desk job wasn't why I came into the Air Force. Tex Hill, who had been a P-40 pilot in the Flying Tigers in China, left the Air Force to start the Flying Tiger Airline. The new CO and his second in command, both full colonels, came out of Washington D.C. Neither had been overseas or in combat. Sunday parades were being scheduled, etc. This is like when I was a cadet."

Before Norb left the service, he was promoted to Major.

"Yes, it was a good time to be in the Air Force. From open cock-pit Stearmans & Waco's in Primary Flying School, thru good prop driven fighter planes thru the first two models of jets. I was very lucky and as I said I had good guardian angel those six plus years." -Norb

Chapter Seven
Home at Last

Norb and Dorothy finally moved back to Bloomer. Their daughter, Wendy was born in September, 1947. Tragedy struck Norb's family again when Dorothy died in October of 1948 after several operations for cancer, both in California and Wisconsin. She was twenty-seven years old.

"Wendy would spend the next two years living with her grandparents on the farm south of Bloomer. My brother, Dick, who was nine years older, lived in Detroit where I had started my college education in 1936. He worked in industrial ovens and heating applications during the war years. He also taught at the university I had attended. On many of his business trips to the West Coast he would ask me to leave the service and join him in a business venture. He and a college friend of ours, Russ Suter, who was a research director at Wyandotte Chemical Company, were developing a process to eliminate the air pollution from many of the heating processes the ovens created. I told him many times I did not care to live in Detroit or any large city.

"After Dorothy's funeral he again asked me to come and look at the basement research work which they had done. If it proved out, I could take it any place I wanted. Wendy was being well cared for and I did not plan to return to California at the time, so I accepted Dick's invite. This visit lasted over two years.

"During that time we had a number of operating units which I installed and started in the field. This job started with a basement demonstration to company management of Reichhold Chemical Company's personnel at Russ Suter's home which was where all the work was being done. This resulted in my being invited to the company's research department to build a small test unit with the Research Director, Stan Hewitt. After successful tests, they ordered the first of sixteen production units. The sheet metal components including the heat exchanger were built by brother Dick's industrial oven company. The catalysts were manufactured by me in Russ' basement.

"On start up Stan Hewitt, the Plant Manager, and I each took eight-hour shifts to babysit the unit for a few weeks' operation. Reichold had plants on the East Coast, in Switzerland and in Sidney, Australia, all of which I would visit years later.

"While the first Reichold unit was in operation, another company with a different problem with lots of air pollution was being tested. This was Phelps Dodge Corporation at Fort Wayne, Indiana. The application here was Wire Enameling. Copper wire of many diameters are coated with various types of varnish and baked in ovens. Each oven had two stacks about ten inches in diameter. The finished product is used in motors, generators, coils, condensers, etc. This plant alone had hundreds of ovens each with two stacks. There were many other plants in this city doing wire enameling.

(*Eau Claire Leader*, January 9, 1955)

"Again, Dick's company built these ovens. They built the sheet metal and I built the catalyst and installed the first and second test units at Phelps Dodge. Later we would furnish catalyst to many other companies such as Ray Magnet Wire, General Electric as well as other foreign companies.

"Later we would build systems that burned the vapors coming off the heated kettles of the varnish and paint manufacturers. We incorporated and formed the company Catalytic Combustion Corporation in February 1950. Now we have orders to fill and need a place to manufacture.

"The former Bloomer Brewery was vacant. I knew the plant building well having worked there every vacation and summers while going to college at Stevens Point. The owner was Al Takenoff, and he rented one small end of the building to me for $30.00 a month. I had carpenters and electricians make some necessary changes while I was home for Christmas in 1949."

In 1955, Catalytic Combustion Corporation was written up in the *Eau Claire Leader Telegram* in January and *Popular Mechanics* in August.

"January 9, 1955 - Bloomer – Three farm boys turned engineer have developed a fume killer that has smog fighters around the world beating a path to their door. Two of the founders of the firm with the jawbreaking name of Catalytic Combustion Corporation, Richard Ruff, 44, and Norbert Ruff, 36, his brother, are from Bloomer. The third, Russell Suter, 42, was a college buddy.

Suter and Dick Ruff, seeking a means of eliminating fumes resulting from baking enamel onto ovens, invented a process and founded a firm which in five years has sprouted from a single employee to a near $250,000 operation. Sales and engineering offices are in Detroit.

Bloomer is the home of the plant in which the catalytic elements, heart of the system, are made by Norb Ruff and where most of the complete systems are built to individual order by the Henneman Blacksmith and Body Shop. They range in size from one that could be held in the palm of the hand to a recently completed giant that filled two railroad flatcars within one inch of the height and width limits. Most units are shipped by truck.

…Ruff [Norb] and his wife have two children, one by his first wife who died while they were living in California after the war. He's an avid hunter and fisherman who has been grabbing his outings in short takes since business began booming for the company. He was the company's lone employee in 1948 and 1949. His brother and Suter were working for Detroit firms. He built a test model and quite a few subsequent units in Suter's basement in Detroit."

Norb holding one of the catalysts.

Plant operations at the old brewery building. Left front: Norman Henneman, the first employee. Behind him is Glen Gullickson, Rear right is Truman Hebert; right front is Norb.

Fifty-six years after becoming incorporated the company is still in Bloomer and is being run by Norb's son, Mark. They outgrew the old brewery building and expanded to two locations in the city. They still sell units all over the world. Norb retired in 1969.

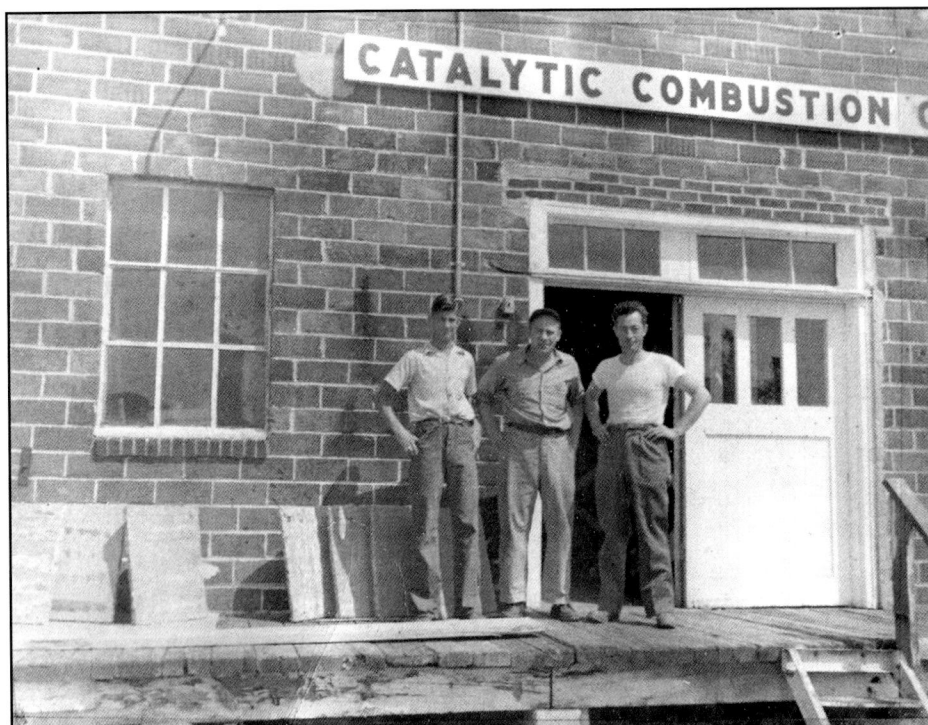

The first Catalytic Combustion Corporation plant in Bloomer
at the old brewery building. Norb rented the building from Al Tankenoff for $30 a
month. L-R: Norb's nephew, Dick Fashingbauer; Al Buchholtz, who was the chemistry
teacher at the high school and worked for Norb during the summers; and Norb.

"Through my brother Dick, I met some of the Quinn daughters who worked in Detroit, but their home was up in the thumb area of Michigan. Dick had a cabin on Saginaw Bay and would give the girls rides up there to their home during the war years. This is where Eileen and I met. Her mother picked me out to be Eileen's husband. We were engaged before I moved the equipment and tools from Russ Suter's basement to Bloomer in March of 1950. We married in Detroit on July 8, 1950.

"Eileen started praying for a family immediately, all to no avail for three years. Then we had four children in five years. I asked her if she knew any other prayers. Wendy was making her home with us and later was joined by Geri, Jackie, Jeanne and Mark.

We have completed 56 years of bliss. I can't give enough credit to Eileen for all the happy years. She has been an ideal wife and mother. Many times my job would call me to various parts of the world – Helsinki, Finland; Balboa, Spain; Germany many times; England and Australia. I was gone as long as seven weeks at a time in 1962, but everything was taken care of at home. Thanks honey."

After first living in the family farmhouse, Eileen and Norb built the house where they still reside. It is located along Mill Pond (now called Lake Como) in the pasture where Norb herded cows so many years ago. Norb still enjoys deer hunting at his cabin in Northern Wisconsin. Although he doesn't get to fish as much as he would like, he has gone on many fishing trips to Alaska with Mark.

To keep his hands in the activity he loves, he has a small business in his basement where he makes and repairs fishing rods. Besides these sports, his family, which now includes six grandchildren, Norb enjoys gardening, especially his tomatoes, sometimes putting out as many as thirty plants which he starts in his house over the winter. In 2002 he and Eileen were honored to be chosen Grand Marshalls for the annual Bloomer Community Parade.

Eileen and Norb on their wedding day, July 8, 1950.

Norb and Eileen, 2006

Unusual Happenings and Close Calls

Many times during our interviews, Norb brought up times when he should have "bit the dust" or "bought the farm." We both agreed he had one very powerful Guardian Angel watching over him. Norb decided to have a section on his "near misses" or "Unusual Happenings" as he calls them. Some of them have already been written, such as his getting hit with a rock when he was four years old; falling through the ice and when his winter belongings were sent home with a telegram about the "late Norbert C. Ruff's personal belongings." Another, in Chapter Four tells about the loss of his flight after he had returned to base with engine trouble. Below are a few more.

"During the summer of 1938 Bob Koehler and I did a lot of flying together. He had a 40-horse power Taylor Craft. Bob was my first cousin, school classmate through grade and high school and best friends. We hunted, fished and built shacks together. Later, in 1950, I was his bestman at his wedding.

"We flew his airplane all over the State of Wisconsin—family reunions down to the Milwaukee area, etc. One summer we decided to fly it up to Hayward [about eighty-five miles due north of Bloomer]. They had a nice little airport up there and a lot of local summer activities. We landed at the airport, tied the plane down and walked into town. Then we walked back and slept in sleeping bags under the wing of the airplane. The next morning we flew back toward Bloomer. It was a nice calm day and we both fell sound asleep at about 5,000 feet. We had the trim pretty well set so we did maintain this altitude, but the wind drifted us about ten miles west of our true course. When we woke up we were over Chetek. Alls well that ends well.

"During WWII Bob was an aircraft mechanic in the Army Airforce. This same little 40 horse power flew across Lake Michigan."

"In the later part of 1946 while at March Field, California, we were flying F-80s. I had parked my airplane after an afternoon flight and walked up to operations with my parachute over my shoulder. Now four of the pilots on the base were going to fly a C-45 up to Minneapolis and back for the weekend. I had been asked earlier if I wanted to join them, but I refused. The pilots were expected to do a certain amount of cross-country flying each year. I had said, 'Sorry, not this time. I'm married now' or something to that affect. While I was walking along one of the pilots said, 'You sure you don't want to go, we got lots of room?' Again I refused. He said, 'My parachute is in for inspection and repack. Can I use yours?' I said, 'Sure' and handed it over to him. Each pilot's name is printed on a panel on the back portion of the rigging. The harness is fitted and adjusted for use by the pilot to his body size. Since the two of us were about the same size, the parachute would work.

"Now Monday morning I checked in at operations and saw a notice on the bulletin board that said the C-45 was 'over due' on a flight from Longbeach, California to March Field. One of the pilots was dropped off at Longbeach on the return from Minneapolis. This distance was only about thirty miles. The airplane was found crashed and burned just off field at March. All aboard were dead. The pilot was the best instrument pilot on the field and the weather had been good. My parachute with my name on it was found in the wreckage. For a little while I was one of the listed aboard the plane."

"In the mid-1960's I was plant manager of Catalytic Combustion, a division of U.O.P. at that time. I was called down to the main offices at Des Plaines, IL. I had reservations to return to

Eau Claire via Wisconsin Air for the next late afternoon's flight at 7:30 pm. Our meeting lasted longer and I missed my flight and had to take a later one at 9:30 pm. The earlier flight, and a Delta flight, collided on the ground at O'Hare Airport in Chicago that day and fifteen people in the Air Wisconsin plane were killed."

"I sure had a real good guardian angel through my life, and I thank God daily for the job well done. My mother had told me she had smallpox during the time she carried me. None of my later smallpox vaccinations ever reacted. When I was six weeks old I caught whooping cough from my older brothers and sisters. At four years of age I had my skull busted by a rock. At seven I spent most of that summer in bed with inflammatory rheumatism which went away after my tonsils were removed. Now the afternoon of the day my 83 year old mother died she told me, 'Norb it was a pleasure raising you.' It sounded more like a burden and worry as I looked back. A mother's love has no boundary. Thanks Mom."

In July of this year Norb was thrilled when Mark took him to Minnesota to meet Ron Fagen. Ron, who started Fagen, Inc., has built 46 ethanol plants and has 26 more under construction, throughout the Midwest, is also an avid pilot and plane restorer. Fagen purchased this P-38, which he had flown to his airport at Granite Falls, Minnesota. The plane, which was restored once in the early nineties, will be restored again.

Mark, Norb and Ron Fagen

The P-38's history is interesting. In 1946 twenty-three year old James Harp bought the airplane from war surplus for $1,250.00, saving it from being scrapped like so many planes from WWII. It was brand new. He wanted to race it in Bendix trophy race of 1946. The race was from Los Angeles to Cleveland, where he took fifth place and won $1,500. Two weeks later he sold the plane for $1,500, earning $1,750 in one summer. The plane then switched hands many times, but was never flown much and barely has 1,000 flying hours.

This P-40 is also owned and was restored by Fagen and his crew. The plane was shown at the Oshkosh Air Show in 2006 where it won Grand Champion Warbird. In Reno it won the Hap Arnold Award for best warbird. This plane also has an interesting history. In November of 1942 the plane was sent to Russia as a lend-lease airplane, where it was shot down by four German Bf-109 fighters in September of 1943. The P-40 stayed

P-40 at the Oshkosh Fly-In, 2006
L-R: Darren Menhusen, Brandon Deuel, Ken Hake, a Tuskegee airman, Erick Hokuf, a Tuskegee airman, Ron Fagen.

where it crashed until Ken Hake of Tipton, Kansas learned about the wreck in August of 1991. He hired two men from the United States to bring the plane to Kansas, where restoration started on the

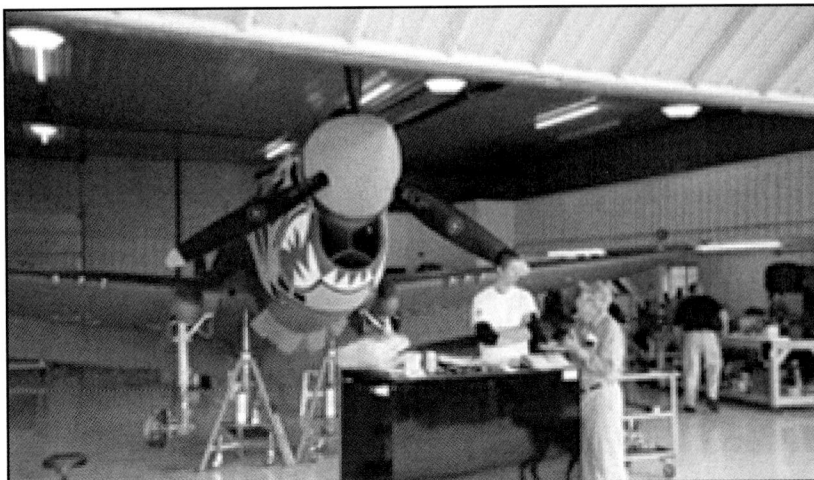

airframe and structural parts. In 2004 structure of the plane was completed. Ron Fagen then purchased the plane from Ken and brought it to Granite Falls, Minnesota. The plane was finished in June of 2006, with the painting, wiring,

Erik Hokuf and Norb discussing the P-40

plumbing and assembling completely redone. The painting was done with the shark face markings that were used with the Flying Tigers in China. Fagen has two other wrecked P-40s, also shot down in Russia, that he will be restoring.

The top picture shows the P-40 where it crashed in Russia. The bottom shows the men getting the plane ready to haul back to the United States.

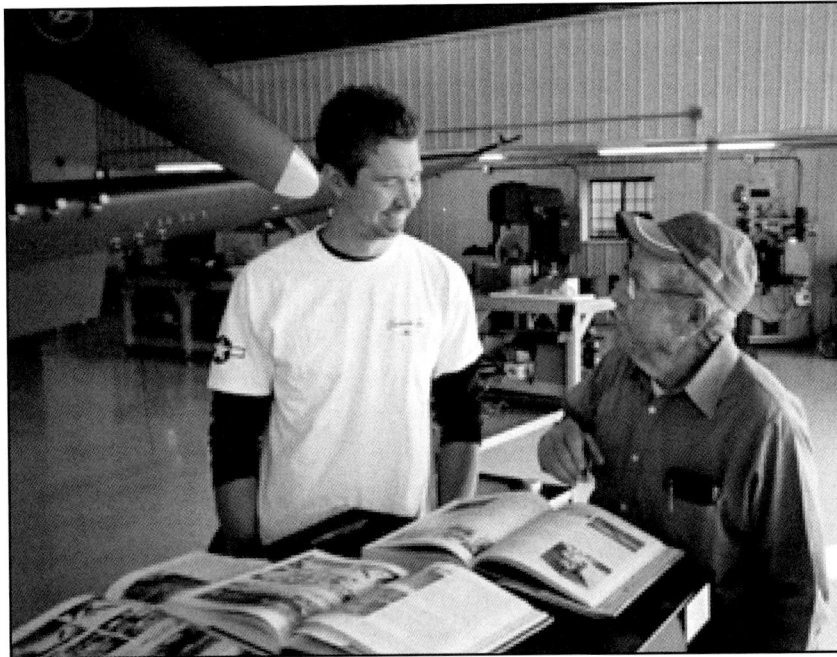

Norb and Erik Hokuf
going over information and
stories in *Attack & Conquer*.

Norb and Mark and the ten point
buck Norb shot at his cabin in
Washburn, Wisconsin in 2004.
He has been hunting there since
the mid-1950s.

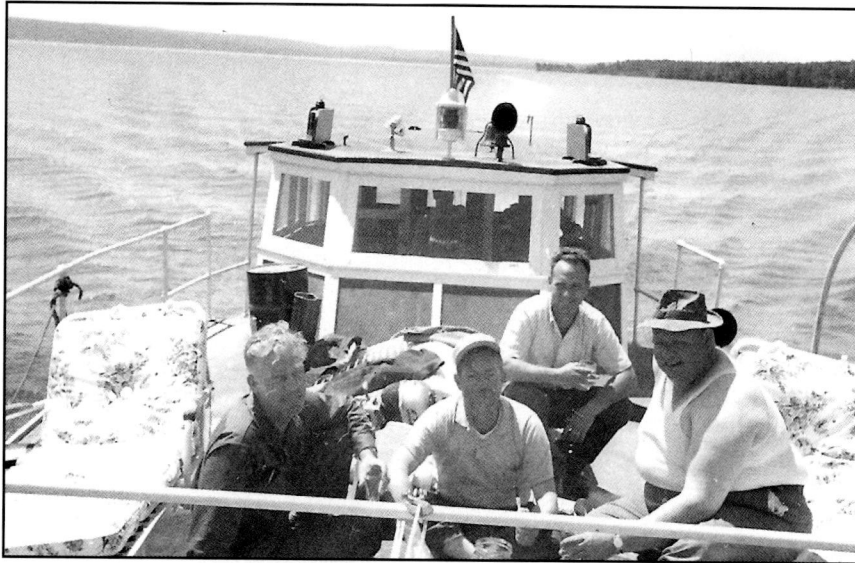

Although this picture was taken many years ago, it shows Norb at one of his
favorite pasttimes, fishing. The boat was bought in 1962 with his brother, Dick,
and friend Ollie Fehr. It was kept at Bayfield, Wisconsin on Lake Superior.
L-R: Dick Ruff, Norb, Don Snippen and Ollie Fehr. Dick passed on the
following year.

Norb shown with some of the
halibut caught while fishing in
Alaska in 2006. The tour,
"Kodiak Sports and Tour" is
owned by Scott and Sonja Phelps
of Kodiak, Alaska

In front of the reconstructed P-38 at the Bong Center in 2006

Families can purchase memorial blocks at the Bong Center. The top three have been mentioned throughout this book. Howard "Bing" Day, another Bloomer boy, was a life-time friend of Norb's and was in the Navy during WWII. He died in 2003.

208

Norb at the Thunderbirds' Hangar at Nellis Air Force Base, Las Vegas at the 2005 80th Squadron reunion.

World War II Honoree

⁞⁞⁞⁞⁞⁞⁞⁞⁞⁞⁞⁞⁞⁞ World War II Veteran ⁞⁞⁞⁞⁞⁞⁞⁞⁞⁞⁞⁞⁞⁞

Norbert C. Ruff

BRANCH OF SERVICE
U.S. Army Air Forces

HOMETOWN
Bloomer, WI

HONORED BY
David & Linda Dresel

ACTIVITY DURING WWII
SERVED FROM 1941 TO 1946. GRADUATED FLYING CADETS IN CLASS OF 41 ON DECEMBER 6, 1941. SPENT JANUARY 12, 1942 TO OCTOBER 1943 IN SOUTHWEST PACIFIC THEATER WITH THE 80TH FIGHTER SQUADRON. FLEW 125 COMBAT MISSIONS IN THREE FIGHTER AIRCRAFT THE P-39, P-400 AND P-38. LATER WAS OFFERED AND INVOLVED IN THE TEST PILOT POSITION IN THE FIRST JET FIGHTERS, THE BELL P-59 AND F-80. RECEIVED THE AIR MEDAL WITH 3 OAK LEAF CLUSTERS, AMERICAN DEFENSE RIBBON, ASIATIC-PACIFIC WITH 3 BRONZE STARS, UNIT CITATION. SERVED IN THE CAMPAIGNS OF BISMARCK ARCHIPELAGO AND PAPUA NEW GUINEA.

Norb's page on the World War II Honoree website.

Norb didn't just get to see the P-38 when visiting with Fagen, but he sat in the cockpit. When I looked at the picture and saw the look on Norb's face I said, "You look like you're in seventh heaven."

He replied, "I just wanted to push forward the throttle and jump the chocks."

After nearly seventy years, the love of the P-38 Lightning has never disappeared.

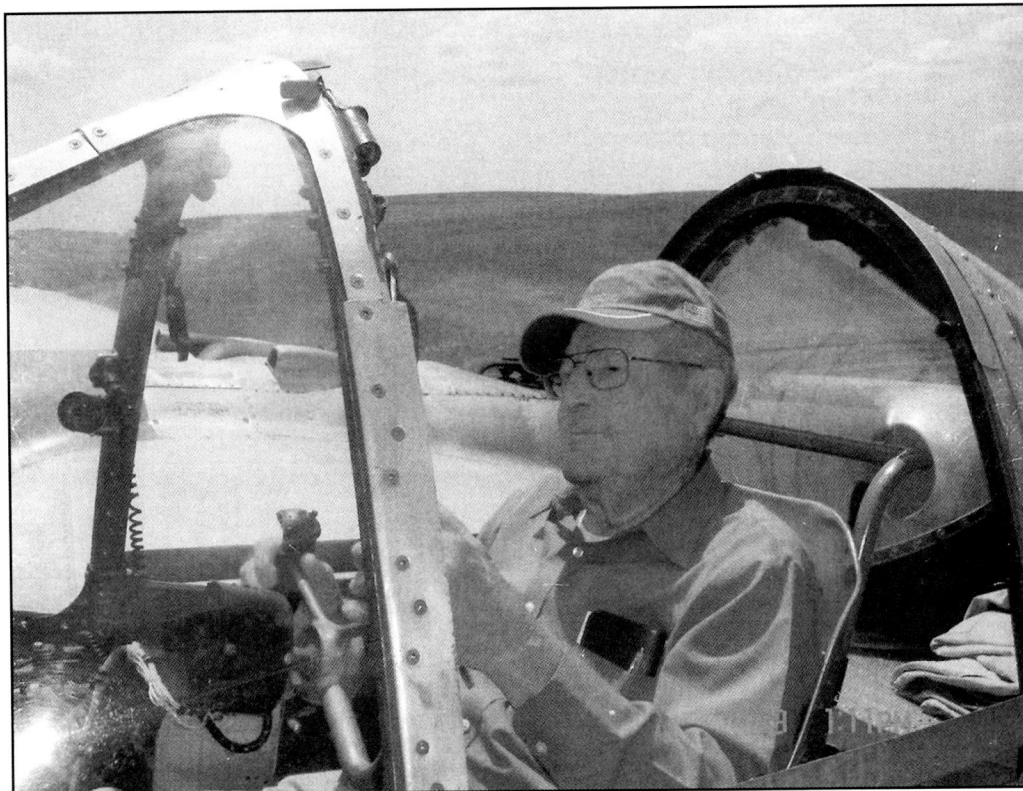

The Story Continues...

Norb, Glen Hope and Marion Kirby at the 80th Squadron Reunion in Fort Worth, Texas in April, 2007. Kirby is holding a bottle of Corio, a Scoth-type whisky sent in from Australia.

Today's 80th pilots with the "old-timers." L-R: Lude, Brandy Maxwell, Norb, Wyatt, Glen Hope, Christopher Wilkowski. Seated: Marion Kirby.

Honoring the WWII Veterans at the banquet. L-R: Glen Hope, Clarence Wolgemuth, Norb, Sid Adelstein, Kirby. Herbert Ross is speaking.

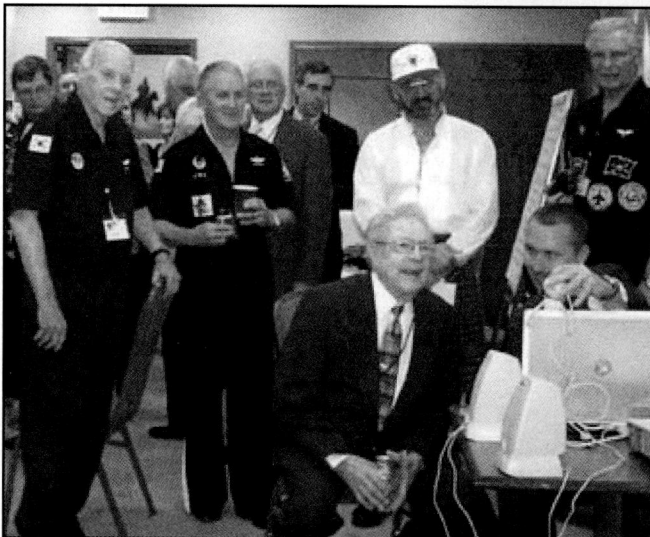

Norb is speaking to the 80th Squadron stationed in Kunsan, Korea during a live remote after the banquet. The men in Kunsan also joined in the sing-a-long.

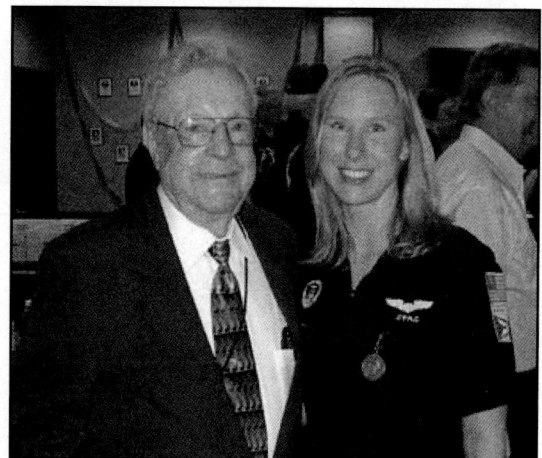

Norb and Brandy Maxwell, a pilot with the 80th Squadron.

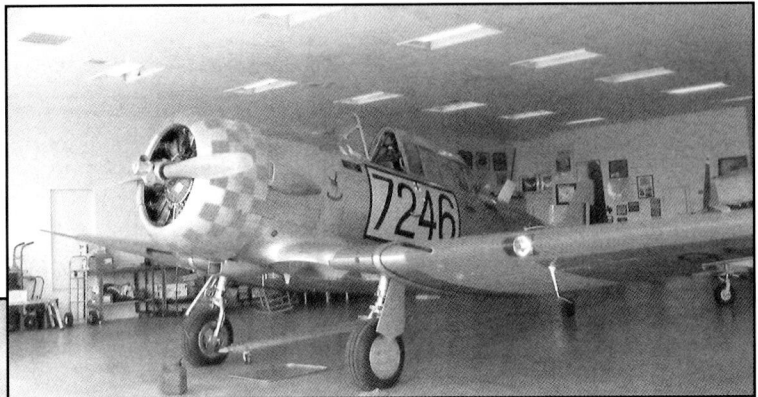

AT6 at left and Stearman below owned and restored by Scott Purdue. He and his wife, Dana invited us to their house to view the planes.

Left: Norb and Scott Purdue checking out the Stearman before going up. Below left: Norb flying high after sixty-six years. Below: Re-creating 1941 picture from page 14.

Above and right: At the Warhawks, Inc. hangar in Granite Falls, the P-38 is taken down to its bare bones. Below: Ron Fagen and his P-38.

On July 23, 2007 the plane was flown to the annual fly-in in Oshkosh, Wisconsin. *Ruff Stuff* is one of only four P-38's flying today with active "superchargers." There was always a crowd waiting to view the plane. The woman standing in the center of the picture is Eileen Ruff.

213

Towing the P-38 to the Warbirds presentation area.

Norb talking about his experiences with the P-38 and the 80th Squadron. The man on the upper left is Kevin Eldridge, the pilot who flew the P-38 and Eric Hokuf, Crew Chief of the rebuilding of the plane.

Just a small part of the crowd at the presentation. This portion was made up of many farmily and friends who made the trip from Bloomer.

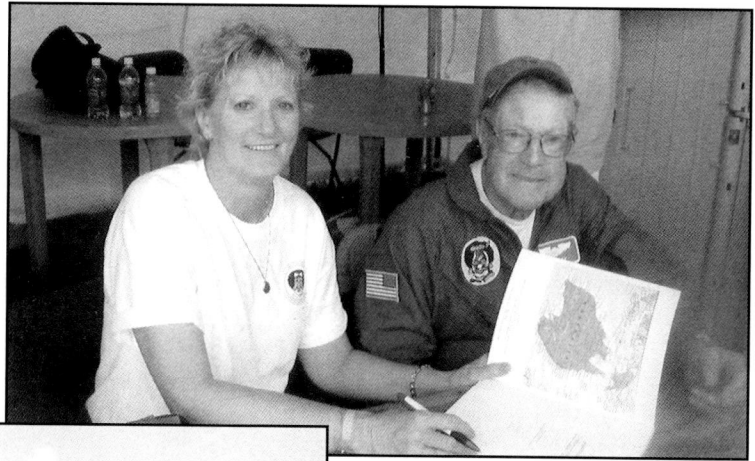

Norb and Tina at a very soggy book signing after the presentation. Good thing a tent was provided.

Norb and his son, Mark, without whom this project would never have been started.

Resources

49ᵗʰ Fighter Group, Ernest R. McDowell, 1989, Squadron/Signal Publications, Inc.

80ᵗʰ Fighter Squadron, The Headhunters, Squadron History, 2d Lt. mark "Pledge" Madaus, Juvat Adjutant 93-94

8ᵗʰ Fighter Group History, www.web-birds.com/5th/8/8th.htm, January 8, 2003

Attack & Conquer, John C. Stanaway & Lawrence J. Hickey, 1995, Schiffer Publishing Ltd.

Attack On Yamamoto, Carroll V. Glines, 1990, Orion Books

Aviation History, March 2000

Beau's Butchers & Boomerangs – Mareeba – The History of the WWII Airfield, 1942-1943, Damian Waters, 2003

Cobras Over New Guinea, Stanaway, *Flypast*, November, 1999

Come Fly With Me, Louis 'Screwy Louie' Schriber

Eagle Against the Sun, Ronald H. Spector, 1985, The Free Press

Everyday Life from Prohibition through World War II, Marc McCutcheon, 1995, Writer's Digest Books

Fight for New Guinea, General Douglas MacArthur's First Offensive, Pat Robinson, 1943, Random House

Fighter Pilots in Aerial Combat, Hard Driving Headhunters, Stanaway, 1984

Flags of Our Fathers, James Bradley, 2001, Bantam

Flying Buccaneers, The Illustrated Story of Kenney's Fifth Air Force, Steve Birdsall, 1977, Doubleday & Company Inc.

Flyboys, A True Story of Courage, James Bradley, 2003, Back Bay Books, Little/Brown & Company

Ghost Soldiers, The Epic Account of World War II's Greatest Rescue Mission, Hampton Sides, 2001, Anchor Books

Hard-Driving Headhunters, The 80ᵗʰ Squadron in World War II, John Stanaway, *Fighter Pilots in*

Aerial Combat, Summer 1984, Fall 1984, Winter, 1984

Kirby Files, Marion Kirby

MacArthur Strikes Back, Decision at Buna, New Guinea, 1942-1943, Harry A. Gailey, 2000, Presidio Press, Inc.

Matson's Century of Ships, Stindt, 1982

P-38 Lightning at War, Joe Christy & Jeff Ethell,

Pacific Sweep, William H. Hess, 1974, Doubleday & Company, Inc.

Pilot Training Manual for the P-38 Lightning

Solo, My Adventures in the Air, Clyde Edgerton, 2005, Algonquin Books of Chapel Hill

The Complete Idiot's Guide to World War II, Second Edition, Mitchell Bard, 2004, Alpha

The 80th Fighter Squadron "Headhunters" Squadron History, as of 2 February, 2001, 80th Fighter Squadron Headhunters Association, Inc.

The Headhunters Headlines

The P-80 Shooting Star, Evolution of a Jet Fighter, E.T. Wooldridge, Jr. 1979, Smithsonian Institution Press

The Plane Wrangler, Air Corps Training Detachment Arledge Field, Stamford, Texas, 1941

They Fought With What They Had, Walter D. Edmonds, 1951, Little, Brown and Company

Troopships of WWII, Charles, The Army Transportation Association

Various web sites on General Bill Mitchell

Victory at Sea, DVD

War & Conflict, DVD

You've Got the Lead, Flight Lead Handbook, written sometime after 1946 when Norb had already left the service.

Numerous personal letters to and from Norbert C. Ruff

Index

223